Cultures of Anti-Racism in Latin America and the Caribbean

edited by Peter Wade, James Scorer and Ignacio Aguiló

University of London Press
Institute of Latin American Studies, School of Advanced Study,
University of London, 2019

British Library Cataloguing-in-Publication Data
A catalogue record for this book is available from the British Library

This book is published under a Creative Commons Attribution-NonCommercial-NoDerivatives 4.0 International (CC BY-NC-ND 4.0) license. More information regarding CC licenses is available at https://creativecommons.org/licenses/.

This book is also available online at http://humanities-digital-library.org.

ISBN:
978-1-908857-55-2 (paperback edition)
978-1-908857-71-2 (.epub edition)
978-1-908857-70-5 (.mobi edition)
978-1-908857-72-9 (PDF edition)

DOI: 10.14296/919.9781908857729 (PDF edition)

Institute of Latin American Studies
School of Advanced Study
University of London
Senate House
London WC1E 7HU

Telephone: 020 7862 8844

Email: ilas@sas.ac.uk
Web: http://ilas.sas.ac.uk

Cover images:
Top: Organización Barrial Túpac Amaru de Jujuy, Argentina, 2016. Photo: ideasGraves. License: CC-BY-2.0.
Bottom: Marcha das Mulheres Negras, 2015. Photo: Janine Moraes, Brazilian Ministério da Cultura. License: CC-BY-2.0.

Contents

	List of illustrations	v
	Notes on contributors	vii
1.	Introduction: Latin American and Caribbean racisms in global and conceptual context *Peter Wade, James Scorer and Ignacio Aguiló*	1
2.	The antinomies of identity politics: neoliberalism, race and political participation in Colombia *Nick Morgan*	25
3.	Photography collectives and anti-racism in Peru and Argentina *Patricia Oliart and Agustina Triquell*	49
4.	Subverting racist imagery for anti-racist intent: Indigenous filmmaking from Latin America and the resignification of the archive *Charlotte Gleghorn*	73
5.	Cultural agency and anti-racism in Caribbean conceptual art *Fabienne Viala*	101
6.	Anti-racism in the classroom and beyond: teacher perspectives from Rio de Janeiro *Gudrun Klein*	125
7.	The last in a country of forgotten people: ancestry, music and identity among Bolivia's Afro population *Lena Schubmann*	147
8.	White *cholos*? Discourses around race, whiteness and Lima's fusion music *Fiorella Montero-Diaz*	167
9.	Bolivia's anti-racism law: transforming a culture? *Henry Stobart*	191
	Index	213

List of illustrations

3.1	'Pachacutec' by Adrián Portugal from the series 'Retratos de peruanos ejemplares', 2005.	60
3.2	'Bailarina' by Adrián Portugal from the series 'Retratos de peruanos ejemplares', 2005.	60
3.3	The two portraits by Colectivo Manifiesto, as altered by anonymous Facebook users.	67
4.1	Hunikui authority addressing the spectator in the prologue to *Já me transformei em imagem* (2008).	79
4.2 and 4.3	Bolinder photo and reenactment in *Nabusímake* (2010).	84
4.4 and 4.5.	Juxtaposing the past of the archive and the future of interpretation in *Sey arimaku* (2012).	90
4.6	Still of Tsa'amri redeployed in *O Mestre e o Divino*	93
5.1	*Moun Brilé* by François Piquet, 'Réparations', Fonds d'Arts Contemporains, Guadeloupe, 2016.	108
5.2	*Whip It Good* was first commissioned by Art Labour Archives and Ballhaus Naunynstrasse, Berlin, 2013.	113
8.1	Joaquín Mariátegui – Bareto's former lead guitarist.	173
9.1	Burning tyres on the streets of Sucre on 25 November 2007 on the morning after the deaths of three *capitalía* protesters.	192
9.2	Gregorio Mamani Villacorta (1960–2011). Depicted playing the charango and wearing *sika bota* leggings and *tinku* [ox-hide] fighting helmet. Image used in music video productions.	200

Notes on contributors

Ignacio Aguiló is lecturer in Latin American cultural studies at the University of Manchester. Broadly speaking, his research focuses on race in contemporary South American cultural production. He is the author of *The Darkening Nation: Race, Neoliberalism and Crisis in Argentina* (2018), which explores the connections between the 2001 financial meltdown in Argentina and the crisis of narratives of whiteness and national belonging, by examining literary texts, popular music, artworks and films. His current research project looks at notions of kitsch and bad taste in contemporary literature, video clips, films and architecture by indigenous artists from Bolivia, Ecuador and Peru, focusing on the racial dimension of the politics of taste.

Charlotte Gleghorn is lecturer in Latin American film studies at the University of Edinburgh. Her research engages with the politics of authorship, aesthetics and film production in diverse contexts across Latin America. From 2009 to 2014, she worked on the European Research Council project 'Indigeneity in the Contemporary World: Performance, Politics, Belonging', hosted at Royal Holloway, University of London, during which time she also collaborated on the international exhibition of indigenous art and performance 'EcoCentrix: Indigenous Arts, Sustainable Acts', at Bargehouse, Southbank, London. She has contributed to several anthologies on women's filmmaking in Latin America, published on Colombian and Mexican indigenous film and video and has co-edited a volume of essays on indigenous performance, *Recasting Commodity and Spectacle in the Indigenous Americas* (2014). She is currently preparing a book manuscript as part of an Arts and Humanities Research Council (AHRC) Leadership fellowship on Indigenous filmmaking in Latin America.

Gudrun Klein obtained her Magister in anthropology at the University of Vienna. She is currently a PhD candidate in social anthropology at the University of Manchester. Her research interests centre on race and ethnicity in Latin America, with a special focus on Brazil. More specifically, her work examines multiculturalist policies and anti-racist narratives in the field of education.

Fiorella Montero-Diaz is currently a lecturer in ethnomusicology at Keele University in the UK, and sits on the board of the British Forum for Ethnomusicology. She first trained as a classical pianist, went on to a degree in sound engineering, and then settled on ethnomusicology. She received an MMus in ethnomusicology at Goldsmiths, University of London, and a PhD in music from Royal Holloway, University of London. Her research focuses on music hybridity, race, class, the elites and social conflict in contemporary Lima, Peru. Fiorella's most recent publications include 'Singing the war: reconfiguring white upper-class identity through fusion music in post-war Lima' (*Ethnomusicology Forum*, 2016), 'YouTubing the "Other": Lima's upper classes and Andean imaginaries' (in *Music, Indigeneity, Digital Media*, 2017) and 'Turning things around? From white fusion stars with Andean flavour to Andean fusion stars with white appeal' (*Popular Music*, 2018). She is co-editing a book entitled *Citizenship in the Latin American Upper and Middle Classes: Ethnographic Perspectives on Culture, Politics, and Consumption* (forthcoming).

Nick Morgan is lecturer in Latin American studies at Newcastle University. His research on Latin American popular culture combines discourse analysis, archival work and ethnography, and focuses on a wide number of sites of cultural production, ranging from telenovelas and the media to the politics of the everyday. As part of an ongoing study of the modalities of social inequality in Colombia, Venezuela and Panama, he has published articles on discourses of race and ethnicity, as well as on nationalism and participatory democracy. His current research project is 'Screening Violence', an AHRC-funded study of the imaginaries of conflict and reconciliation in Algeria, Argentina, Colombia, Indonesia and Northern Ireland.

Patricia Oliart works at Newcastle University where she is senior lecturer in Latin American studies. She holds a BA in social sciences, an MA in Latin American studies and a PhD in human geography. From 1994 to 2003 she worked in Peru as lecturer, consultant and researcher in the areas of gender, ethnicity, cultural change, and education in urban and rural areas in the Andes and Amazonia. She was member of the Institute of Peruvian Studies and lecturer at the Universidad Nacional Mayor de San Marcos. Her current research analyses cultural production (mainly music and photography) as a field for political interventions in the context of neoliberal cultural transformations in Latin America. Since 2015 she has been co-coordinator with Jorge Catalá-Carrasco of the EU-funded H2020 MSCA-RISE 48-month project 'Cultural Narratives of Crisis and Renewal', with partners in Spain, Holland, Argentina, Chile and Peru.

Lena Schubmann holds a BA in international relations from King's College London and an MPhil in Latin American studies from the University of Cambridge. Her research focuses on indigeneity and identity politics in Latin America as well as international climate policy. Since 2013, she has been a member of the German Academic Scholarship Foundation. In 2017, she co-organised the academic conference 'Global Politics of Knowledge: Lessons from the South', hosted by the University of Cambridge. Recent publications include 'The gendered road to Paris 2020: potential of the EU-LAC Partnership for Gender-Inclusive Climate Action' (LACalytics, 2018) and 'Decolonizing the state? Plurinationalism and state formation in Bolivia' (*Strife Journal*, 2018). Lena currently works for the World Food Programme of the United Nations in Guatemala.

James Scorer is senior lecturer in Latin American cultural studies at the University of Manchester, where he is also co-director of the Centre for Latin American and Caribbean Studies. He is the author of *City in Common: Culture and Community in Buenos Aires* (2016), and the co-editor of *Comics and Memory in Latin America* (2017). His research focuses on cultural explorations of the relationship between place and political identities in Latin America. He has worked and published on urban imaginaries, principally those of Buenos Aires, on photographs of pre-Columbian ruins, including those taken by Martín Chambi, and on Latin American comics. As part of the latter, he is currently the lead investigator of the international network entitled 'Framing Urban Communities: Comics and the City in Latin America', which is funded by The Leverhulme Trust.

Henry Stobart is reader in music/ethnomusicology in the music department of Royal Holloway. He studied tuba and recorder at Birmingham Conservatoire, completed a PhD at Cambridge University and, following a research fellowship at Darwin College Cambridge, was appointed as the first lecturer in ethnomusicology at Royal Holloway in 1999. After extensive research of rural musical practices in the Bolivian Andes, subsequent research has focused on indigenous music video (VCD) production, music 'piracy', and the cultural politics of this region. More recently, he co-directed the National Science Foundation-funded project 'Cultural Property, Creativity, and Indigeneity in Bolivia', with Michelle Bigenho (Colgate University, USA), with whom he was also awarded an American Council of Learned Societes collaborative research fellowship to research heritage declaration issues in Bolivia. His books include *Music and the Poetics of Production in the Bolivian Andes* (2006) and five edited or co-edited volumes, among them *Music, Indigeneity, Digital Media* (2017) and *The New (Ethno)musicologies* (2008).

Agustina Triquell is a lecturer at Universidad Nacional de San Martín in Buenos Aires. She holds a BA in social communication and a PhD in social sciences. Her doctoral research focused on the way photographic images build up subjectivities in different social contexts. She has worked with various NGOs related to human rights and cultural diversity in Córdoba and Buenos Aires. Her research focuses on photographic images and their circulation in the public sphere, as well as photographic memories of the recent past. She participates in collective projects regarding art, public archives, and social intervention in cities in Argentina and Latin America. Agustina is the author of *Fotografías e historias: la construcción narrativa de la memoria y la identidad en el álbum fotográfico familiar*, winner of the 2011 CdF Latin American Photographic Research Prize (Montevideo, Uruguay). She currently works at the Citizenship and Human Rights Program at the Instituto de Desarrollo Económico y Social (IDES).

Fabienne Viala is a reader in Hispanic and Caribbean studies at the University of Warwick. From 2015 to 2018, she was director of the Yesu Persaud Centre for Caribbean Studies and the president for the Society of Caribbean Studies, UK. She has published books and articles on the post-1945 European and Latin American new historical novel, Cuban literature, French and Anglophone Caribbean cultures, black literature and visual art in Puerto Rico, and the legacies of slavery in the French, English and Spanish Caribbean. She is the author of *The Post-Columbus Syndrome: Identities, Cultural Nationalisms and Commemorations in the Caribbean* (2014). Her research focuses on the ways in which Caribbean conceptual art offers new approaches to agency and restorative justice and participates in the debate on global memory studies.

Peter Wade is professor of social anthropology at the University of Manchester and recently held a British Academy Wolfson Research Professorship (2013–16). His publications include *Blackness and Race Mixture* (1993), *Race and Ethnicity in Latin America* (2010), *Race, Nature and Culture: An Anthropological Perspective* (2002), and *Race and Sex in Latin America* (2009). He recently directed a project, funded by the Economics and Social Research Council and the Leverhulme Trust, on 'Race, Genomics and *Mestizaje* (mixture) in Latin America'. An edited book from the project is titled *Mestizo Genomics: Race Mixture, Nation, and Science in Latin America* (2014). His most recent books are *Race: An Introduction* (2015), and *Degrees of Mixture, Degrees of Freedom: Genomics, Multiculturalism and Race in Latin America* (2017). With Mónica Moreno Figueroa, he is currently co-directing a project on 'Latin American Antiracism in a "Post-Racial" Age'.

1. Introduction: Latin American and Caribbean racisms in global and conceptual context

Peter Wade, James Scorer and Ignacio Aguiló

The inspiration for this volume came from two lines of enquiry: what role art, broadly conceived, might play in anti-racism; and whether Latin American and Caribbean racial formations can be seen as specific within a broader global context. Cultural productions and performance have long been domains in which ideas and feelings about the racial and ethnic dimensions of the social order have been expressed and dramatised, whether to reinforce or challenge the status quo. Especially since the advent of the 'politics of recognition', but also before that, questions of naming and representation have been central concerns in regulating and contesting hierarchies, and the arts constitute a terrain – albeit unequal – on which different ideas about the significance of names, identities and representations can jostle for space and traction. Our intent in *Cultures of Anti-Racism in Latin America and the Caribbean* is to map some of the ways art, and the affective dimensions of human experience with which it engages, relate to racism and anti-racist struggles.

We address this intersection for a region where racial and ethnic differences and hierarchies have always been a concern, and where racism and anti-racism have become more widespread and explicit following the turn towards multiculturalism that began in the late 1980s. The ambivalent and somewhat precarious nature of this growing concern can be glimpsed from an article in *The Guardian* that reported on the presence of racist caricatures in several Latin American countries (Lakhani, 2015). Mexico's cartoon character Memín Pinguín and black-face TV personalities such as Peru's Negro Mama, Brazil's Adelaide character in the comedy show *Zorra Total* and Guatemala's Black Pitaya (played by comedian-turned-president Jimmy Morales) are prominent examples of such visual racism, to which can be added Colombia's Soldado Micolta (see Morgan's chapter in this volume). These representations have only recently been questioned in these countries, usually by black activists, but they are also sometimes defended as harmless fun and even as an expression of racial

---

P. Wade, J. Scorer and I. Aguiló, 'Introduction: Latin American and Caribbean racisms in global and conceptual context', in P. Wade, J. Scorer and I. Aguiló (eds.), *Cultures of Anti-Racism in Latin America and the Caribbean* (London: Institute of Latin American Studies, 2019), pp. 1–23. License: CC-BY-NC-ND 2.0.

tolerance (Moreno Figueroa and Saldívar, 2016). It is precisely these tensions and ambivalences that we explore in this volume.

In this book we take racism to be a system of structures, practices and ideas rooted in the colonial domination by European powers of other parts of the world. That understanding differs from typical dictionary definitions of racism, which define it as a set of beliefs about the superiority of one 'race' over another. Our approach sees racism as a system that distributes power, privilege, welfare and security among people, distinguished, classified and stratified in terms of ideas about their physical nature and their behaviour, seen as durably linked together within and across generations. Scholars today would typically use the terms 'biology' and 'culture' to refer to nature and behaviour – and they might well relate 'racism' to classifications based only on biology – but we prefer to use 'nature' and 'behaviour' to highlight that racial classifications usually elide biology and culture, naturalising the latter (Wade, 2002).

Many scholars share our emphasis on the colonial origins of racism, particularly recent coloniality theorists, who see racism and colonial relations (including those that persist after the end of formal colonialism) as underpinning concepts and projects such as 'modernity' and 'civilisation' (Mignolo, 2011; Quijano, 2007; Restrepo and Rojas, 2010). Earlier scholars also tried to tackle the ways that racism – and ideas about racial and ethnic difference – functioned in hierarchical social relations, an approach evident in the work of the Marxist African American scholar Oliver Cox (1948) or in Latin America in the 1970s with studies influenced by Marxist-inflected perspectives on dependency (see Wade, 2010). All these approaches share with today's critical theory of race the insight that racism is an integral part of the functioning of a global order structured by a colonial history and postcolonial capitalism (Goldberg, 2008); and that, while it is necessary to accept the post-structuralist view of racial identities as being in a constant process of construction and re-elaboration, it is also necessary to see how that process is imbricated with the constant construction and reproduction of inequality, including in the distribution of knowledge. The chapters in this volume follow such approaches but are also influenced by the way that, especially from the 1990s but with roots in African American women's discourses in the 1970s, today's theorists are more aware of the ways that racism goes hand-in-glove and is inflected by class, gender and sexuality (Collins, 1990; Wade, 2009). Several chapters in this book, for example, address the intersectionality of race and gender.

In the remainder of this introduction we reflect on the specificity (or not) of the racial formations of the region that is our focus: Latin America and the Caribbean. We explore to what extent the region's features might prove both relevant and also instructive to other postcolonial societies, even or perhaps especially when those features are configured in very specific ways. This section will also introduce some of the racial histories of Latin America and the Caribbean to readers less familiar with the region. We then analyse the history and meaning of key terms – race, racism and anti-racism – in the region as a way of highlighting some of the similarities and differences in racist and anti-racist discourses in different countries and at different historical moments. In the following section, we ask what should be included in the term 'racism', exploring three conceptual questions: a) should racial discrimination be encompassed in a generic concept of discrimination?; b) does discrimination against indigenous peoples in Latin America count as racism, even if they tend to avoid the term?; c) is racism the same as racial discrimination? In the final section, we turn to the role of the arts in anti-racism, exploring this first in general terms and then in relation to our region of interest, before discussing how the book's chapters deal with these matters.

Latin American racial formations in a global context

Claims about the racial exceptionalism of Latin America and the Caribbean have been common in certain circles – mostly among elites and nation-builders, but by no means confined to them. Drawing on the region's racial history of encounters between pre-Columbian indigenous societies, white colonial settlers and black slaves, these claims have rested on ideas about processes of *mestizaje/mestiçagem* (race mixture, understood as cultural as well as sexual reproduction), processes related both to later ideas of hybridity and transculturation that became common currency within Latin American anthropology, literary theory and cultural studies, and also to the concurrent figure of the mestizo. They argue that societies in which mixture was constitutive of colonial formation and subsequent postcolonial nation states have managed to avoid racism or at least soften its grip. Racial categories are said to have become vaguely bounded and flexible in societies in which mestizos are usually the majority, which in turn is said to make racial segregation difficult to achieve, even if class segregation is clearly very present. Moreover, it is frequently said that the difference between indigenous people and mestizos is primarily drawn in terms of cultural difference, not a 'racial' one (by which is meant 'not phenotypical'). Always implicit – and often explicit – in these arguments is a comparison with other regions perceived to be the home of racism, typically the United States, but also apartheid South Africa and Europe (Seigel, 2009).

One critical approach to such exceptionalism holds that such arguments are mere ideology (in a restricted sense of the word), a mask created by political elites that hides the reality of racism and racial exclusions, which social scientists have shown to exist in Latin American racial formations (Hernández, 2013; Rahier, 2014). This approach rejects exceptionalism and makes Latin America look like other racially stratified societies. A slightly different critique is that these ideas are more than just a mask because, like all hegemonic ideologies (using a broader sense of the term), they resonate with the lived experience of many people – which also means they are not just an elite ideology, even if elites are particularly active in their promotion (Da Costa, 2014; Sue, 2013; Wade, 2005). As such, *mestizaje* has a dual character: it creates a lived experience in which racial conviviality and elements of racial democracy *co-exist* simultaneously with racial hierarchy and racism. The very sites of mixture within which racial democracy can be enacted are also those where racial hierarchy is inscribed (Moreno Figueroa, 2012; Wade, 2009, p. 175). This approach rejects the exceptionalist claim that Latin American societies are especially non-racist, but nonetheless contends that processes and ideas of *mestizaje* give them a certain particularity, meaning they should be seen as a series of variants on hemispheric themes of histories of conquest, colonialism, enslavement, nation-building, racism and multiculturalism. These societies should be seen as a 'series of variants' precisely to avoid a homogenising view of a 'Latin American model' of racial formation that ignores the huge differences between, say, Brazil and Argentina, or Chile and Puerto Rico, while still recognising that all these societies relate, in some way, to ideas about *mestizaje*.

It may be that other regions of the world are increasingly approximating some version of such Latin American variants. If a feature of racial formations built around the idea of *mestizaje* is that racial difference and racism can be minimised and rendered illegitimate as matters of public concern, then claims that certain societies are now entering a 'post-racial' phase are based on similar acts of minimisation and delegitimation (Lentin, 2011, 2014; Mukherjee, 2016; Redclift, 2014). Recent processes that underlie claims of post-raciality include the following: the scientific rejection of race as a viable biological category – rejections that, tellingly, have happened again and again since at least the 1910s;[1] the political rejection of Nazi racism, which made 'race' a toxic term in some European societies, leading to the dominance of discourses of ethnicity and cultural difference (Stolcke, 1995); the dismantling of Jim Crow segregation and South African apartheid; increasing rates of race mixture in many postcolonial societies, alongside more official recognition of mixed-race identities;[2] and the turn towards multiculturalism since the 1970s, which institutionalised the recognition of difference, albeit in ways that arguably glossed over racialised inequalities and talked of difference in cultural terms that delegitimated references to racism.

These processes have meant that it has become increasingly possible to make claims about the declining significance of race, to quote the title of Wilson's famous 1978 book about the effects of racial desegregation on the United States, in which he made the argument, restated in a recent article, that 'in the economic realm, the black experience has moved historically from economic racial oppression experienced by virtually all African Americans to

---

1   For a recent example see a press report on research on genes for skin colour (Zimmer, 2017).
2   Interethnic marriage has increased in the UK, France and the United States (Fryer, 2007; Maxwell, 2012; Office for National Statistics, 2014; Wang, 2012). Recognition of mixed-race identities has also increased (Ifekwunigwe, 2004; Root, 1996).

the economic subordination of the black poor'. Wilson (2011, p. 57) was not denying the significance of race or racism, but he was saying that they were no longer the 'primary determinant of life chances for blacks' and that they had been surpassed by class stratification. The recent resurgence of explicit racism in the United States and Europe, symbolised for many by the election of Donald Trump, may seem to contradict this trend. However, it is important to stress that claims about post-raciality do not necessarily depend on simply denying race or racism; they can also use techniques of minimisation and delegitimation. Supporters of Trump and UKIP, for example, will often react to accusations of racism by inverting the charge and accusing their accusers of being racist because they 'unfairly' play the race card and 'unjustly' blame racism for social inequalities when the focus should rather be on working hard and getting ahead.

Claims of post-raciality in Europe and the United States tend to signpost features that have also been highlighted in Latin America: the importance of class in defining life chances in the absence of stark racial segregation; high levels of race mixture; and the idea that culture is often more important than race (read 'phenotype') as a way to talk about difference (Da Costa, 2016). The way anti-racism in Latin America tackles these issues, therefore, is relevant to other contexts in which post-racial claims are being made. The notion of the 'white ally', for example, which is discussed in several chapters in this book, raises the thorny question of whether the solidarity and support offered by the white ally are authentic and reliable when s/he has not actually lived the same affective and emotional experiences as a non-white person: there is a difficult balance between claiming that empathy or vicarious experience can suffice, and claiming that only an authentic experience of suffering can create sufficient affective traction. In the case of Latin America, this tension might be mediated by the idea of *mestizaje/mestiçagem*. It may be easier in Peru or Brazil, for example, to traverse the affective terrain between white and black or indigenous when the intermediate figures of the *cholo* (which implies some mixture, at least cultural if not biological) and the *moreno* or *pardo* (terms also implying mixture) are in play.

This is a tricky argument to get right. In Brazil, there has been a concerted attempt by the black movement, and subsequently the state itself, to construct a category of *negro* that embraces both black (*preto*) and brown (*pardo*) and that stands opposed to white. This is designed to counteract precisely the way in which *mestiçagem* can work to minimise racism. But state anti-racism and multiculturalism can easily remain highly superficial, vaunting the value of intercultural interactions in ways that are strongly reminiscent of the nationalist glorifications of *mestizaje*, at the same time as violence continues to be visited mercilessly on black and indigenous leaders. In light of this, paying attention to the productive possibilities contained within the ideas and practices of *mestizaje* is always a double-edged sword. Yet there may be ways in which these productive possibilities can be exploited to generate broad anti-racist alliances, building on elements of racial conviviality in everyday life. This kind of conviviality – identified and valued in a British context by Gilroy (2004) and hinted at in some recent work on cosmopolitanism (Werbner, 2015) – may well be easier to foment in a Latin American context where *mestizaje* can provide affordances for crossing racial boundaries, even if, as noted, these potentialities are permanently haunted by the opposite possibility that a racial hierarchy will re-emerge. Indications of both potentialities can be glimpsed in examples of Afro-indigenous interactions around land claims, such as in Colombia (Ng'weno, 2007) or Brazil (French, 2009), in which racial boundaries are both crossed and unsettled by alliances and also polarised by competition at the same time. Anti-racism, then, can be made a part of everyday life and can, countering the claims made by racists, help to undermine racism, not least when allied to the everyday experiences of crossing racial difference that is one dimension of *mestizaje*. But the opposite possibility is always there: that racism can also be denied in the interests of maintaining white/mestizo privilege and reproducing the hierarchies that form the other dimension of *mestizaje*.

Before moving on to think about the relationship between culture and racism within Latin America and the Caribbean and, more specifically, the role that cultural production might play in discourses and practices of anti-racism, we now offer some reflections on the terms at stake.

Race, racism and anti-racism in Latin America and the Caribbean

What do the terms race, racism and anti-racism encompass in the context of the region? Historically, the term *raza*, as applied to humans rather than the domestic animals or plants to which the term was first applied in 14th-century Europe, gained most currency in the Spanish-speaking world in the 15th century. This was in the context of Iberian statutes about *limpieza de sangre* (purity of blood), which discriminated against people who had *raza de judío o moro*, that is, Jewish or Muslim blood or ancestry; the term referred to a type of genealogical connection, not a class of people, as it did in later centuries (for example, *la raza blanca*).

In the American colonies, the term continued to have this genealogical meaning, but was not commonly used; the term *casta* [caste, breed or type] was more usual (Martínez, 2008), evidenced by the famous *casta* paintings that provided a visual guide to racial categories and their concurrent social standing. During this period people also spoke in terms of the *calidad* [quality] of a person in ways that included elements of ancestry and appearance (McCaa, 1984). In Europe of the mid 1700s, the word race also appeared infrequently and often in reference to such categories as a race of Visigoths (Montesquieu), a race of Laplanders (Buffon) or a race of financiers (Hume), all defined as much by behaviour and lineage as by physique. In late 18th-century North America, Jefferson did refer to 'races of black and red men', but even these were defined in terms of a constitution that integrated what would later be separated out as moral and physical (or cultural and biological) elements.[3]

Despite the earlier absence of the term itself, however, race was a key organising concept for understanding human diversity in both Europe and the Americas, and by the mid and late-19th century it had become common to use the word *raza* to talk about categories of humans. Domingo Faustino Sarmiento in *Conflicto y armonías de las razas en América* (1883) and José Martí in *Nuestra América* (1891) both did so and, some decades later, the usage was still common. Examples include books such as *Raza chilena* (Palacios, 1918 [1904]), *Los problemas de la raza en Colombia* (Jiménez López et al., 1920) and *La raza cósmica* (Vasconcelos, 1997 [1925]), while Molina Enríquez and José Ingenieros used the word frequently in, respectively, *Los grandes problemas nacionales* (2004 [1909]) and *Sociología argentina* (1918 [1908]). Even at this time, when eugenics reigned throughout the region, Latin American understandings of *raza* – and of eugenics – tended to mix biology and culture, such that a *raza* was understood as much in terms of a shared history, environment and way of life as in terms of a shared biology (Stepan, 1991). For that reason Ernesto Guevara (2005, p. 196) could, in a speech nominally given in 1952 and reproduced in *Diarios de motocicleta*, toast a united Latin America by celebrating the fact that beyond national differences its peoples form 'una sola raza mestiza que desde México hasta el estrecho de Magallanes presenta notables similitudes etnográficas'.

Today the term is both commonplace and taboo (Hartigan, 2013; Wade, 2017, pp. 228–33). It is still routinely used to describe breeds of animals and plants, but one can easily come across references to people '*de la raza negra/blanca/indígena*', and in downtown Mexico City there is a monument named La Raza near an eponymous metro station. And, despite the broad turn within Latin America towards more critical views of European colonisation, some countries, such as Colombia and Honduras, continue to commemorate the day – 12 October – that Columbus landed on the Caribbean island of Guanahani, referring to it as Día de la Raza.[4] In this everyday usage, *raza* still carries the meaning of shared cultural as well as biological heritage: it is common to hear people talk about *la raza dominicana*, for example. The concepts of nation and race overlap a great deal, as they did for Hume in his 1742 essay 'Of National

---

3   See Wade (2015, pp. 65–7).

4   Celebrations of the Día de la Raza were common in Latin American countries after the president of the Unión Iberoamericana, Faustino Rodríguez-San Pedro, proposed the date in 1913. However, in recent years, 12 October has been renamed in most countries in the region to highlight racial tolerance and/or indigenous resistance to colonialism. In Argentina, for example, the day is now officially known as *Día del Respeto a la Diversidad Cultural*, and in Nicaragua it is the Día de la Resistencia Indígena, Negra y Popular.

Characters'. The word does also, however, carry connotations of racism, racial discrimination and racial hierarchy. For this reason, it is increasingly superseded and rarely used in public political discourse (see, for example, Sue, 2013, pp. 31–7). Brazil is probably the major exception here, with *raça* and *racial* being widely used in policy and politics, especially since the admission by President Fernando Henrique Cardoso in the mid 1990s that racism was a reality in the country, with the resultant turn towards race-based affirmative action.

That the word *raza* today easily connotes the spectre of racism speaks to the fact that what was, from the mid 19th century, deemed in some Euro-American intellectual circles to be a simple fact of life – racial hierarchy – was deemed by others to be immoral and evil, a view which gained traction in the 20th century, even as eugenics was building up steam. The word racism first appears in English and in French in the early 1900s, according to the *OED* and the *Trésor de la langue française*, although it does not figure in the Real Academia Española's 1925 dictionary.[5] It is a decidedly modern word, and from the start carried a negative charge, linked to US racial segregation and European Fascism.

Of course, people had, and still have, other words for labelling aspects of what might later be called racism. For example, W.E.B. Du Bois (1897) talked of 'prejudice', which he described as 'personal disrespect and mockery, the ridicule and systematic humiliation, the distortion of fact and wanton license of fancy, the cynical ignoring of the better and boisterous welcoming of the worse, the all-pervading desire to inculcate disdain for everything black'. In Cuba, during the wars of independence of the 1890s, Cuban rebels referred to 'the venomous tongues' and 'the prejudices, suspicions, mistrusts and false slanders of the Caucasian group' who felt 'hatred for blacks'. In the context of the 1912 violence that targeted Afrocubans, there were references to 'racist rebellion' and 'race war' (Helg, 1995, pp. 70, 214). Martí in *Nuestra América* talks of '*el odio de razas*' (race hatred) and the Colombian indigenous leader Manuel Quintín Lame also talks of *odio* in his 1939 autobiographical text originally titled *Los pensamientos del indio que se educó dentro de las selvas colombianas*, published later as *En defensa de mi raza* (Lame Chantre, 1971). In *A Voz da Raça*, the newspaper of the Frente Negra Brasileira, published between 1933 and 1937, the word *racismo* is not found, but the term *preconceito de raça* is frequently used and lamented as an obstacle to Afrobrazilian integration.[6] The Afrocolombian politician, Natanael Díaz, titled a 1948 essay 'Discurso de un negro colombiano sobre la discriminación racial' – although he talked mainly about US discrimination against Latin Americans, a common preoccupation

---

5   Early uses of racism were similar to a typical present-day definition, which says racism is the belief that all members of each race have specific characteristics and abilities, and that these distinguish each race as inferior or superior to other races.

6   See the digitised collection of the newspaper, accessible at http://bndigital.bn.br/acervo-digital/voz-raca/845027 (accessed 27 Feb. 2019).

of Colombian intellectuals touching on questions of racism, such as the lawyer and educator Rafael Bernal Jiménez, who in a 1946 text decried any such 'racist criterion' as unsuited to the Colombian context (Pisano, 2012, pp. 37, 55).

In recent decades, the use in Latin America of the term racism – and allied terms such as racial discrimination – has been uneven. First, racism in a broad sense was frequently targeted by black social movements from the 1960s onwards, which took inspiration from the US and South African black resistance movements. The word racism itself was not often used. For example, a 1985 book by the founder of Colombia's black human rights organisation, Cimarrón, uses the word racism but far less frequently than the words racial discrimination and racial hatred (Mosquera, 1985). Brazil's Movimento Negro Unificado, founded in 1978, was initially called Movimento Negro Unificado Contra a Discriminação Racial, although potted histories of the organisation on the internet usually describe it as fighting against racism. Meanwhile, indigenous movements have often been more circumspect in their use of these terms, partly because they have tended to mobilise around culture and 'ethnicity': discussions about racism and racial discrimination and prejudice in Latin America more often than not continue to evoke ideas about Afrodescendant people.

With the multicultural turn of the 1990s, political and legal reforms throughout Latin America redefined the nation as pluriethnic and multicultural, extending existing rights and recognising new ones for indigenous peoples (Van Cott, 2000). Initially, only a few countries encompassed Afrodescendant people in these reforms, but over the last 25 years this number has been growing – for example, nowadays most countries do at least count Afrodescendants in their censuses (Loveman, 2014). In this context, black communities in several Latin American countries started to define themselves in cultural terms in order to appear legible to state agendas that recognised the historical cultural difference exemplified, in the state's eyes, by indigenous peoples: this happened in Colombia and Honduras, for example, where black mobilisation focused on land rights for rural black communities (Hooker, 2005). In this conjuncture, questions of racism, which had inspired the Afrocolombian black movement, were temporarily sidelined. As with the term race, Brazil was an exception to this trend because, while the reforms there included measures for black rural communities, they were primarily directed at urban black populations and their exclusion (Htun, 2004).

More recently, racism – and anti-racism[7] – has been taking centre stage. The Afrocolombian movement, for example, has shifted a little towards the fact that the majority of black Colombians do not live in rural areas but rather in cities, where exclusion from markets is of more concern than land rights.

---

7   The precise word *anti-racismo* is not often found in Latin America; the use of the prefix anti- is often said to be an Anglicism. Instead, one sees phrases such as *la lucha contra el racismo* [the struggle against racism].

The state has responded by supporting publicity campaigns with names such as the Campaña Nacional Contra el Racismo (2009), and in 2015, as part of the International Decade of Afrodescendants declared by the UN (2015–24), Hora Contra el Racismo and Ponga la Cara al Racismo. In many countries, racism has been banned and even criminalised, usually in terms of acts of racial discrimination or hate. In Brazil, the 1951 Afonso Arinos Act defined exclusions motivated by 'racial or colour prejudice' as a misdemeanour, while the 1989 Caó Law defined as a crime any discrimination due to race or colour (or ethnicity, religion or nationality). Bolivia passed a 2010 Law Against Racism and All Forms of Discrimination and in 2011 Colombia legislated against 'acts of racism and discrimination' (Law 1482). Many countries do not have specific laws against racism, but instead outlaw acts of 'discrimination' in general, on grounds of age, colour, race, disability, sex, cultural and ethnic origin, language, pregnancy, religion and so on. Mexico, for example, has a state agency, Consejo Nacional para Prevenir la Discriminación (CONAPRED), which addresses a wide range of discriminations. Likewise, Argentina has the Instituto Nacional contra la Discriminación, la Xenofobia y el Racismo (INADI), in which, as the name indicates, racism features alongside other forms of discrimination. In addition, indigenous movements remain ambiguous about their use of the concept of racism. The Colombian regional organisation, CRIC (Consejo Regional Indígena del Cauca), uses the terms racism and racial discrimination fairly frequently on its website, while the Ecuadorian movement, CONAIE, refers to them much less often and only in passing as part of a list that includes xenophobia and other forms of discrimination.[8]

Racism and discrimination

This exploration of the use of specific terms raises a number of conceptual issues. First, should racial discrimination be encompassed in a generic concept of discrimination? Second, does discrimination against indigenous peoples in Latin America count as racism, even if they tend to avoid the term? Third, is racism the same as racial discrimination?

These questions require a clear grasp of what racism is – a question that, as the different understandings of the term highlighted in the previous section indicate, has been answered in diverse ways (Banton, 2015; Goldberg, 1993; Miles and Brown, 2003; Wade, 2002). As we stated above, however, we see racism as a product of colonial and postcolonial relations of domination and inequality in a global world order. In turn, we take racism to be the product of two intersecting processes (Wade, 2015). The first set of processes concerns *modes*

---

8   See https://conaie.org and http://www.cric-colombia.org (both accessed 27 Feb. 2019). It seems, anecdotally, that when violence (symbolic or actual) against indigenous people is involved, there may be a greater tendency to refer to racism (Calla and Muruchi, 2011; Casaús Arzú, 2014).

of classification of people (and other life-forms). Classification can use diverse criteria, but one set of linked features refers to a perceived internal embodied essence, thought to derive in some way from the relationship of the body to the environment (understood to include elements that we would today separate out as natural, cultural and supernatural); this essence is transgenerational (that is, hereditary in a broad sense, encompassing cultural and sexual reproduction), and somewhat durable, albeit not fixed; and it is perceived to correspond to observable physique, constitutional qualities and behaviours. These ideas about people are very widespread across space and time, and they are not all usefully thought of as racial. The version of them most typically associated with race and racism is that which involves ideas about 'blood' or biology determining other non-biological qualities (intelligence, moral qualities, culture, and so on). This particular and limited version is characteristic of 19th-century Euro-American racial theory.

The second set of processes involves historical processes of conquest of one geographical area by another. The defining case for race is European colonialism, starting in about the 15th century. But there is a good case for thinking about Japanese colonialism too (Weiner, 1995), and Russian colonialism is another relevant area (Zakharov, 2013). These colonial processes created a context in which a specific set of ideas about human difference became articulated to structures of power difference and economic domination. In the New World, Iberian concepts of *limpieza de sangre* formed a crucible in which ideas about religious belief and practice, seen as partly carried in the blood, were gradually transmuted into ideas about human behaviour and constitution more generally (Hering Torres et al., 2012; Martínez, 2008). In the process, specific historically constructed categories of people emerged – typically in Latin America and the Caribbean, *negros*, *indios*, *blancos*, *mestizos*, and so on. Thus racism is the product of both the articulation of a set of ideas about human difference and also a set of processes of the construction and reproduction of power difference.

This approach suggests some answers to our three questions. First, racism is not the same as other forms of discrimination, which do not involve this same articulation. Racism has a particular history, which it still carries today, for example, in the form of specific sets of stereotypes about black, indigenous, white and mestizo people (among others); and in ideas about where they all sit in relation to each other in the value and power hierarchies that organise nations, wider regions and the globe. Second, discrimination against indigenous peoples counts, in analytic terms, as racism because it is rooted in this history. It does not matter that indigenous people are usually classified on the basis of language, residence, dress and so on, rather than biology – although this standard understanding of indigenous people as defined in terms of ethnicity rather than race does not do justice to the role ideas about physical appearance and biology do actually play in racism against indigenous (and mestizo) people (Hale, 2006, pp. 24–5; Moreno Figueroa, 2010; Nelson,

1999, pp. 206–44; Roberts, 2012). What matters is that the category *indio/indígena* derives from a colonial history, and that the difference between this category and others is understood in terms of ingrained transgenerational characteristics. Third, racism is not identical to racial discrimination, insofar as the latter tends to focus the attention on individual acts and attitudes, while the former should refocus our gaze towards culturally embedded systems of belief and value, and socially pervasive structures of discrimination and privilege. Together they are the complex product of these colonial histories and may be reproduced independently of individual acts which can easily be labelled as racial discrimination. In this sense, it is interesting that the term racism is increasingly appearing in public discourse – although this does not remove the possibility that it is being recognised in a purely tokenistic way.

This empirical and conceptual context indicates that racism is arguably gaining more traction than previously, both as a concern for social movements (even if they do not use the term itself) and for the state (even if it too avoids the term and may seek to ignore its structural dimensions). We can now move onto the more specific focus of this book and its authors, namely what role do creative practices play in combatting racism?

The role of cultural production in anti-racism

As noted at the beginning of this introduction, a key source of inspiration for this book was the idea that creative practices of various kinds offered a specific window onto racism, anti-racism and thinking about racial difference more generally. Much anti-racism tends to be channelled into certain domains of action: a) social policy, involving a bureaucratic logic in which racialised disparities are measured using statistical methods, leading to concrete policies designed to correct the inequalities; b) law, entailing the prohibition and perhaps criminalisation of racist acts, such as racial discrimination and racially motivated hate speech or attacks; and c) education, aimed at raising awareness of the biological non-existence of race, the social constructedness of race, the possibility of unconscious racism and the moral imperative of liberal tolerance, building on abstract ideas of human equality and the value of fairness. All these important realms of action have in common an underlying rationality of a Weberian bureaucratic kind, in which means and ends are clearly defined and their relationship assessed with utilitarian criteria of efficiency, with the aim of establishing structures to regulate human agency. However, although racism may have an element of utilitarian motivation ('we want to protect our jobs/schools/neighbourhoods/morals'), it is also driven by some profoundly non-rational and visceral emotions, rooted in the psychic dynamics of the mutual constitution of self and other, and involving sentiments of hate, fear, suspicion, envy, desire and pleasure. In this sense, rational responses to racism may always be missing a vital trick: 'There is always "more than reason", whether this be power, nonnegotiable and axiomatic value differences, or the never-ending assertions of conflict and alterity' (Benhabib, 1996, p. 14). As Stoler (2004, p. 5) argues, sentiment should be seen as part of 'the substance of politics' rather than as a mere embellishment of it.

Despite the incursions of neoliberal managerialism into the arts sector, creative artistic practice arguably operates in a different way to bureaucratic rationality, a way that allows it to engage more readily with the emotive side of racism. In Sommer's words, cultural agency can create 'wiggle room' in the interstices of social structures, whether these are the structures that reproduce racial hierarchy or the anti-racist structures set up by the operation of bureaucratic rationality. This wiggle room – though always subject to appropriation and re-colonisation by dominant forces – has the potential to enhance self-confidence and strengthen ethical subject formation, by suggesting new structures of feeling (Sommer, 2005). Art and politics have been seen to articulate powerfully because artistic practices and representations have an affective intensity, which goes beyond the purely propositional logic that may also be extracted from them by an analytic gaze (Beasley-Murray, 2010; Flynn and Tinius, 2015; Sommer, 2005, 2014; Thompson, 2014).

Specifically within Latin America and the Caribbean, alongside other acts of resistance to racial oppression, including slave rebellions, indigenous uprisings, the work of race-based NGOs and state legislation, cultural production has a long history of anti-racist discourse. Just as, say, *casta* paintings, foundational literary texts and anthropological photography all played a part in establishing and reinforcing the racialised organisation of society, artists and writers have long used culture as a means of attempting to wrest back control of racial discourses and visualities. In Peru, for example, artists, photographers and writers in the first half of the 20th century tried to rebalance the dominance of Limeño discourses of white Hispanic superiority by inscribing indigenous populations and their cultural practices into notions of national and regional identities (De la Cadena, 2000). At roughly the same time, in the Francophone Caribbean, the authors associated with the *négritude* movement were using literature to express a radical critique of colonialism and to rethink black identity in pan-African terms. In Mexico, muralism acted as a channel to denounce racism in different ways, from earlier works by Diego Rivera, David Siqueiros and José Clemente Orozco to Zapatista murals, like the one destroyed by the Mexican army in the municipality of Taniperla (and later reproduced in other cities in the world as a gesture of solidarity). These few well-known examples demonstrate the rich tradition of anti-racist art in 20th-century Latin America and the Caribbean, and situate the cultural products discussed in this volume – most of them, contemporary – in a historical perspective. As will be shown, some of the artistic manifestations analysed in this book engage in critical dialogues with the ways in which race has featured – both in progressive and regressive forms – in older forms of Latin American artistic production.

As mentioned, a central argument of this volume is that the mobilisation of affect by cultural products allows for new ways of thinking about anti-racist strategy. An example of this affective traction is provided by Montero-Diaz's chapter on 'white *cholos*' – as she calls young music fusionist innovators from Lima's upper class who experiment with genres, traditionally rejected by this self-same social sector due to their association with urban mestizos. She traces the routes through which musical empathy crosses racial difference and redounds on privileged people, encouraging them to question their own positions and assumptions. But she also shows how the desire for social change expressed by white upper-class musicians is simultaneously inscribed through racial prejudice or ignorance. The precarious nature of this empathy is suggested by the way poorer musicians challenge white *cholos* on the grounds that they have never personally suffered hardships of poverty and racism and thus cannot produce 'authentic' musical forms associated with, say, marginality and the street. Montero-Diaz also highlights the imbricated nature of race and gender when describing the young white female percussionist who felt the need to assert herself against the stereotypical portrayal of percussionists in this style of music as working-class black men. That her legitimacy was also undermined by her sex is unsurprising given the complex intersections of accumulated meanings that construct the image of the working-class black man, located in what Collins (1990) calls a matrix of domination.

Similar concerns over the portability (or not) of racial affects emerge from Klein's chapter about how people invest time and energy in anti-racist education. She examines the recent implementation of legislation in Brazil that makes the teaching of Afrobrazilian history compulsory in secondary schools, focusing on the experience of a group of teachers who also negotiate their own racial identity and involvement in anti-racism in a context of the well-established criticism of Brazil's myth of racial democracy. Klein highlights the importance of looking at the everyday practices of those tasked with carrying out anti-racism, and shows that commitment to this agenda emerges from personal experiences. But she further demonstrates that this domain can encompass the possibility of a non-black person 'becoming black' through a process of coming to consciousness about the operation of racism in Brazil and thus their own position of privilege, a process which is at least as empathetic and affective as it is rational.

The potential of affect within anti-racist cultural production is evident in Viala's analysis of artists of Caribbean origin who try to turn spectators into implicated viewers, or even actors, through the mobilisation of empathy, re-enactment and irony as techniques to induce audience members to participate in a sense of restorative justice. Reflecting on current demands for reparations in relation to Caribbean slavery, Viala argues that contemporary art offers a privileged body of work to explore anti-racism precisely because its practices of visuality encourage affective encounters. She traces how three artists, who address different dimensions of colonial power structures, use images, objects and acts of cremation, whipping and bondage to draw audience members into a visceral encounter with the history of enslavement without falling into the trap of victimisation. Viala too is aware of the gendered nature of race: though both the female Jeannete Ehlers and the male Ano resignify tools of slave torture in their artwork, Ehlers's appropriation of the whip to challenge 'codes of white-male supremacy' has a rather different resonance to a black man wearing a representation of an iron collar. Enslavement for black men was highly charged with gendered and sexualised meanings – around emasculation and control – and these have been subject to many reassertions of black masculinity (Nagel, 2003). In Viala's examples, however, it is the woman who taps right into the root of sexualised racial domination by the very fact of her gender, a reminder of the dense historical matrix of accumulated meanings that constructs the figure of the subordinate black female. Being more than the sum of its parts, this matrix has a particular power to provoke affective reactions.

Gleghorn's chapter likewise explores techniques of engaging an audience, here via innovative cinematic techniques that take aim at viewers' habitual, perhaps emotionally charged, reading practices, which may unpredictably undermine explicitly anti-racist messages aimed at the rational consciousness. She shows how some contemporary indigenous filmmakers choose to deploy archival footage from a past, but not entirely foreign, era, which unselfconsciously depicts racial inequality and hierarchy. As such, these films exemplify the critical dialogues, mentioned above, in which current artistic manifestations converse with older forms of racist cultural production. More importantly, the technique deployed engages with affect, using subtle images of the past to perform a series of 'aberrant readings' that resignify racist imagery from the present.

Oliart and Triquell make a similar argument about the photographs used by Colectivo Manifiesto, an Argentinian artistic collective whose members are intent on constructing alternative narratives and images of political sociality, based on representations of people usually classed as socially and racially marginal. The images try to capture the embodied presence of the inhabitants of the *villas* (areas of informal housing) of Córdoba, the country's second most populous city, who are stereotyped as *negros* – a term used in Argentina to racialise the urban poor, who are usually of mestizo background. The photographers found that they needed to add text to the photos to stave off the purposefully racist appropriations to which unadorned images could be subjected on social media. Oliart and Triquell also show how, in Peru, the photographer Adrián Portugal produces images of people associated with typically working-class neighbourhoods and cultural forms, such as cumbia music. His portraits of lower-class people in public events (protests, concerts) seek to challenge the connections between the mestizo precariat of Lima and racial and social violence and marginalisation. Portugal uses photography to recentre these individuals in Peruvian society by labelling them exemplary citizens, who nevertheless draw their visceral strength and embodied visual power from the multitudes that surround them in the images.

Oliart and Triquell's account of Portugal's photographs also addresses the intersection of race and gender. They argue that, by positioning the female 'exemplary Peruvian' cumbia dancer centre-stage, the photographer gives her an agency that challenges prevailing sexist attitudes. But the depiction of the male 'exemplary Peruvian' – an indigenous hero riding on the shoulders of other men and demanding attention from the authorities – is very different to the scantily-clad female body being observed by the largely male audience. Both figures say something about the assertion of racialised identity, but their juxtaposition highlights the gendered aspects of that assertion, which reinforces dominant gender images.

Stobart's account of the Bolivian indigenous musician, Gregorio Mamani, also interrogates these thorny questions of the affective directions of artistic practices. He argues that the 2006 election of Evo Morales potentiated indigenous identity practices around 'native' culture, such as music, dance and dress. One result of Evo's election was that Gregorio, who had produced music videos supporting Evo during his electoral campaign, was appointed director of the Municipal and Community Empowerment Service for the province of Chuquisaca. The light-skinned elites' feelings of threat and fear at the election of Morales were channelled in part through campaigns to have Sucre, provincial capital of their regional power base, replace La Paz as the national capital. These *capitalía* protests in 2008 famously involved incidents of explicitly racist violence and the humiliation of local indigenous people. But native cultural expressions have also been commodified for, and stylistically adapted to, middle-class and tourist tastes with the active participation of artists such as Mamani, who defended their 'authenticity' in exclusivist and protectionist ways. The question then arises of the extent to which the promotion of indigenous identity and culture simply hardened racial antagonism and encouraged consumerist appropriation. Nevertheless, Stobart, like others in this book, finds grounds for more positive assessments. While certain sectors of the population, who feel their privilege is becoming precarious, might react with fear, resentment and violence, others feel less threatened and are interested in creating intercultural collaborations, often around specific political and cultural projects, such as supporting the election of Evo or running music and dance groups for young people.

An intriguing case, which offers scope for more detailed research, is that of the Afrobolivian king, analysed by Schubmann in her essay on music and identity in Bolivia. It is an exceptional, even unique, case in modern Latin America. The story of the king makes explicit reference to traditions of African kingship, although the Afrobolivian king's attire is reminiscent of European regal symbols rather than African ones, which may conceivably establish a link with the colonial-era 'kings' of black lay religious orders.⁹ This fits with a strategy of highlighting African origins and thus Afro distinctiveness in the nation, which is common in the context of Afrodescendant mobilisations in Latin America. But the particular figure of the king raises questions about the affective traction of a regal figure in a republic based on the overthrow of monarchical rule, not least in a country where a nominally socialist president is in charge. The recognition of the king by the La Paz prefecture is ambiguous and ambivalent: on the one hand, it is a mark of respect (conceding royalty, no less); on the other, it is almost a joke (what can royalty mean in this context?); on the one hand, it recognises autonomy (regal sovereignty); on the other, it is a clear tactic of co-optation in which the tokenism is indicated by the simple fact of recognising a 'king'.

*****

The contributions to this book highlight the ongoing and crucial role that artistic and cultural production can play in enacting and promoting anti-racist discourse and practice in Latin America and the Caribbean. Whether in terms of reappropriating racist legacies by refashioning the material past of instruments of slavery or the visual prejudices of the anthropological archive linked to indigeneity, or in terms of demonstrating how notions of whiteness, blackness, indigeneity and mixedness can be taken up and shared as part of a process of affective encounters, artistic cultural production has a specific role to play within anti-racism. At the same time, however, there are clear signs that cultural productions can be co-opted or misdirected by white elites, the market or the state more broadly and incorporated into low-intensity versions of multiculturalism that celebrate diversity without fully acknowledging or addressing the persistence of racism and inequality in the region.

In this respect, the contribution to anti-racism made by the law in general and cultural policy in particular is indeterminate. While Klein argues that ethno-educational legislation provides opportunities for supporters to 'leverage its legal authority', she acknowledges that they have to be 'creative and come up with innovative ways' to make it work. Stobart is even more ambivalent: he appreciates that indigenous people can now use 'legal weapons [around intellectual property rights] previously employed to exclude them' and he speculates that young middle-class mestizo people in Bolivia may now be more open to egalitarian interactions with their indigenous maids; but overall he concludes that the situation has not moved much beyond the notion of the *indio permitido*. In contrast, Morgan sees multiculturalist laws in Colombia as ineffective in the face of intensifying extractivism, land-grabs and violence. This indicates the general finding that discourses of anti-racism have the

---

9   See, for example, Jean-Baptiste Debret's 1828 watercolour of *Coleta para a manutenção da igreja de Nossa Senhora do Rosário* at https://goo.gl/images/TCsNz6 (accessed 28 Feb. 2019).

potential to obfuscate other demands more specifically focused on class, gender and citizenship.

All those wishing to use cultural production to address the structural inequalities of racism in Latin America, the Caribbean and beyond, will need to concentrate on resolving those tensions. In this regard, we have suggested that Latin America and the Caribbean may be a useful site of cognition for thinking about anti-racism more widely. The region clearly demonstrates that racism and racial conviviality readily co-exist. Ideas about race mixture are always double-edged, in that they can be a specific manifestation of racism, based on a hierarchy of degrees of mixture and closeness to whiteness. But there may also be ways in which the productive possibilities contained within the ideas and practices of *mestizaje*, above all when conceived as a process not dominated by whiteness, can be exploited to generate broad anti-racist alliances, building on elements of racial conviviality in everyday life.

Bibliography

Banton, M. (2015) *What We Now Know About Race and Ethnicity* (Oxford: Berghahn Books).

Beasley-Murray, J. (2010) *Posthegemony: Political Theory and Latin America* (Minneapolis, MN: University of Minnesota Press).

Benhabib, S. (ed.) (1996) *Democracy and Difference: Contesting the Boundaries of the Political* (Princeton, NJ: Princeton University Press).

Calla, A. and K. Muruchi (2011) 'Transgressions and racism: the struggle over a new constitution in Bolivia', in L. Gotkowitz (ed.), *Histories of Race and Racism: The Andes and Mesoamerica from Colonial Times to the Present* (Durham, NC: Duke University Press), pp. 299–310.

Casaús Arzú, M. (2014) 'Las expresiones de odio y racismo en la opinión pública guatemalteca durante el juicio por genocidio contra el general Ríos Montt', *Interdisciplina,* 2 (4): 75–96.

Collins, P.H. (1990) *Black Feminist Thought: Knowledge, Consciousness and the Politics of Empowerment* (New York: Routledge).

Cox, O.C. (1948) *Caste, Class and Race: A Study of Social Dynamics* (New York: Doubleday).

Da Costa, A.E. (2014) *Reimagining Black Difference and Politics in Brazil: From Racial Democracy to Multiculturalism* (New York: Palgrave Macmillan).

— (2016) 'Thinking "post-racial" ideology transnationally: the contemporary politics of race and indigeneity in the Americas', *Critical Sociology*, 42 (4–5): 475–90.

De la Cadena, M. (2000) *Indigenous Mestizos: The Politics of Race and Culture in Cuzco, 1919–1991* (Durham, NC: Duke University Press).

Du Bois, W.E.B. (1897) 'Strivings of the negro people', *Atlantic Monthly*, 80: 194–8.

Flynn, A. and J. Tinius (eds.) (2015) *Anthropology, Theatre, and Development: The Transformative Potential of Performance* (Basingstoke: Palgrave Macmillan).

French, J.H. (2009) *Legalizing Identities: Becoming Black or Indian in Brazil's Northeast* (Chapel Hill, NC: University of North Carolina Press).

Fryer, R.G., Jr. (2007) 'Guess who's been coming to dinner? Trends in interracial marriage over the 20th century', *Journal of Economic Perspectives*, 21 (2): 71–90.

Gilroy, P. (2004) *After Empire: Melancholia or Convivial Culture* (London: Routledge).

Goldberg, D.T. (1993) *Racist Culture: Philosophy and the Politics of Meaning* (Oxford: Blackwell).

— (2008) *The Threat of Race: Reflections on Racial Neoliberalism* (Malden, MA: Wiley-Blackwell).

Guevara, E. (2005) *Diarios de motocicleta: notas de un viaje por América Latina* (Buenos Aires: Planeta).

Hale, C.R. (2006) *Más que un indio (More than an Indian): Racial Ambivalence and Neoliberal Multiculturalism in Guatemala* (Santa Fe, NM: School of American Research Press).

Hartigan, J. (2013) 'Translating "race" and "raza" between the United States and Mexico', *North American Dialogue*, 16 (1): 29–41.

Helg, A. (1995) *Our Rightful Share: The Afro-Cuban Struggle for Equality, 1886–1912* (Chapel Hill, NC: University of North Carolina Press).

Hering Torres, M.S., M.E. Martinez and D. Nirenberg (2012) *Race and Blood in the Iberian World* (Berlin: Lit Verlag).

Hernández, T.K. (2013) *Racial Subordination in Latin America: The Role of the State, Customary Law, and the New Civil Rights Response* (Cambridge: Cambridge University Press).

Hooker, J. (2005) 'Indigenous inclusion/black exclusion: race, ethnicity and multicultural citizenship in contemporary Latin America', *Journal of Latin American Studies*, 37 (2): 285–310.

Htun, M. (2004) 'From "racial democracy" to affirmative action: changing state policy on race in Brazil', *Latin American Research Review*, 39 (1): 60–89.

Ifekwunigwe, J.O. (ed.) (2004) *'Mixed Race' Studies: A Reader* (London: Routledge).

Ingenieros, J. (1918 [1908]) *Sociología Argentina* (Buenos Aires: L.J. Rosso).

Jiménez López, M., L.L.d. Mesa, C.T. Umaña, J. Bejarano, S. Araújo, L. Caballero, et al. (1920) *Los problemas de la raza en Colombia* (Bogotá: El Espectador).

Lakhani, N. (2015) *Guatemala Election Puts Latin America's Aaffinity for Racist Caricatures in Spotlight* [cited 9 Jan. 2018], available at: https://www.theguardian.com/world/2015/oct/21/guatemala-election-latin-america-racist-caricatures (accessed 4 April 2019).

Lame Chantre, M.Q. (1971) *En defensa de mi raza*, with an introduction and notes by Gonzalo Castillo Cárdenas (Bogotá: Rosca de Investigación y Acción Social).

Lentin, A. (2011) 'What happens to anti-racism when we are post race?', *Feminist Legal Studies*, 19 (2): 159–68.

— (2014) 'Post-race, post politics: the paradoxical rise of culture after multiculturalism', *Ethnic and Racial Studies*, 37 (8): 1268–85.

Loveman, M. (2014) *National Colors: Racial Classification and the State in Latin America* (New York: Oxford University Press).

Martí, J. (1891) 'Nuestra América', *La Revista Ilustrada de Nueva York*, 10 Jan.

Martínez, M.E. (2008) *Genealogical Fictions: Limpieza de Sangre, Religion, and Gender in Colonial Mexico* (Stanford, CA: Stanford University Press).

Maxwell, R. (2012) *Ethnic Minority Migrants in Britain and France: Integration Trade-Offs* (Cambridge: Cambridge University Press).

McCaa, R. (1984) 'Calidad, clase and marriage in colonial Mexico: the case of Parral, 1788–90', *Hispanic American Historical Review*, 64 (3): 477–501.

Mignolo, W. (2011) *The Darker side of Western Modernity: Global Futures, Decolonial Options* (Durham, NC: Duke University Press).

Miles, R. and M. Brown (2003) *Racism* (London: Routledge).

Molina Enríquez, A. (2004 [1909]) *Los grandes problemas nacionales*, (Alicante: Biblioteca Virtual Miguel de Cervantes).

Moreno Figueroa, M. (2010) 'Distributed intensities: whiteness, mestizaje and the logics of Mexican racism', *Ethnicities*, 10 (3): 387–401.

— (2012) '"Linda morenita": skin colour, beauty and the politics of mestizaje in Mexico', in C. Horrocks (ed.), *Cultures of Colour: Visual, Material, Textual* (Oxford: Berghahn Books), pp. 167–80.

Moreno Figueroa, M. and E. Saldívar (2016) '"We are not racists, we are Mexicans": privilege, nationalism and post-race ideology in Mexico', *Critical Sociology*, 42 (4–5): 515–33.

Mosquera, J. de D. (1985) *Las comunidades negras de Colombia* (Medellín: Editorial Lealon).

Mukherjee, R. (2016) 'Antiracism limited', *Cultural Studies*, 30 (1): 47–77.

Nagel, J. (2003) *Race, Ethnicity, and Sexuality: Intimate Intersections, Forbidden Frontiers* (Oxford: Oxford University Press).

Nelson, D.M. (1999) *A Finger in the Wound: Body Politics in Quincentennial Guatemala* (Berkeley, CA: California University Press).

Ng'weno, B. (2007) *Turf Wars: Territory and Citizenship in the Contemporary State* (Stanford, CA: Stanford University Press).

Office for National Statistics (2014) *2011 Census analysis: what does the 2011 Census tell us about inter-ethnic relationships?* [cited 31 Oct. 2017], available at: https://www.ons.gov.uk/peoplepopulationandcommunity/birthsdeathsandmarriages/marriagecohabitationandcivilpartnerships/articles/whatdoesthe2011censustellusaboutinterethnicrelationships/2014-07-03 (accessed 4 April 2019).

Palacios, N. (1918 [1904]) *Raza chilena: libro escrito por un chileno y para los chilenos* (Santiago de Chile: Editorial Chilena).

Pisano, P. (2012) *Liderazgo político "negro" en Colombia, 1943–1964* (Bogotá: Universidad Nacional de Colombia).

Quijano, A. (2007) 'Coloniality and modernity/rationality', *Cultural Studies*, 21 (2–3): 168–78.

Rahier, J.M. (2014) *Blackness in the Andes: Ethnographic Vignettes of Cultural Politics in the Time of Multiculturalism* (New York: Palgrave Macmillan).

Redclift, V. (2014) 'New racisms, new racial subjects? The neo-liberal moment and the racial landscape of contemporary Britain', *Ethnic and Racial Studies*, 37 (4): 577–88.

Restrepo, E. and A. Rojas (2010) *Inflexión decolonial: fuentes, conceptos y cuestionamientos* (Popayán: Editorial Universidad del Cauca).

Roberts, E.F.S. (2012) *God's Laboratory: Assisted Reproduction in the Andes* (Berkeley, CA: University of California Press).

Root, M.P.P. (ed.) (1996) *The Multiracial Experience: Racial Borders as the New Frontier* (Thousand Oaks: Sage).

Sarmiento, D.F. (1883) *Conflicto y armonías de las razas en América* (Buenos Aires: Imprenta de D. Tuñez).

Seigel, M. (2009) *Uneven Encounters: Making Race and Nation in Brazil and the United States* (Durham, NC: Duke University Press).

Sommer, D. (ed.) (2005) *Cultural Agency in the Americas* (Durham, NC: Duke University Press).

— (2014) *The Work of Art in the World: Civic Agency and Public Humanities* (Durham, NC: Duke University Press).

Stepan, N.L. (1991) *"The Hour of Eugenics": Race, Gender and Nation in Latin America* (Ithaca, NY: Cornell University Press).

Stolcke, V. (1995) 'Talking culture: new boundaries, new rhetorics of exclusion in Europe', *Current Anthropology*, 36 (1): 1–23.

Stoler, A.L. (2004) 'Affective states', in D. Nugent and J. Vincent (eds.), *A Companion to the Anthropology of Politics* (Oxford: Blackwell), pp. 4–29.

Sue, C.A. (2013) *Land of the Cosmic Race: Race Mixture, Racism, and Blackness in Mexico* (New York: Oxford University Press).

Thompson, J. (2014) *Humanitarian Performance: From Disaster Tragedies to Spectacles of War* (Calcutta: Seagull Books).

Van Cott, D.L. (2000) *The Friendly Liquidation of the Past: The Politics of Diversity in Latin America* (Pittsburgh, PA: University of Pittsburgh Press).

Vasconcelos, J. (1997 [1925]) *The Cosmic Race: A Bilingual Edition* (Baltimore, MD: Johns Hopkins University Press).

Wade, P. (2002) *Race, Nature and Culture: An Anthropological Perspective* (London: Pluto Press).

— (2005) 'Rethinking mestizaje: ideology and lived experience', *Journal of Latin American Studies*, 37: 239–57.

— (2009) *Race and Sex in Latin America* (London: Pluto Press).

— (2010) *Race and Ethnicity in Latin America* (London: Pluto Press).

— (2015) *Race: An Introduction* (Cambridge: Cambridge University Press).

— (2017) *Degrees of Mixture, Degrees of Freedom: Genomics, Multiculturalism, and Race in Latin America* (Durham, NC: Duke University Press).

Wang, W. (2012) 'The rise of intermarriage: rates, characteristics vary by race and gender' (Washington: Pew Research Center), available at: https://www.pewresearch.org/wp-content/uploads/sites/3/2012/02/SDT-Intermarriage-II.pdf (accessed 15 May 2019).

Weiner, M. (1995) 'Discourses of race, nation and empire in pre-1945 Japan', *Ethnic and Racial Studies*, 18 (3): 433–56.

Werbner, P. (ed.) (2015) *Anthropology and the New Cosmopolitanism: Rooted, Feminist and Vernacular Perspectives* (London: Bloomsbury).

Wilson, W.J. (2011) 'The declining significance of race: revisited and revised', *Daedalus*, 140 (2): 55–69.

Zakharov, N. (2013) *Attaining Whiteness: A Sociological Study of Race and Racialization in Russia* (Uppsala: Uppsala University).

Zimmer, C. (2017). 'Genes for skin color rebut notions of race, researchers say', *New York Times*, 12 Oct., A9.

2. The antinomies of identity politics: neoliberalism, race and political participation in Colombia

Nick Morgan

The focus of this research is what might be thought of as Colombia's official culture of anti-racism, a term that seems decidedly out of place in a country where racism continues to be such an obvious everyday reality. Yet in some ways it is an apposite categorisation. After all, Colombia is a country in which the constitutional recognition of the rights of Afrocolombian and indigenous communities has led to nearly a third of the national territory being assigned to the jurisdiction of the traditional authorities of these minority groups (Paschel, 2016b, p. 57). An anti-discrimination law focusing particularly on racism, passed in 2011, the International Year of Afrodescendants, allows for the imprisonment of offenders for up to three years. State and municipal institutions have programmes emphasising the need for 'inclusion', a rather nebulous term, to be sure, but nonetheless one which implies the need to recognise the rights of minorities and promote their representation in public life. The *manuales de convivencia* that exist in all of Colombia's schools, both public and private, contain sections promoting tolerance and respect for ethnic or racial minorities. In short, the political and juridical foundations of the Colombian state enshrine the principle of equal rights and equal status of minority groups in a pluriethnic and multicultural state.

This framework has been shored up by other forms of official recognition. The designation of 21 May as the day of *afrocolombianidad*, albeit a rather weak move in a country where most days seem to have some profession or group attached to them, has been followed by official anti-racist programmes such as the Hora contra el racismo [Hour against Racism] and Ponga la cara al racismo [Face up to Racism], which have in turn been framed within the Afro Decade campaign launched by the ministry of the interior as part of a UN initiative. With its slogan 'Recognition, Justice and Development 2015–24', the programme aims at 'making visible the rights of Afrocolombians', a form of words that reworks the longstanding complaint about Afrocolombians' lack of visibility on the national stage in order to focus on the need to respect the rights they have already been afforded under the constitution and subsequent legislation.

N. Morgan, 'The antinomies of identity politics: neoliberalism, race and political participation in Colombia', in P. Wade, J. Scorer and I. Aguiló (eds.), *Cultures of Anti-Racism in Latin America and the Caribbean* (London: Institute of Latin American Studies, 2019), pp. 25–47. License: CC-BY-NC-ND 4.0.

The national media appear to have accepted and amplified these measures. Indeed, for some time now, casual everyday racism has been increasingly subject to critique in the public space created by the media. In 2012, Bogotá city councillor Jorge Durán Silva was forced into a humiliating apology after describing a rowdy meeting as a 'blacks' tea party', while in 2015, Caracol TV, one of Colombia's two main private TV channels was forced to retire the polemical blackface character, Soldado Micolta, played by mestizo comedian Roberto Lozano, from the popular comedy show *Sábados Felices*, after a complaint by the activist group Chao Racismo.

Most recently, Maurice Armitage, the mayor of Cali, a city with a large Afrocolombian population, found himself at the centre of a media storm for the racist tenor of comments made during an interview with TV news programme CM&, in which he linked football violence to the civic strike in the nearby port of Buenaventura, on the overwhelmingly black Pacific coast. His claim that Cali was 'an explosive city' where 'we have a million blacks and live with them in peace, we love them a lot but we have to be careful with this kind of violence', as a prime example of the 'othering' of the black population, while associating it unequivocally with violence (*El Espectador*, 2017). What made this statement even more embarrassing was that Ray Charrupí, president of Chao Racismo, had been taken on as a consultant by Armitage in an attempt to deal with the city's endemic racism, which has received increasing media attention in recent years. To make matters still worse, Armitage's administration had only just denounced *caleño* journalist Daniel Vivas's racist Twitter feed denigrating the annual Petronio Álvarez festival celebrating music from the Pacific littoral. 'What's that smell of shit?', tweeted Vivas. 'Ah, yes, the Petronio Álvarez has started' (Aldía, 2017). The tweet was promptly deleted, but a deluge of outrage ensued. Vivas's equally racist blog was removed by *El Tiempo* (2017), Colombia's main daily, after complaints by readers, leading to the editorial team issuing a statement noting that 'this newspaper reiterates its respect and admiration for the country's cultural traditions, which enhance its ethnic diversity and construct a pluralist and democratic identity'.

The public outcry, steered and editorialised by the media, exemplifies the everyday dynamics of an official or mainstream anti-racism, an assemblage of institutional arrangements and discourses, which has found an echo in the mainstream networks of cultural exchange. The political consequences of this nexus, whose emergence is the fruit of a long and arduous struggle by anti-racist activists within the Afrocolombian and indigenous population, as well as the adoption of anti-racist discourses by international institutions such as the World Bank, have been significant since its establishment through the constitution of 1991. Most strikingly, the disavowal of racism, once the default position of national institutions, has been replaced by an acceptance of its prevalence, alongside a blanket condemnation of all discriminatory practices.

Of course, not only do these examples themselves reveal the casual racism that continues to disfigure everyday life in Colombia but even at the moment of condemnation both the media and institutions frequently reproduce racist tropes. Institutions, after all, are made up of people, many of whom unreflectingly share commonly held racist assumptions. At the very least, stereotypical ways of thinking about race continue to make their appearance in public campaigns, exemplified by an anti-racist campaign organised in 2015 by the local administration in Bogotá. It showed the figure of an indigenous woman anchored by the slogan 'Don't discriminate, I'm in your blood', in the process reproducing a longstanding metaphor about the biological foundations of identity. Furthermore, as is so often the case, the fine intentions of official documents may exist in the statute books without being put into practice in everyday life. Between 2012 and 2016, for example, only one person was convicted under the anti-discrimination law, although 873 cases were brought. Most of the material pertaining to the Afro Decade campaign on the ministry of the interior's website is cut and pasted from UN documents, as the site itself acknowledges. When it comes to the specific contribution of the state to this process, we are simply informed that the Santos administration's development plan, based on the three pillars of peace, equity and education, will 'obviously' help all Colombians, since it has a multi-ethnic focus (DACN, 2015). In fact, it seems that the relationship between institutions and the ethnic minority population is often characterised by co-option and tokenism, as Afrocolombians and indigenous people remain underrepresented in Congress. Meanwhile those who have taken over ministerial portfolios have done so in areas that fit existing stereotypes about ethnic minorities, such as culture and the environment. Most importantly, by every available indicator these communities live shorter and more impoverished lives, receive worse public services, are offered poorer quality education and health care, and have provided a disproportionate number of victims of the violent encounters that have come to be known simply as the armed conflict.

The chasm between these social realities and the official adoption of an explicitly anti-racist stance invites us to explore the latter's role in the reproduction and contestation of power in one of the most unequal states in the most unequal region of the world. After all, the New Granadan social order, whose legacy continues to haunt contemporary Colombia, was founded on a hierarchy of difference that is now understood through the lens of race and ethnicity. For all that Malcolm Deas (1997, p. 358) notes that mid 19th century Colombia was 'in many respects [...] a more mobile, freer, less caste-bound, less deferential, more democratic society than its neighbours', the fact remains that the abject poverty that marked the lives of most of the million inhabitants of Nueva Granada at the time of independence, in stark contrast to the leisured classes, had not been alleviated at the turn of the 20th century. Colombia, its population then four million, remained one of the poorest and most unequal countries in the hemisphere. In spite of the economic lift-off of the 1920s and 30s, and the emergence of a middle class as a result of the increasing prosperity of the country from mid-century on, this fundamental inequality has not been overcome in two hundred years of republican history. While there was a modest redistribution of resources between the 1960s and the early 1980s, the advent of neoliberal economic policies put paid to Colombia's nascent welfare state in the 90s. World Bank figures for 2014 suggested Colombia had a GINI of over 53, rising to a staggering 86 in rural areas, putting it ahead of Brazil, Paraguay and Honduras in terms of inequality (World Bank, 2014; UNDP, 2011). Other estimates vary but, by any measure, Colombia's disparities in income and access to resources remain extraordinarily large.

Given that anti-racism sets out to combat the effects of particular historic forms of inequality, to talk about this struggle without considering the broader picture of inequality in the country is to miss an important point, as if the social order experienced by the mestizo majority were somehow fundamentally democratic and just. Furthermore, the prejudices associated with racism are not confined to attitudes to those who are identified as part of the black and indigenous populations, but permeate society as a whole. Indigenous-looking and dark-skinned mestizos still experience discrimination, and the imbrication in the social imaginary of notions of race and class continues to legitimise both racism and elitism. Combatting racism, in other words, is not simply a matter of integrating previously marginalised populations into a prevailing democratic order, but of challenging the sedimented history of inequality that continues to structure the contemporary political scene. In this respect, Paschel (2016a, p. 50) is right to note that anti-racist mobilisation may 'take multiple forms', singling out intellectuals, political leaders and activists like the Afrocuban Rafael Serra and the Afrocolombian Diego Luis Córdoba, 'who organized around regional identity and under a socialist platform'.

This is not to say that struggles over ethnicity should be abandoned in favour of class. On the contrary, my contention is that notions of race and class cannot properly be separated in the Colombian context. The left's failure to take ethnicity properly into account revealed a political blind spot, as revolutionary movements took for granted a vision of the mestizo nation that ignored the specificity of racial discrimination. All forms of politics are in a sense forms of identity politics, in that, rather than representing stable pre-constituted social phenomena, identities are articulated, claimed, and further developed through conflict. However, just as in the case of class, an emphasis on ethnicity to the exclusion of other factors is likely to obscure other patterns of dominance and subordination. In what follows, therefore, I focus on the case of Afrocolombians in order to consider the influence of the official recognition and condemnation of discrimination on recent political struggles in Colombia. In particular, the questions of the role current institutional arrangements envisage within the political system for ethnic minorities, of how these groups are constituted as political subjects, and how their relationship not only with the state but with other social actors has developed since 1991, are of crucial importance in contemporary political conflicts. The case studies that make up the second part of this chapter therefore, centre on how *afrocolombianidad* is constructed as a political identity in specific contexts, and in particular considers its role in attempts to construct a counterhegemonic movement capable of challenging the deep-seated inequalities that continue to shape everyday life.

Gramscian hegemony and identity politics

The framing of these questions places them within the general idiom of Gramscian hegemony theory, which will provide the overarching conceptual point of reference here, though it will not be taken as a precise model to be followed. As has often been pointed out, Gramsci's approach was very much an ad hoc one, and the many insights that can be gleaned from the hundreds of pages of notes written in Mussolini's jails do not represent a complete conceptual system. What Gramscian thinking does allow, however, is an approach that emphasises the multiplicity of factors through which modern societies have come to be, as Hall (1980) put it, structured in dominance, and the heterogeneous nature of both elite and subaltern groups, who forge their identities through struggle. It emphasises the importance of violence in the reproduction of power, a point often underplayed in understandings of Gramsci that focus on the role of consent, but which has a particular resonance in the Colombian context. It also concerns itself with the cultural dimension of power, whose importance is evident in the way social relationships become naturalised through forms of 'common sense' that contain the seeds of resistance, or as Gramsci (1971, p. 627) puts it, 'prejudices from all past phases of history ... and intuitions of a future philosophy'. In the process, it captures the fragmented, incomplete, and often contradictory nature of social being.

Colombia offers an intriguing case study for hegemony theory and the role of identity politics. Some might claim that the country's turbulent history is proof of a failure of hegemony, and therefore of the state's lack of legitimacy. Yet the stability of the country's social structure, which has been capable of tolerating relatively high levels of political violence, shows that in spite of the problems of legitimacy faced by the state, the reproduction of power and privilege has nonetheless been secured. The Gramscian concept that best captures, perhaps, Colombian politics over the turn of the century is 'passive revolution' (p. 288). This term refers to periods in which the alliance of groups that dominates a given polity faces a crisis. A passive revolution provides a temporary fix for the crisis by initiating change without substantially threatening the interests of the alliance of groups that exerts leadership in a particular social formation. In the Colombian case, the crisis was posed by the need to dismantle the last vestiges of the import substitution model, already largely abandoned in the 80s, and reposition the Colombian economy within corporate globalisation. The fix came through the promotion of extractive industry, industrial agribusiness, and the provision of services, particularly in the financial sector. In short, the passive revolution under way since the late 80s has effected a significant transformation of the local political economy without confronting the problem of inequality. The current negotiated surrender of the Revolutionary Armed Forces of Colombia (FARC) can be thought of as a part of this ongoing process, offering as it does enormous opportunities for a deepening of a neoliberal development model while posing real perils for popular movements.

This notion also affords insights into the constitution of 1991, which is seen as a milestone for its construction of a political and legal framework that institutionalises a form of multiculturalism, partly in terms of recognition and partly in terms of redistribution (Fraser, 1995). In spite of its limitations and ambiguities, it is generally interpreted as a progressive document that seeks to effect a shift in the status of historically excluded groups. Over the last decade a sector of the Colombian political class, essentially those groups supporting ex-president Alvaro Uribe, has been at war with a constitutional settlement perceived as too liberal, too permissive and too democratic. However, the constitution has long been the object of vigorous attacks from the left, who have criticised it as a neoliberalising document that paved the way for the privatisation of parts of the Colombian state, in a process described by Harvey (2004) as accumulation through dispossession. In the words of Mejía (2007, p. 236, my translation), 'Colombia's elites managed [...] through the imposition of a neoliberal model of development, to constitutionalise lies and cloak their historic strategy of domination in the seductive clothing of the social state of law and participatory democracy'.

The expansion of participatory programmes and the recognition of Afrocolombian and indigenous rights, therefore, need to be understood in the context of the neoliberalisation of the economy and the refusal of traditional elites to relinquish their privileges. This restructuring was not simply an elite conspiracy, imposed from above, but part of a series of struggles that have shaped a political scene which is not exactly what any group would have chosen, but which consistently favours the interests of a dominant bloc. As Mejía (2007, p. 236) notes, social democratic, multicultural, and neoliberal currents all coexist within the final document, the product of negotiations between very different political constituencies that included the Liberal party, the recently demobilised guerrillas of M-19, and Álvaro Gómez's right-wing Movement for National Salvation. Among its progressive features are the special rights afforded to what it designates as black and indigenous communities, offering them relative autonomy within territorial boundaries recognised by the state. These institutional shifts represent a significant break with the history of Colombian constitutionalism. Hitherto, republican appeals to citizenship and equality before the law helped to legitimise a national ideal of *mestizaje* that denied racism in the name of mixing, while continuing to discriminate not only against Afrocolombian and indigenous Colombians but also dark-skinned mestizos, whose features too clearly betrayed their proximity to the less favoured sources of race mixture. The constitutional protection of property and privilege discriminated against precisely these social identities, overrepresented among the poor. Indeed, the racism that characterises Colombian society is dependent on the reproduction of a particular kind of inequality that continues to stratify the nation in sociracial terms. In this respect, rather than accepting that, as Paschel (2016a, p. 47) puts it, 'class inequalities were arguably more salient than racial inequalities in the everyday lives of ordinary people', it should be argued that forms of discrimination based on race and class were mutually reinforcing to the extent that they were impossible to separate, even though neither is reducible to the other. In short, racism and elitism went hand in hand, as they do to this day, and it is this nexus, inherently racist in spite of its ambiguities, that was implicitly rejected by the constitutional recognition of minority rights.

A key aspect of the shift was the constitutional granting of special legal privileges on the basis of bound serialities. The distinction between bound and unbound serialities comes from the work of Benedict Anderson and Partha Chatterjee, who use the notion to distinguish between collective identities that are voluntarily adopted and those that are imposed by others. For Anderson (1998, p. 117), unbound serialities are those forms of collective identity that are open to all, 'such open-to-the-world plurals as nationalists, anarchists, bureaucrats, and workers', whereas bound serialities refer to identities whose membership is limited by categories such as race or ethnicity. From this perspective, unbound categories such as citizenship are potentially liberating, whereas bound serialities are understood as backward-looking and fundamentally exclusive, out of step with the universalising vision of a democratic politics. Furthermore, he is suspicious of attempts to divide the social field in this manner, as they allow the state to impose categories that allow it to control and manage populations.

Chatterjee, in contrast, sees bound serialities as a fact of political life – in some respects as *the* fact of political life – as the institutions of the state engage with populations divided into specific demographics. Borrowing a notion of Foucault's, both Anderson and Chatterjee contrast the universal ideals of democratic politics with governmentality. For his part, Chatterjee (2004, p. 4) identifies 'a conflict that lies at the heart of modern politics in most of the world', namely

> the opposition between the universal ideal of civic nationalism, based on individual freedoms and equal rights irrespective of distinctions of religion, race, language, or culture, and the particular demands of cultural identity, which call for the differential treatment of particular groups on grounds

of vulnerability or backwardness or historical injustice, or indeed for numerous other reasons.

This opposition, furthermore, 'is symptomatic of the transition that occurred in modern politics [...] from a conception of democratic politics grounded in the idea of popular sovereignty to one in which democratic politics is shaped by governmentality' (p. 4). In a further contrast to Anderson, Chatterjee sees the terrain of governmentality, marked by a specific set of relationships between institutions and 'populations', as the most significant space of popular politics, as opposed to the mechanisms of representative democracy that are the preserve of civil society which, in a return to Marx, he sees as 'the closed association of modern elite groups, sequestered from the wider popular life of the communities, walled up within enclaves of civic freedom and rational law' (p. 4).

As James Clifford (1998, p. 364) notes with regard to Anderson, this binary opposition tends to oversimplify the political field and risks freezing 'a moralized binary', and a similar critique might be made of Chatterjee's inversion of Anderson's position. However, the debate resonates in the Colombian context, not least because it captures something of what is at stake in the development of political identities. The allocation of specific rights to members of certain bound serialities introduced a new level of complexity into the country's politico-juridical structure, envisaged, in the manner described by Chatterjee, as a form of historic reparation. Afrocolombian and indigenous communities were guaranteed some measure of representation in Congress and limited autonomy in the territorially bounded communities recognised by the state. These communities received recognition and a degree of redistribution, while simultaneously being treated as a supplement, a historic remnant best dealt with in isolation. While special measures were envisaged for ethnic communities, a broader emphasis on participation sought to open the political process up to a more engaged citizenry. Thus, both the universalising possibilities invoked by unbound serialities and the dynamics of population classification and management present in their bound counterparts are apparent in the constitution. With regard to the former, the rhetoric of participation has proliferated in dozens of polities around the globe in the last fifty years but it has a specific history in Colombia, where the closed nature of the political system, particularly in the National Front period (1958–74), was frequently invoked by left-wing insurgencies as a justification for taking up arms. The constitutional settlement of 1991, therefore, sought to open up the democratic process, allowing a voice to all in 'the decisions that affect them', as article two proclaims. The constitutional emphasis on participation justified the development in the following years of a myriad of participatory spaces within the Colombian polity. However, these were overwhelmingly devoted to processes of popular consultation at a local level. Expressions of participatory democracy with genuine decisive power, such as participatory budgeting, have been confined in the main to a few timid experiments in some of the country's major cities.

It is striking, however, that programmes supposedly aimed at all citizens have generally been perceived in terms of bound serialities, though not those outlined in the constitution. Just as 'black' or indigenous populations were regarded as special cases, participatory programmes were targeted at marginalised communities, rather than the population as a whole. The word *comunidad*, so often invoked in these contexts, in practice designates vulnerable, territorially defined communities, whose influence on the national scene has historically been limited. Participation, in other words, has always been aimed at precise populations, identified by the state as victims of historic marginalisation, including, in the Bolivarian idiom, not only Afrocolombians and indigenous communities but 'the poor of all colours'. To borrow Chatterjee's frame of reference, it is one of the two main forms of engagement between the populations and the world of politics (the other being clientelism). Furthermore, the practical experience of participation in Colombia has more to do with governmentality than democracy, as local administrations have incorporated the notion into their practice across a broad range of dependencies. Contrary to the spirit of the constitution, vulnerable communities – often places where Afrocolombian and indigenous-looking people are overrepresented – have found it difficult to turn these relationships into an exercise in engaged citizenship. Instead, participatory programmes have represented a means for institutions to manage the demands and expectations of a categorised and classified population, while simultaneously legitimising their own systems of governance.

Beyond the political and juridical provisions of the new settlement, the promises of inclusion appeared in a fractured and sometimes violent political landscape. Passive revolutions are often accompanied by violence, and Colombia has been no exception. In the post-1991 period, just as land-titling for minority communities was taking place, an alliance between global corporate interests and local clientelistic networks deployed both paramilitary and state violence in order to carry out the greatest agrarian counter-reform in Colombian history. This simultaneously furthered a development model based on extractive industry and the promotion of industrial agribusiness, a process that has been going on throughout the global south. These groups, particularly powerful in the regions, are strongly represented in Congress, and have captured many branches of Colombia's hybrid state (López, 2010). In the words of Machado et al. (2017, p. 1075), the result is

> a paradoxical context where on one hand the country's ethnic and cultural diversity are recognised and, on the other, the imposition of an extractive economic model continues to cause displacement and devastating environmental conflicts, forcing communities to constantly defend their territories, rights, *cosmovisiones* [worldviews], and lifeways.

This is the broad political context which frames attempts to understand the place of institutional anti-racism and Afrocolombian activism in the struggle for equality. What, then, is the role of identity politics in the attempt to counter the ongoing top-down transformation of Colombian society? In order to explore this question, I want to consider three specific cases. My involvement with each took place during an extended period of fieldwork in Quibdó, the departmental capital of Chocó, where I was researching the municipal administration's attempts to forge a political alliance with urban communities that were mainly but not exclusively Afrocolombian. During this study of the relationship between the municipality and vulnerable communities in Quibdó's Comuna Dos [Second District], my focus was not the notion of *afrocolombianidad*, nor in fact Afrocolombian rights, but on problems of participation more generally in an urban area where specific differential rights did not apply. In the process, however, I was able to consider the way that ethnicity was constructed in a document outlining the political programme proposed by the local administration, and I will start with a brief discussion of how this document sets out to construct a unified political subject. Following this, I will refer to two specific events, the First Congress of the Pueblo Negro, Afrocolombiano, Palenquero and Raizal, held in Quibdó in August 2013, and the Cumbre Agraria, held in Bogotá in March 2014.

The *Quibdó MIA* development plan

Quibdó has in many respects been a symbol of poverty and the failure of the central state in its treatment of Afrocolombians. Unlike the rest of the Pacific lowlands, where the littoral is an adjunct of administrative centres located on the other side of the western *cordillera*, Chocó is at least nominally self-governing, having become a department in 1947, and being governed by a local Afrocolombian political class. This has allowed politicians and the media in the metropolitan centres to tap into the racist imaginary by claiming that the problems of the department are the result of local corruption, as if the scandals that periodically rock the rest of the country were mere figments of the imagination. In 2012, however, a new administration took over the running of the municipality, and promised to do politics differently. The programme of new mayor Zulia Mena, whose own political capital had been accrued through a long history of Afrocolombian activism, offered participation for the most marginalised sectors of the population in the construction and execution of a programme that would prioritise the needs of the most vulnerable in a city where over 80 per cent of the population have unsatisfied basic needs. Crowded with refugees from paramilitary offensives in the rest of the department, whose arrival put an increasing burden on already deficient public services, and surrounded by rivers contaminated by illegal gold mining, Quibdó was a challenging political context in which to promote participation.

Intriguingly, however, the new administration was also the first to foreground the identitarian tropes associated with the institutionalisation of a discourse of *afrocolombianidad*.

The Mena administration's development plan, *Quibdó MIA*, articulates a complex and contradictory political subject. Unusually for documents of this sort, it sets out a historical context, noting that centuries of exploitation, impoverishment and lack of opportunity have left the Afrochocoan population in a state of near 'mental incapacity' (Mena, 2012, p. 16), though there is no corresponding reference to the plight of indigenous communities. The cause of this suffering is identified as the 'absentee-extractivist economic model' (p. 16), in the ascendant during the institution of slavery, that expropriates local resources leaving nothing behind. The programme proposes to counter this historical dispossession by turning Quibdó into 'a world capital of biodiversity' (p. 12). At the same time, it promises to end corruption as 'the mechanism for achieving individual and collective interests' (p. 18), and 'diminish the traps of poverty' (p. 13).

The political subject that underpins this plan is the 'MIA' (mestizo, indigenous, Afrocolombian) of the programme's title, referred to at times as a 'multi-ethnic people', a term that foregrounds popular sovereignty while recognising the bound serialities that come into play in a municipality whose rural area includes collectively titled lands administered by Afrocolombian community councils and indigenous *cabildos* [traditional authorities]. Even when referring to the urban area, however, where no such special rights prevail, there is a tension in the document between the desire to produce a unified popular subject and the assertion of ethnic difference, apparent through the use of the word 'imaginary', which at various points in the text stands in for the notion of culture. Thus, the document sees its collective subject 'originating in the acceptance, integration and harmonization of the three existing ethnic imaginaries [...] and their achievements as ethnicities in the unique and logical construction of an idea of development that will make possible the bio-psycho-social wellbeing of the population'. Part of this process is the struggle to 'position eco-values and identity founded on spiritual beliefs as the means for constructing a just, peaceful, harmonious and united society, rich in morality' (pp. 15, 25).

The focus on traditional values in the pursuit of prosperity sounds somewhat in keeping with the 'utopian thinking' researcher-activist Ulrich Oslender (2016, p. 218) regards as necessary in the Pacific region, the more so because his citation of Lefebvre brings to mind the latter's work on the city. Unlike the cases imagined by Oslender, however, the document's invocation of its collective political subject suggests the problems inherent in the institutionalisation of identity politics within the Colombian political scene. In an environment where being *afrocolombiano* rather than mestizo is the norm, it reproduces the multiculturalism of the constitution by seeking to create a united popular subject, while simultaneously appealing to bound serialities.

The emphasis on cultural identity, however, blurs the distinction between bound and unbound forms of groupness, in the process removing much of the politics from the text. The solution to the problems of the region is presented as lying in the cultural values of its inhabitants. Furthermore, the presentation of the ethnic identity of an emergent collective subject as a political solution in its own right avoids engagement with the contemporary political economy of the department. The brief history of Afrochocoans, with its dependency-theory-infused critique of extractivism, confronts the political economy responsible for the vast inequalities that shape daily life in the department. Yet it also consigns the worst effects of exploitation to the past. The responsibility for the poverty of the department is assigned to the absentee white or mestizo proprietors and landowners of the past, rather than the current mestizo population, regional elites, or even the central government, which the administration claims to represent. Indeed, as far as the future is concerned, the document echoes the discourse of neoliberal competitiveness and comparative advantage that underpins the state-sponsored model of development, with its promises of securing outsourced contracts – '*procesos de tercerización, de off shore, de maquila*' [processes of sub-contracting, off-shoring and assembly-line production] (Mena, 2012, p. 57). This aside, the commodification of the environment and the attitudes to it of local communities is presented as the only hope for a better life, a decidedly forlorn one at that, given the administration's 19th-century obsession with the 'locomotives of progress'. For all the talk of poverty, injustice and corruption, the document exemplifies how ethnic identity politics can be absorbed within institutional structures in ways that remain perfectly functional to Colombia's ongoing passive revolution. The invocation of identity politics in this context, therefore, serves to legitimise the goals of a particular set of political entrepreneurs rather than express the demands of a social movement. Some community organisers saw it as a kind of political ventriloquism, in which the architects of *Quibdó MIA* simultaneously interpellated the population and claimed to speak for it. In the parts of the city where we worked there was little appetite for identitarian discourse as a mobilising factor, partly because to claim *afrocolombianidad* or indigeneity brought no special benefits in the urban setting, but also because so little was offered in practical terms.

The First Congress of the Pueblo Negro

The complexities surrounding the constitution of a political subject were apparent on a larger stage in the Primer Congreso Nacional del Pueblo Negro, Afrocolombiano, Palenquero y Raizal in 2013, an event partly scheduled to take stock of the impact of law 70, 20 years after its implementation. The activists of the organising committee were well aware of the pitfalls involved in the attempt to construct a specifically Afrocolombian political subject, capable of setting a collective agenda, mobilising support, and applying pressure on the state to achieve its goals. The division between bound and unbound serialities once again provides insights into the challenges they faced. The cumbersome title of the congress is suggestive of what is at stake in the struggles over naming that have taken place within Afrocolombian social movements. The key concept is that of the people, introducing the idea of popular sovereignty, but this universal political subject is immediately bound, first by the term '*negro*' [black], and then by '*afrocolombiano*'. The first of these might be taken as a simple reference to phenotype but it is in fact a highly loaded term, steeped in the long history of racism in Colombia. The tension between the two terms is in part a result of the disagreement between those who reject '*negro*' as irredeemably derogatory and therefore racist and those who see it as an expression of identity that can be reclaimed from its discriminatory connotations. The former prefer to emphasise the importance of shared ancestry through the use of the term '*afrocolombiano*', presented as the key factor in the definition of this collective subject. As the National Conference of Afrocolombian Organisations (CNOA, n.d.) puts it, 'we consider the Afrocolombian people to be constituted by women and men descended from Africans born in Colombia'.

This nomenclature too is tied to the ways in which the state has allotted specific rights to officially recognised ethnic groups. Thus, to self-identify as *negro* can be either a generic or a highly specific act. It is the term the mestizo majority imposes on people with a particular phenotype throughout the country, but it is also a common form of self-identification among Afrocolombians. Most people in Quibdó, for example, identify as *negro*. On the other hand, when hitched to the territorially defined notion of 'community', *negro* is a constitutionally recognised ethnicity affording specific rights. As a result of demands from activists, both *palenqueros*, descendants of a small but culturally significant maroon community not far from Cartagena, and *raizales*, speakers of an English-based creole in the Caribbean islands of San Andrés and Providencia, are identities recognised by legislation (specifically article 310 of the constitution for *raizales*; decree 4181 of 2007 and decree 2163 of 2012 for both *raizales* and *palenqueros*). Unlike the generic notion of blackness, which could be applied to or be claimed by any black citizen without affording any particular rights, each is both culturally and territorially bound. Both *negro* and *afrocolombiano* can be applied to these groups, though the latter's identification with the English-speaking Caribbean makes the nationalising aspect of the word *afrocolombiano* problematic. The deliberate use of each of these terms, then, was a highly politicised choice, simultaneously recognising the heterogeneity of blackness within Colombia, declaring unity within difference, and advancing political claims within the juridical framework of the state.

The Congress was envisaged as a space in which Afrocolombian organisations would refine their goals and clarify their dealings with the state. In fact, some *quibdoseños* suggested that this was a gathering of all those who position themselves as interlocutors of the state, as representatives and community leaders, to be sure, but above all as brokers. As in the case of *Quibdó MIA*, some people felt that these actors appropriated the voice of the black or Afrocolombian population, excluding absent perspectives, in the pursuit of personal advancement. This was in many ways an unfair claim because alongside the traffickers of influence were many activists with a long trajectory in the struggle for Afrocolombian rights. If things had been otherwise, the event would never have taken place, as the process of canvassing opinion, compiling the agenda, and organising transport and accommodation was dependent on a reservoir of good will.

At the same time, this critique recognised both the partially co-opted nature of these spaces, and the lack of participation of most of the community, a problem not exclusive to ethnic minorities. It also reminds us, as Paschel (2016a, p.3) notes, that while Afrocolombian organisations in Colombia 'were essential to the making of black political subjects' they were 'small and under-resourced networks of activists […] with few political allies, unpopular with, and largely unknown to, the masses'. Grass-roots scepticism about the movement – echoed by activists who occasionally wondered whether it made sense to talk about a movement – was clear in a sarcastic remark made by a Quibdó woman: 'I hear they brought a thousand *negros* to Quibdó for this Congress – why did they do that when there are already plenty of *negros* here?' The provocative use of the word *negro* questions activists' insistence on the political significance of particular forms of nomenclature. Redolent of the commonly held scepticism about 'politics' in Colombia, such attitudes play a key role in discouraging activism and political mobilisation. In the particular case of Afrocolombians, they are indicative of the relative weakness of identity politics on the national scale, especially when the obvious incentives to mobilise around identity are missing. This was particularly true of attempts to foreground urban issues such as racism in large cities with mestizo majorities. In these contexts, Afrocolombians might be identified as needing representation, but the bound seriality of *afrocolombianidad* brings with it no specific rights. Furthermore, from the perspective of Quibdó's poorest *barrios*, even struggles against racism had little immediate bearing on the lived experience of communities struggling for jobs and basic public services in a city where the administration itself was Afrocolombian.

The division between different actors struggling for Afrocolombian rights is partly due to the relationships constructed through constitutional legislation. As Bolívar (2004, p. 17) notes, law 70 did little to establish the mechanisms through which Afrocolombian community councils, the organisations exercising jurisdiction over collectively titled lands, could interact with each other and with regional society, framing them instead as interlocutors of the state. The need to build a cohesive movement was frequently mentioned in the Congress. Tensions between activists, however, came to the surface very quickly. After the fanfare surrounding the presidential visit, the following day's opening of the Congress for business was a tumultuous affair. Following ritual invocations of spiritual and ancestral forces, the start to proceedings was delayed by an hour as a delegation from Valle, dominated by powerful regional broker Rosa Solís, approached the stage, arguing loudly about the order of proceedings, and haranguing the rest of the auditorium. Solís has been an influential figure in establishing more than 20 community councils in the wake of law 70, and part of a high-level consultancy group with Afrocolombian communities set up by the Uribe administration, a group later dissolved by order of the constitutional court. A controversial figure, Solís is seen by many as the quintessential example of the broker who has made both a name and a living as a trusted interlocutor of the state (La Silla Vacía, 2012).

Similar scenes were repeated on the final day, and were seen by the organisers as humiliating for the movement as a whole, and the general conclusions drawn up by the CNOA underline the negative effects of competition for influence within their organisations, often referred to as the desire for 'protagonism'. Under the 'lessons learned' section of the Congress proceedings, the first three examples of negative practice were 'the institutionalisation of the movement through the strategy of divide and corrupt', 'the projection of an image of organisational chaos which the State takes advantage of to ignore its obligations to the black people', and the fact that 'the *negro*, *afrocolombiano*, *raizal* and *palenquero* social movement has no presence in decision-making spaces' (Vivanco and Ramírez, 2014, p. 9). The final point underlined the key problem that, as elsewhere in participatory spaces in Colombia, community engagement was limited to processes of consultation.

In the case of ethnic communities, however, the legal requirement for consultation represented a form of leverage. The question of how to engage with the state hinged on a single practical point, the controversial topic of *consulta previa* [prior consultation]. This legal figure, adapted from the International Labour Organisation's convention 169 (1989), was a fundamental feature of legislation surrounding the granting of land title, and the main gift of the new legislative framework to officially recognised minorities. In effect, it means that development affecting collectively held lands has to receive the informed consent of the communities concerned before going ahead. What should be a political trump card, however, has constantly been undermined through a wide range of dubious practices, from official denial of the existence of ethnic communities in specific territories to badly managed and unrepresentative processes which have rubber-stamped projects with powerful backers in the private or public sector. The Congress therefore aimed to produce a set of protocols protecting community rights. Furthermore, it was agreed from the outset of the Congress that the list of demands emerging from each of the thematic committees was to carry a warning at the top of the page noting that the deliberations of these committees were not to be regarded as an exercise in prior consultation. From this perspective, the Congress was characterised by the failure of the administration's strategy of flattering the Afrocolombian movement for its political significance, while seeking an accommodation that would allow it to pursue both its goal of disarming the FARC and furthering its development goals.

For activists, the Congress offered an opportunity to build a more united movement. In many respects, the rhetoric of solidarity covered up a movement dogged by infighting over which sectors, and even which leaders, should be regarded as proper interlocutors of the state. In particular, the collective recognition of the movement's own relative weakness led to a simple recommendation on the need for solidarity: 'we need to make statements in favour of other social and communitarian movements, because alone we will get nowhere' (Vivanco and Ramírez, 2014, p. 9). There is a clear recognition that identity politics alone cannot produce a political subject capable of challenging the deepening of Colombia's passive revolution, a process that more than any other threatens the life opportunities of Afrocolombians.

The Cumbre Agraria of 2014

It is precisely this appreciation that led to the participation of ethnic activists in the Cumbre Agraria, Campesina, Étnica y Popular (the agrarian, peasant, ethnic and popular summit) of 2014. In fact, while the Congress was taking place, Colombia was in an almost unprecedented state of turmoil. The free trade agreement with the US that had come into law in 2012 forced agricultural workers to buy US seeds and pay exorbitant prices for fertiliser. In a desperate response, peasant organisations, including members of indigenous and Afrocolombian communities, blocked major roads in 25 of the country's 31 departments, bringing the heavy goods haulage that is the lifeblood of Colombian commerce to a grinding halt. President Santos' unfortunate declaration that 'there is no such agrarian strike' was belied by blocked highways, as the strikers were joined by hauliers protesting at fuel prices. Daily images of the activists' confrontations across blazing barricades with the notorious Colombian riot police made news bulletins across the country, garnering unprecedented support for their cause among the urban population. Even the private media channels, generally hostile to social protest, toned down their coverage and presented the strikers in a neutral and at times even positive light. For a while, this nascent movement represented the most obvious threat to the dominant model of development.

In the face of the government's failure to respond to the strikers' demands, a meeting of the Cumbre was scheduled to take place in Bogotá in March,

2014. A huge organisational effort brought more than 30,000 delegates to the Coldeportes coliseum over a rainy March weekend in Bogotá. Here, too, the agglutinative title of the event is striking. Clearly aimed at the creation of a rural popular front seeking to articulate distinct demands in order to create a single, more powerful political actor, such an attempt was particularly significant because in the years after 1991 peasant leaders were concerned that the ethnicisation of collective land-titling had left mestizo peasants and colonists on the agricultural frontier in limbo. Indeed, as Duarte (2015, p. 450) notes, one of the effects of the constitution and its attendant ethnic legislation was that the mestizo peasant became 'the bearer of third class rural citizenship compared to the ethnic populations'. And as Bolívar (2004, p. 219) notes in her comments on Sotomayor's work in the 90s in Silvia, Cauca, 'the process of constructing a cultural identity and redefining themselves as indigenous has led to a cultural "invisibility" of the peasant which […] could be useful to the government in neutralizing peasant struggle'.

Indeed, whereas indigenous and Afrocolombian groups tended to be presented as guardians of the environment, mestizo colonists were more likely to be framed as destructive *raspachines* [coca growers] and guerrilla sympathisers. However, the legal scaffolding established by the constitution, with its offer of rights on the basis of bound seriality, led peasants to seek recognition as a collective subject in similar terms, with the legislation on the establishment of peasant reserve zones being passed a year after law 70. It is significant that an element of these claims is the desire to protect peasant culture, with the National Association for Peasant Reserve Zones emphasising the importance of 'positioning our cultural identity' and ensuring 'the survival of our cultural identity' (Prensa Rural, 2014). This is in itself a hint that the state's recognition of the bound serialities of ethnic minorities has been noted by other groups seeking political recognition. It is also a reaction against the increased visibility of ethnic communities with a recognised cultural identity, and peasant communities whose cultural distinctiveness was ignored. As Bolívar rightly suggests, post-1991 legislation 'inverted the differences, the negative representations, and the lack of connection between those groups that could be identified as culturally distinct, and the poor mestizos, now devoid of support and protection' (Bolívar, 2004, p. 220). Thus, as Montenegro (2016, p. 175) notes, 'it is not the same to struggle for a piece of land as it is to exercise territoriality, understood as the establishment of economic, political and cultural relationships in the territory, as well as territorial forms of ordering and government'. Furthermore, whereas the state has seen peasant reserve zones as areas in which it can strengthen its presence, for the peasant movement the political autonomy of the ethnic communities represents a model. Montenegro (p. 176) cites Robert Daza, then president of the National Agrarian Coordinating Committee (Coordinador Agrario Nacional), who claimed that 'while the historic struggle of the peasantry has been for land the scenario of struggle has recently been extended to the defence of and the right to territory'. For his part, Andrés Gil, representative of Marcha Patriótica, was even clearer in his declaration that 'we don't just want land, we want territoriality to carry out an exercise in self-government' (Telesur, 2014). These demands, with their denunciation of the multiple threats posed by state promoted megaprojects, extractive industry, and agro-industrial monocultures such as oil palm and bananas, represent a direct threat to the dominant development model.

Competition between the different ethnic and peasant movements debilitates all of them in the face of global capital's assault on the Colombian countryside. Thus, the presence of the Black Communities' Process (PCN), an organisation that has played a key role in struggles of Afrocolombian rights in the southern part of the Pacific littoral, and the National Indigenous Organisation of Colombia (ONIC) at the summit was a significant strategic departure. This was the first time that a unified list of demands had been presented to the state by such a broad range of organisations. At this moment of solidarity, however, another concern weighed on the minds of delegates. If the Congreso Afrocolombiano had focused on prior consultation and its relationship to the state, the Cumbre was haunted by the peace negotiations in Havana, and the widely shared sense that the movement's demands were not being represented. The constant demand for 'peace with social justice', repeated in committee after committee like a political incantation, suggested a deep anxiety about the post-accord world. Given that radical structural reforms likely to challenge privilege were absent from the agreements, social justice still had to be fought for.

Though it would be naive to imagine that the social movements involved in these struggles had no channels of communication with the FARC and the National Liberation Army (ELN), the relationship was more problematic in the case of ethnic organisations. The notion that the guerrilla groups have always existed in a predatory relationship with traditional authorities is an exaggeration, increasingly apparent in the wake of the FARC's disarmament, as extractive industry and logging have gone into overdrive in the power vacuum left by the insurgents. Even so, if the peasant movement felt marginalised by its lack of constitutional recognition, ethnic movements have long had a fraught relationship with the armed left and, indeed, with the left in general, which tended to deny the specificity of ethnic struggles not only by focusing strongly on class but by unreflectingly repeating the nostrums of nation-building *mestizaje* (Arocha, 1998; Bolívar, 2004, p. 220). In recent times, the presence of armed actors in collectively held ethnic territories has had an ambiguous effect, at best.

If any more proof were needed, the negotiations in Havana, haggling over the details of the insurgency's defeat, were taking place without the participation of ethnic communities. This absence was also a significant indicator of the priorities adopted by the Santos administration. At the 2013

Congress, the Afrocolombian movement established a body, the Autoridad Nacional Afrocolombiana [National Afrocolombian Authority], precisely in order to establish a channel of communication with the negotiators in Havana. These efforts were initially ignored or rebuffed and the ethnic chapter of the Havana peace accords of 2016, currently being discussed by communities across Colombia, was very much an afterthought. It was only 12 hours before the presentation of the final document that an addition to the sixth chapter of the agreement was approved, establishing an 'ethnic focus' (similar to the 'gender focus' that runs throughout the document) during the implementation of the accords, essentially a recognition by both the state and the insurgency that the rights associated with ethnic difference would be respected in the post-accord world. What is striking in this case is that ethnic identity politics should be so low on the agenda for both the state and the FARC.

In spite of these doubts, the march from the coliseum to the symbolic seat of national government in the Plaza Bolívar was an expression of a utopian dreaming, not least because of the crowds warmly applauding the march. Briefly, it was as if the Uribe years, marked by what Eduardo Restrepo (personal communication, 2004) once described as the 'paramilitarisation of the Colombian mentality', no longer had any purchase on the imagination. Writing two years after the Cumbre, José Santos of the PCN (2016, p. 88) argued for a utopian solution to the national conflict 'through the construction of an intercultural territory, which respects the territorial structures of each of the peoples, united in a single entity. All under the same umbrella, which we could call the United Interethnic Territory of Colombia'. This dream, however, is unlikely to be realised. As Santos's text was being published, the leadership committee wrote to the president of the republic, denouncing 'the systematic strategy of delay and attrition […] on the part of the government's delegation', and the fact that 'there are no effective results that demonstrate your government's supposed political will to peace' (*Desde Abajo*, 2016). Worse still, the social movements proposing an alternative vision to the model were paying a high price. In March 2017, delegates of the Cumbre occupied the buildings of the Ministry of the Interior to protest at the murder of activists in the peasant, Afrocolombian and indigenous movements. By their own reckoning, 120 had been killed in just over 14 months. This particular struggle against the model is being lost in a bloody fashion, and at the time of writing there is no end in sight for the violence. As a result, Colombia's passive revolution shows no sign of being challenged in the short term.

Conclusion

The official promotion of identity politics in Colombia contains a fundamentally contradictory idea, namely that the inclusion of Afrocolombians and indigenous groups is possible without a radical restructuring of the distribution of wealth and power. Indeed, the very notion of inclusion becomes untenable, as in order to be able to contemplate an end to racism and the elitism that goes with it, the very entity comprising these groups would have to be transformed into something radically different. The granting of rights on the basis of bound serialities, whether these are based on race, ethnicity, territory, or a mixture of all three, apparently engages with indigenous and black Colombians while banishing them to the margins, to places where they are out of sight and out of mind for the urban majority. Yet these groups are not safe, even where they 'belong', because those territories that were deemed *baldíos* [public lands], empty and unclaimed, turned out to be places that dominant groups had plans for after all.

Needless to say, the public expressions of anti-racism found so frequently in the media are never linked to this perspective. It is not uncommon for the news bulletins to include a three-minute news item on an Afrocolombian woman being denied service in a bar, while the murder of representatives of black and indigenous communities goes unremarked. The most that can be expected is that such occurrences are reported on as random events, inexplicable tragedies, as resistant to explanation as a hurricane or an earthquake. There are, it seems, acceptable and unacceptable forms of identity politics, and those that seek common cause with others in the struggle against Colombia's entrenched inequality are too challenging to be allowed a voice within a national conversation managed by Bogotá-based media companies, owned by the conglomerates that drive economic policy.

Gramscian perspectives are often praised for their subtlety. In this study, however, I have used the notion of passive revolution bluntly, partly to provoke and partly to underline the gravity of the present conjuncture. Of course, as Restrepo (2013, p. 15) notes, the state is not a monolithic entity against which all struggle can be measured, something that a detailed Gramscian analysis would emphasise. The same can be said for neoliberalism. And, as Oslender (2016) and others have shown convincingly, people do find spaces for struggle, even within the neoliberal horizon, winning breathing spaces and small victories for their communities. But Gramsci's work reminds us that 'in its contradictory structure, [the state] condenses a variety of different relations and practices into a definite "system of rule"' (Hall, 1986, p. 18). Identity politics is part of this regime and tends to be functional to it, as much by accident as by design. Gramsci's thinking underlines that all hegemonic projects have their day, but his emphasis on the need to apply an unshrinking 'pessimism of the intellect' to political analysis warns against an excessive faith in emancipatory processes. With this in mind, the notion of passive revolution reminds us that the struggle against entrenched privilege in a country as unequal as Colombia is likely to be long and difficult. Local elites have historically proved adept at reshaping institutional arrangements in their favour and the current conjuncture suggests that social movements will continue to face very testing times in the years to come.

Bibliography

Aldía (2017) '"Periodista" insultó el festival Petronio Álvarez y tiene indignados a todos en Twitter', http://www.aldia.co/viral/periodista-insulto-el-festival-petronio-alvarez-y-tiene-indignados-todos-en-twitter (accessed 28 Aug. 2017).

Anderson, B. (1998) 'Nationalism, identity and the world in motion: on the logics of seriality', in P. Cheah and B. Robbins (eds.), *Cosmopolitics: Thinking and Feeling Beyond the Nation* (Minneapolis, MN: University of Minnesota), pp. 117–33.

Arocha, J. (1998) 'Inclusion of Afro-Colombians: unreachable national goal?', *Latin American Perspectives*, 25 (3): 70–89.

Bolívar, I. (2004) 'Estado y participación: ¿la centralidad de lo político?', in M. Archila and M. Pardo (eds.) *Movimientos sociales, estado y democracia en Colombia* (Bogotá: Universidad Nacional de Colombia), pp. 207–33.

Chatterjee, P. (2004) *The Politics of the Governed: Reflections on Popular Politics in Most of the World* (New York: Columbia University Press).

Clifford, J. (1998) 'Mixed feelings', in P. Cheah and B. Robbins (eds.), *Cosmopolitics: Thinking and Feeling Beyond the Nation* (Minneapolis, MN: University of Minnesota), pp. 362–70.

CNOA (n.d.) '¿Quiénes somos?', https://convergenciacnoa.org/quienes-somos/ (accessed 8 Aug. 2017).

DACN (2015) 'Colombia es Decenio Afro', http://dacn.mininterior.gov.co/decenio-afro/colombia-es-decenio-afro (accessed 7 Dec. 2017).

Deas, M. (1997) 'Violent exchanges: reflections on political violence in Colombia', in D. Apter (ed.), *The Legitimization of Violence* (London: Palgrave), pp. 350–404.

Desde Abajo (2016) 'Pliego cumbre agraria, campesina, étnica y popular', https://www.desdeabajo.info/fondo-editorial/item/28932-pliego-paro-31-de-mayo-de-2016.html (accessed 8 Aug. 2017).

Duarte, D. (2015) '(Des)encuentros en lo público. Gobernabilidad y conflictos interétnicos en Colombia' (Paris, France: IHEAL, Paris III doctoral thesis).

El Espectador (2017) 'Gabinete afro, la prueba de que Armitage no es racista', http://www.elespectador.com/noticias/nacional/maurice-armitage-la-palabra-negro-para-mi-no-es-despectiva-articulo-709502 (accessed 15 July 2017).

El Tiempo (2017) 'El retiro de un blog ofensivo', http://www.eltiempo.com/colombia/otras-ciudades/el-tiempo-retira-blog-ofensivo-sobre-el-festival-petronio-alvarez-123804 (accessed 25 Aug. 2017).

Fraser, N. (1995) 'From redistribution to recognition? Dilemmas of justice in a "post-socialist" age', *New Left Review*, I (212): 68–93.

Gramsci, A. (1971) *Selections from the Prison Notebooks* (London: Lawrence and Wishart).

Hall, S. (1980) 'Race, articulation and societies structured in dominance', in UNESCO (ed.), *Sociological Theories: Race and Colonialism* (Paris: UNESCO), pp. 305–45.

— (1986) 'Gramsci's relevance for the study of race and ethnicity', *Journal of Communication Inquiry*, 10 (2): 5–27.

Harvey, D. (2004) 'Accumulation by dispossession', *Socialist Register*, 40: 56–75.

La Silla Vacía (2012) 'Rosa Solís, el dolor de cabeza de los grandes proyectos del Gobierno', http://lasillavacia.com/historia/rosa-solis-el-dolor-de-cabeza-de-los-grandes-proyectos-del-gobierno-32410 (accessed 15 Feb. 2018).

López, C. (ed.) (2010) *Y refundaron la patria* (Bogotá: Arco Iris).

Machado, M., D. López Matta, M.M. Campo, A. Escobar and V. Weitzner (2017) 'Weaving hope in ancestral black territories in Colombia: the reach and limitations of free, prior, and informed consultation and consent', *Third World Quarterly*, 38 (5): 1075–91.

Mejía Quintana, O. (2007) 'Elites, etnicidades y constitución: cultura política y poder constituyente en Colombia', in G. Hoyos Vásquez (ed.), *Filosofía y teorías políticas entre la crítica y la utopía* (Buenos Aires: CLACSO), pp. 235–56.

Mena, Z. (2012) 'Plan de desarrollo Quibdó MIA: unido, equitativo y acogedor' (Quibdó: Concejo Municipal).

Montenegro, H. (2016) 'Ampliaciones y quiebres del reconocimiento político del campesinado colombiano: un análisis a la luz de la Cumbre Agraria, Campesina, Étnica y Popular (Cacep)', *Revista Colombiana de Antropología*, 52 (1): 169–95.

Oslender, U. (2016) *The Geography of Social Movements: Afro-Colombian Mobilization and the Aquatic Space* (Durham, NC: Duke University Press).

Paschel, T.S. (2016a) *Becoming Black Political Subjects: Movements and Ethno-Racial Rights in Colombia and Brazil* (Princeton, NJ: Princeton University Press).

— (2016b) 'The limits of inclusion', *Berkeley Review of Latin American Studies*, Spring/Fall: 56–9.

Prensa Rural (2014) 'El campesinado de ANZORC expresa su descontento por la escasa implementación del Acuerdo de Paz', http://prensarural.org/spip/spip.php?article22235 (accessed 18 Dec. 2017).

Restrepo, E. (2004) Personal communication. Roundtable discussion, Universidad Nacional de Colombia, Bogotá, Oct. 2004.

— (2013) *Etnización de la negridad: la invención de las 'comunidades negras' en Colombia* (Popayán: Universidad del Cauca).

Santos, J. (2016) 'Conflictos por el uso del suelo: territorios indígenas y afrodescendientes', *Bitácora* (Universidad Nacional de Colombia), 26 (2): 87–9.

TeleSur (2014) 'Noticiero', https://www.youtube.com/watch?v=mXGhDr15tNw (accessed 31 Jan. 2018).

UNDP (2011) *Human Development Report 2011. Sustainability and Equity: A Better Future for All* (New York: United Nations Development Programme).

Vivanco, D. and D. Ramírez (2014) 'Compilación de Documentos I, Congreso Nacional del Pueblo Negro, Afrocolombiano, Palenquero y Raizal, 23 a 27 de agosto de 2013 Quibdó, Colombia' (Cali: CNOA).

World Bank (2014) 'GINI index (World Bank estimate)', http://data.worldbank.org/indicator/SI.POV.GINI (accessed 28 Aug. 2017).

3. Photography collectives and anti-racism in Peru and Argentina

Patricia Oliart and Agustina Triquell

This chapter examines the context, format and content of a set of photographs by Adrián Portugal, a member of Supay Colectivo de Fotografía based in Lima, Peru, and two photographic productions by Colectivo Manifiesto, based in the city of Córdoba, Argentina.[1] Although different in purpose, these interventions into systems of racialised social representations are manifestations of anti-racism, which challenge the stereotypes and practices that mark groups of the population as different, undesirable and even dangerous. With their images, these photographers deliberately reinforce ideas, aesthetic expressions and forms of living in Lima and Córdoba, which challenge the status quo by actively defying clichés about 'the other', the urban poor. As Sassen (2013, p. 213) states, the incompleteness of cities makes them 'a space where the powerless can make history'. By recording acts of 'innovation under duress' performed by 'the powerless' (p. 210), these photography collectives embrace a role as trustees of history-making actions that need to be recorded and, in doing so, they inspire political imaginaries about the social transformations that could take place in their countries (Pinney, 2016).[2]

The documentary photography that both collectives practise is at the crossroads between the arts, photojournalism and political activism. Both Supay and Manifiesto use collaborative forms of production and open-access platforms to disseminate their work, in order to intervene actively in their societies' system of representation. Both collectives are part of a large network of numerous photographers in the region and beyond, who are engaged in a high degree of reflexivity about their practice and social position. Having taken a critical stance against social injustice and discriminatory practices,

1 The collaborative work for this article was possible in the context of the RISE–MSCA H2020 project 'Cultural Narratives of Crisis and Renewal', http://www.culturalnarratives.co.uk (accessed 4 March 2019).

2 This is how Pinney (2016) summarises the ideas of Didi-Huberman (2008) and Azoulay (2012) when discussing whether documentary photography can play a politically liberating role.

P. Oliart and A. Triquell, 'Photography collectives and anti-racism in Peru and Argentina', in P. Wade, J. Scorer and I. Aguiló (eds.), *Cultures of Anti-Racism in Latin America and the Caribbean* (London: Institute of Latin American Studies, 2019), pp. 49–72. License: CC-BY-NC-ND 4.0.

they use their lenses to document the presence, concerns, actions and lives of the disenfranchised and emerging groups of people in urban and rural areas, unashamedly practising a partisan photography and siding with and serving social movements (Marzo, 2006; Azoulay, 2010; Carreras, 2010; Gonzales Granados, 2016).

A fascinating and complex ideological landscape is currently emerging in Latin America (Hershberg and Rosen, 2006; Goodale and Postero, 2013). On the one hand, discourses of solidarity, civic engagement and the quest for social justice became official during the emergence of the so-called Pink Tide regimes, attracting the support of young people, but also generating opposition from more radical autonomous movements. On the other hand, even though aspects of neoliberalism have had a strong cultural grip on Chile, Peru and Colombia since the 1990s, some Latin Americans consider neoliberal discourses around cultural diversity or women's rights to be too progressive (Vich, 2014). It is true that the questioning of racism and racist practices is 'part and parcel of the effective management of cultural diversity' (Bonnett, 2000, p. 3), and most Latin American countries have experienced constitutional changes recognising cultural diversity and outlawing discrimination based on race or ethnicity. However, none of this guarantees the transformation of the pervasive and widespread racist values, attitudes and practices found in all social echelons and among state officials, nor does it protect indigenous peoples from dispossession and abuse at the hands of the state. Furthermore, the legal sanctioning of discrimination tends to consider individual cases, meaning victims of discrimination, have to face the state alone with their complaints.

The range of anti-racist practices in this context is broad. At one end, it involves adopting an egalitarian form of life that aspires to eradicate racial prejudice and hierarchies based on phenotype, and to challenge the racialisation of cultural difference in everyday life. At the other end, it involves active participation in campaigns and organisations denouncing racial discrimination and defending the rights of indigenous groups and Afrodescendants. They all aim to care for and heal the wounds of racism, by taking a clear stance against it (Mbembe, 2016). The photographic interventions of Supay and Manifiesto stand in different places in this spectrum of anti-racist practice. Nevertheless, they also share important features. Both collectives are socially diverse; their members are typically not activists in any specific identity- or class-based movement in the cities where they live and work. However, in their production they are critical of practices of exclusion that link class and phenotype, and they engage in photography projects that stir criticism or destabilise prejudice or common racialised discriminatory assumptions about the 'urban poor'. In spite of their differences, they are representative of a generation of Latin American photographers who join in the production of challenging narratives about democracy and citizenship. Their work contributes to the struggle against racism as their photography affirms the presence of groups of the population 'where they are not supposed to be'.

This chapter first presents documentary photography as the central activity of the collectives studied. There is a discussion of conditions of production for documentary photography and the role that photography plays in contemporary social movements. Then two cases are presented: the series *Retratos de peruanos ejemplares* [portraits of exemplary Peruvians] by photographer Adrián Portugal from Colectivo Supay, and the intervention of Colectivo Manifiesto around the Marcha de la Gorra [March of the Cap] in 2014 and 2015. For each case, the context is first outlined for anti-racist expressions in neoliberal Peru and Argentina. The chapter concludes with a discussion of the role that photography collectives may play in transforming ingrained racialising practices by intervening in and expanding the repertoire of images in the visual cultures of both countries.

Documentary photography collectives

A passage from the pioneering book *Podría ser yo* (Jelin et al., 1987) describes a moment when a woman stops photographer Alicia D´Amico as she is about to take a close-up in her kitchen: 'Will you even photograph the dirt on my pans?' The woman's discomfort challenged the photographer's interest in the detail of what the woman might consider the intimate, imperfect, dirty, concealable details of her kitchen, usually free from an external gaze.

This scene provokes reflection on the photographer's gaze and on who is seen and what is put on display in the traditional repertoire of themes in documentary photography. By revealing the conditions of production of an image, Jelin and Vila elicit a reflection on the tensions and exchanges in the encounter between the photographer and those who pose, or are inadvertently recruited, for that fleeting moment.

Reflection about these interactions is relevant for a practice that has 'the real' as its point of reference. This referential condition – this weight, says John Tagg (2003) – assigns documentary photography a ubiquity in the fields of science, law and, particularly relevant here, the narration of the social world. A second dimension of the documentary condition that deserves attention involves the establishment of a canon, an aesthetic and a way of articulating one image with another, a way of recounting and describing worlds, which, even though it is situated in time and bound to follow technological developments, still conforms to the identifiable narrative forms of photojournalism. And the third dimension concerns the circuits in which images are consumed, which also define the documentary condition. For most of the 20th century, the outlets were magazines, competitions and festivals. The spread of online platforms in this century has produced a proliferation of outlets for documentary photography, where images circulate freely. This has also generated an eclectic array of uses of documentary photography, as it becomes part of art projects, relational interventions and even advertising.

Over the 20th century, documentary photography evolved as a practice amidst numerous debates that found parallels in discussions of the use of photography in anthropology. Dominated by a 'hermeneutics of suspicion' about the medium and the role of power relations in regimes of representation (Azoulay, 2010), the debate has moved to the current focus on the act of taking photos, understanding photography as an event of performative engagement. According to Azoulay, the photographic event includes four elements: the photographer, the camera, the objective and the spectator, creating among them a double temporality. One relates to the camera and the other to the photograph (or its hypothetical existence). For the author (2015, p. 18), 'an ontological description of photography has to suspend the simple syntax of the sentence divided into subject, verb, predicate and adjective – *photographer photographs a photograph with a camera*' and, instead, promote a political ontology, 'an ontology of the many, operating in public, in motion. It is an ontology bound to the manner in which human beings exist – look, talk, act – with one another and *with objects*', thus a photograph is the 'act of many', 'a trace of a space of human relations'.

From its origins, documentary photography favoured social issues and showed an interest in promoting change in situations of disaster, poverty, stagnation and humanitarian crisis (Edwards, 2015; Freixa Font et al., 2015; Ritchin, 2013). This tradition started very early on and developed in both the post-war European context and in the United States – within the framework of projects such as the Farm Security Administration. The reception of documentary photography in Latin America had specific features. Up until the 1980s a considerable corpus of documentary photography adopted a tone of denunciation and criticism of the wealth and power that disadvantaged the exploited and the disenfranchised, in common with other aesthetic expressions such as literature and film (Lindstrom, 1998; Rosenberg, 2016). The intention was to prick consciences, produce knowledge, and promote action associated with the struggles and activism of social organisations and calls for revolution. Thus, images presumed wide audiences that included the protagonists captured in them, and they operated with a logic in which it was common sense (Caggiano, 2012) to produce stories about the exploited and disenfranchised.[3]

However, the uncomfortable realities that became visible to wider audiences were soon part of a miserabilist paradigm that generated visual repertoires which, by typically portraying barefoot boys and girls, disorderly neighbourhoods,

---

3   Reflective work about the role of visual representations also took place, as in the case of 'Cine de la Base' by Raymundo Gleyzer. This group, which emerged as a distribution team for the film *Los Traidores* (1973) by Gleyzer and Melian, considered that screening the film was in itself a political act, for it sparked discussions that would lead viewers to action, and at that time in Argentina this meant involvement in guerrilla groups).

violent gestures, sad faces, and violent and defiant looks, transformed poverty into a spectacle and a commodity (Rosenberg, 2016). In the 1970s, Luis Ospina and Carlos Mayolo – filmmakers from the Cali group in Colombia – famously took a decisive stand against this type of representation. *Agarrando pueblo*[4] is a short fake-documentary film that presents the making of a documentary – a film within a film – about poverty in Cali, caricaturing a filmmaker working for a German production company. Although they focused on what they called '*pornomiseria*' cinema,[5] their criticisms extended in principle to documentary practices more generally, both in photography and in moving image. The criticism raised the question of who is behind the lens.

Participatory photography is a form of documentary photography that developed in the 1970s to intervene in regimes of visual representation and, by the 1990s, it was part of the experience of grassroots urban and rural organisations in various parts of the world. In these contexts, members of community organisations receive cameras to produce images of their surroundings that are relevant to them, in an attempt to provide access to the subjectivity of those not normally behind the camera lens. On the one hand, Martha Rosler (2007, pp. 266-7) recognises that this type of image production provides an opportunity to access 'what the subjects want to show themselves', although she is also sceptical about the efforts put into many of these projects to foster the development of the communicative abilities that can bring 'the photographer' to the fore. More importantly, she is concerned about how relying on the mere fact of giving the camera to project participants underestimates the decisive influence of the institutions sponsoring the projects, and of the contexts of reception. On the other hand, based on her study of Talleres de fotografía social (TAFOS) in Peru, Tiffany Fairey (2017) agrees with the need to question the romantic view behind these projects, but also recognises that the long-term impact on the participating communities and the individual photographers is unpredictable in its potential for social change. These perspectives make evident how documentary photography becomes a privileged arena where politics, aesthetics, expression and perception come together, because of the value attributed to the photographic image as historical evidence, political tool and cultural and artistic manifestation (Poivert, 2002).

The development of digital technologies and the widespread use of online platforms for the dissemination of images and social uses of photography has raised the issue of how to create visual stories. Antigoni Memou (2013)

---

4   See the full movie with English subtitles at https://www.youtube.com/watch?v=szqPmaZ7KdQ
5   If poverty had stimulated independent cinema to denounce and analyse injustice, the market transformed it into an exotic attraction for the very system that generated it. Its profitability hampered any possibility of analysing poverty, instead reinforcing demagogic approaches to social injustice (Mayolo and Ospina, 1977). For more information, see Luis Ospina's website: https://www.luisospina.com/archivo/grupo-de-cali/agarrando-pueblo/ (accessed 4 March 2019).

explains how various events in the world of social movements have converged to produce this shift. Among them are the unmediated access to the world that online platforms provide, and the crisis of the mainstream press, which is perceived to have lost independence and to serve particular interests. These circumstances have granted photography enormous currency for contemporary social movements, particularly those sharing alter-global or anti-globalisation agendas.[6] This agenda has shaped an interest in politics for a whole generation of young people, inspiring them to become social actors (Glasius and Pleyers, 2013), and this includes artists from diverse disciplines.

In a global context in which political parties have also lost appeal for the new generations, collectives – associations of five to twenty people united around friendship, similar ideas or interests in particular activities – have emerged as an alternative means to channel political interests and artistic practice. Photography collectives have appeared across the globe, challenging earlier forms of photographic work, proposing new dynamics and modes of production of images and a different pedagogy. Although it is not the first mode of collaborative production in photography, such collectives are now a very vibrant phenomenon in Latin America, and have aroused increasing interest in the last 15 years.[7] New technologies call for the integrated use of video, sound and text articulated together in multimedia formats. Editing then becomes the fundamental task in the process of producing photographic images. This has brought to the fore a grammar where selection, culling and sequencing have displaced the importance of the defining 'precise moment' for a photographic shot, proposed by Henri Cartier-Bresson.

Going back to the need to create visual stories, contemporary Latin American documentary photography collectives work to articulate their members' diverse views into a single story, giving special importance to the logic of placing one image next to another for the plural construction of meaning. They decide on the sequence of images through collective deliberation, discussing and negotiating their interpretations and opinions. While it is not possible to generalise, in the practice of the collective photographic projects that we have studied, photographers understand the production of the visual stories they create as much more than the sum of their parts (pictures, text, audio). Their commitment is to produce a narrative with multiple voices, transforming the

6   Memou (2013, p. 86) points to the Zapatista movement as a key inspiration in the quest for 'winning the game of visibility' and creating a counter narrative about social movements through photography.

7   Since 2010 the Spanish curator Claudi Carreras has organised three versions of E.CO (Encounter of Collectives) with Ibero-American photography collectives in Madrid, São Paulo and Santos. The network of Latin American photography collectives has also met in Argentina and Uruguay, hosted by MAfIA in Buenos Aires in 2014, and by REBELARTE in Montevideo in 2016. Collectives have also collaborated in special projects, such as the alternative coverage of the 2014 World Cup in Brazil, organised by Media Ninja, or the national coverage of La Marcha de la Gorra 2016, organised by Colectivo Manifiesto.

individual act of looking into a debate or conversation between different gazes (Freixa Font et al., 2015). Editing becomes a central task: it is the moment when the collective narrative emerges, when they share images from each camera in one folder, processing and sequencing them after intense deliberation and collective experimentation, gaining depth and complexity. Sharing images and building a common language is also linked to the global spread of common-pool peer production, which relies on the sharing and coordination of the creative energy of a collective and avoids hierarchical structures (Benklers, 2006). As part of a wide and dense network of cultural agents in Latin America, contemporary photography collectives quickly process social events to produce and swiftly share and circulate aesthetic representations (Sommer, 2006; Scheper Hughes and Dalla Dea, 2012). They are part of alternative online photojournalism endeavours, such as Media Ninja in Brazil. Colectivo Manifiesto is a frequent collaborator of *La Tinta*, an online news platform in Argentina, and photographers from Supay collaborate with *Ojo Público* and *La Mula*, which are investigative journalism platforms in Peru.

Racism and anti-racism in Peru

At a meeting held with indigenous leaders and activists in Manaos, Brazil, in 2000,[8] indigenous Brazilian sociologist Azelene Kaingang from Matto Grosso said that the most serious challenge to racism is a non-racist indigenous person. Stating that racism needs two sides in order to exist, she further explained that if your everyday practice and ways of being in the world contest the belief that race defines social hierarchies and is a justification for disenfranchising certain people, the symbolic power that racists hold loses ground. According to Bonnett (2000), the possibilities of challenging racism in this way, by simply making anti-racism part of a way of life, are even stronger when the state has officially questioned racism and its effects in society, as in the case of Peru.

Two completely different regimes explicitly targeted racism in Peru. The progressive military dictatorship of 1968–75 carried out an agrarian reform under the motto: *Campesino, el patrón no comerá mas de tu pobreza* [peasant farmer, the landowner will no longer feed off your poverty]. They made Quechua an official language and gave centre stage to indigenous and Afrodescendant cultures, celebrating diversity and linking development with liberation from all forms of oppression, including the colonial and neocolonial heritage and the oligarchic regime. The next time issues of race occupied a central role in official political discourses was during the presidential elections of 1990, when Fujimori said he was a *chinito*[9] confronting a *blanquito* (Mario

---

8   The meeting took place as part of the project 'Envisioning the Challenges of Indigenous Peoples in the New Millennia', funded by OXFAM America and the Ford Foundation.

9   In Peru people featuring the epicanthic fold are called *chino* [Chinese] regardless of ethnic background or origin.

Vargas Llosa) to become a 'president [who is] just like you'.[10] The 1993 constitution condemned racial discrimination, and it was during Fujimori's second regime that racism was considered a punishable crime.[11] In 2000, during a vibrant speech about the liberating force of market economy, Beatriz Boza, director of the consumers' protection agency Instituto Peruano de Defensa de la Competencia y de la Protección de la Propiedad Intelectual (INDECOPI), stated that consumers should recognise that money had to have the same purchasing power for all Peruvians. In January 2017, during the presidency of Pedro Pablo Kuczynski, law decree 1323, article 323, established incarceration of at least two years for public servants who committed discriminatory acts based on race or ethnicity. Furthermore, Kuczynski's minister of culture, actor and film director, Salvador del Solar, embarked on a personal campaign criticising racism in football matches and in the media, retweeting posts from such anti-racist sites such as 'Alerta contra el racismo' [racism alert] and others, to denounce discriminatory actions as they occurred. An exception to this trend took place during the second presidential period of Alan García (2006–11) when the racialisation of political opposition came back into official discourse in a dispute about granting local and foreign investors access to indigenous territories, which had tragic results and generated overwhelming resistance (Drinot, 2011). But perhaps this hiatus made evident that, despite the restructuring effect of 1970s agrarian reform on the oligarchic order, and the top-down implementation of cultural diversity policies from the 1990s, the incorporation of indigenous and Afrodescendant Peruvians into the official national imaginary has not been fully achieved. To date, for many Peruvians the only possible language that can be used towards indigenous or Afrodescendant Peruvians is that of violence and exclusion. Officially defunct or not, racism has not ceased to be the ultimate justification behind overt and violent dynamics of dispossession and disenfranchisement.

The way in which *cholos*[12] resist racism in Peru is by trespassing on (or rather, ignoring) the limits it is supposed to impose on them. '*Se acabó la vergüenza*' [the time for being ashamed is over] is an expression often found in YouTube comments when praising the success of musicians, sports people, writers or cooks of apparently indigenous origin, who have become famous in the mainstream media. It reflects nicely a historical sense of transformation

---

10 Fujimori's campaign made the white educated elites 'the other' pitted against 'the people', the latter encompassing *cholos, indios, negros, pobres, provincianos*, i.e. people with no access to power (Oliart, 1998).

11 And yet it was the same regime that implemented an abusive programme of involuntary sterilisations among indigenous women (using deceit or force) to bulk up numbers in order to mark the success of a national health policy designed to give women access to reproductive rights (Oliart, 2008).

12 This polysemic term is used in Peru to name a culturally mestizo person of indigenous origin, or a supposedly mixed-race person whose cultural behaviour is closer to her indigenous roots. It is used as an insult, as an expression of endearment, and as a proud sign of cultural identity.

that yields multiple forms of self-representation where people occupy social and cultural territories that were previously denied to them because of their assumed (and 'undesirable') closeness to indigenous origins. Supay Fotos and Adrián Portugal actively contribute to the visual repertoire that celebrates this transformation.

Supay Fotos

Six photojournalists, who met in the course of their work in Lima more than a decade ago, became friends and formed Supay Fotos collective, creating their webpage supayfotos.com in 2007.[13] They were all graduates of communication studies from two private universities in Lima. The practice of photojournalism had given them unique access to areas of the city, and to cultural and social activities that would otherwise have been unknown to them, alerting them to a wide array of micro-universes that sparked their curiosity and passion. The collective became a platform to share and work on photography projects that reflected their individual interests, and also to elaborate collectively on the experience of encountering these diverse and compelling worlds. The mainstream media were not an adequate outlet for the exploration of the different visual language that emerged from that experience. Working as a collective, the Supay Foto members found the autonomy needed to edit their own images and they took on the challenge of developing a common language through joint projects. Publishing their work on the webpage allowed them to enter the international circuit of festivals and exhibits in the Americas and Europe, with both individual and collective projects. Ernesto Benavides, Max Cabello, Roberto Cáceres, Marco Garro, Adrián Portugal and Giancarlo Shibayama are well recognised as documentary photographers who combine working for national and international magazines with helping to produce visual campaigns for public and private institutions, as well as creating their individual and collective exhibits and publications. The collective language they have developed conveys a close, attentive and lucid approach to difficult aspects of Peruvian life, such as socio-environmental conflicts around mining, post-conflict memory, human trafficking or youth marginality. However, while being critically engaged with these and other issues, their language is at the same time playful, refreshing and celebratory of defiant collective and individual expressions of urban and rural popular culture.

The way Supay Fotos members describe how photojournalism granted them the chance, first, to be in all corners of Lima and, later, to travel around the country, reminds us of Jan Masschelein's (2010) definition of walking as a transformative process. Drawing on Michel Foucault, Walter Benjamin and Judith Butler, Masschelein defines it as 'a displacement of the gaze that enables

---

13   Material for this section comes from diverse interviews with Supay in the media, available online, and from Oliart's interviews with Adrián Portugal (in April 2015 and June 2017).

experience not just as a passive undergoing (being commanded), but also as blazing a trail or path, a kind of cutting a road through' (p. 45). This experience of walking, of being there, leads to 'being or becoming attentive, to expose oneself open to the world [...] so that it can present itself to us'. To walk is a liberating experience that allows us to gain a critical distance, expose ourselves to the present, 'a concrete space of practical freedom: a space of possible self-transformation' (p. 47).

The photographers of Supay were born between the 1970s and the 1980s. At the turn of the century, many members of their generation participated in Peruvian politics for the first time in the massive street protests opposing the authoritarian and corrupt regimes of Alberto Fujimori (1990–5, 1995–2000). Rather than an alternative political programme, what mobilised thousands of university students was an ethical standpoint. They rejected the corruption of the state apparatus, authoritarianism and its attack on institutions of the state, the manipulation of the press, the repeated human rights abuses, and the electoral fraud. Thousands of university students joined other social and political actors and took to the streets. Adrián Portugal, a member of Supay born in 1977, said he 'started participating in street protests at the time of the marches against Fujimori. It was all so evident, the outrage was generalised, there was a sense of urgency, you had to be involved.' The deep crisis of the regime ended with a transitional government, general elections and a sense of empowerment for the people who participated in the protests, a few artists among them. After the end of the armed conflict (1980–93) and the return to democracy, the work of many artists from the generation of the Supay Fotos photographers shows a sense of freedom and renewal in their relationship with Peruvian society. They want their work to reflect a different relationship with the national territory and ways of circulating in it; they also want to question established aesthetic boundaries between social and cultural groups and to negotiate a different relationship with indigenous Peruvians (Oliart, 2014). The work of Supay Fotos is respectful, inquisitive and critical; it shows 'attention, presence and generosity' (Masschelein, 2010, p. 48). And it is with these attributes that they approach the people and places they photograph.

Adrián Portugal and his 'Portraits of exemplary Peruvians'

Adrián Portugal's individual work focuses on urban popular culture and people's enjoyment of specific activities that generate a world around them. According to him, these worlds, organised around activities that people enjoy collectively, are spaces of freedom that generate their own sense of order. When discussing his work, Portugal explains how choosing and presenting a topic constitutes 'a declaration of principles, a viewpoint about a particular theme' that comes through with more clarity in the editing and mounting process. This elaboration of a theme, where Portugal says he finds his voice, is different from his attitude and body language while taking photos, 'where your ego disappears, [it] needs to disappear'. One of his most celebrated works is the series 'Agua Dulce', a beach frequented by people living in some of the poorest districts south of Lima. Other projects in his portfolio include break-dancing boys in the city centre, a beauty contest in Cantagallo (a Shipibo community that has been settled in Lima since 2000) and his book on Iquitos, the largest city in the Peruvian Amazon. The pages that follow discuss two of the eight images that form part of another of Portugal's projects, the series 'Portraits of exemplary Peruvians' which he introduces thus:

> In school, they teach us that exemplary Peruvians are the heroes who gave their lives for the country. They come to us as people from another era: they belong in history books. This series suggests the idea that there are exemplary Peruvians around every corner. How would you recognise them? They are common people who, in a country like ours, full of violence and beauty, pursue a dream and try to build it in their own terms. Thanks to some inexplicable personal qualities, they transform the world that surrounds them. It is true, they are not that common. They embody strength and fantasy. Even if they have not won wars, every day they win a fight against the poisonous side of our cities: pettiness, boredom, routine. If we look at them closely, we may come to admire them.

The pair of Portugal's heroes discussed here are 'Pachacutec' (see fig. 3.1) and 'Bailarina' (see fig. 3.2) or 'cumbia power', as the photo circulating online has been dubbed. The first photo shows a dweller of Pachacutec, a settlement in the middle of the desert north of Lima, dressed as an Inca (presumably Pachacutec) amidst a protest in Lima, who is demanding that the authorities pay attention to his remote neighbourhood.[14] The second photo shows a young, strong and committed woman, dancing cumbia for a large audience. Both 'exemplary Peruvians' are surrounded by their communities in acts of support and celebration.

Pachacutec is carried on the shoulders of the crowd, while performing a defiant act of either showing the way to the celebrating crowd, or pointing at the enemy. Ciudadela Pachacutec is in the district of Ventanilla, in the Province of Callao, bordering northwest Lima (it takes about two hours to get to central Lima from there). It comprises 136 associations of dwellers occupying the sandy hills formed by branches of the Andes reaching down to the sea, crossing the desert from the east. It was accorded the status of *ciudadela* [small city] in 1989. Some of the associations in Pachacutec, however, do not have legal recognition due to their illegal occupation of the desert. Even though they will not be considered in the planning of roads and services, such as water or electricity, until their legal status is resolved, residents of these precarious settlements continue building their houses. This fact makes access to services much slower

---

14 The name Pachacutec or Pachacuti Inca means 'he who overturns time and space' (Cameron, 1990, p. 58).

Figure 3.1. 'Pachacutec' by Adrián Portugal from the series 'Retratos de peruanos ejemplares', 2005 (by permission of the artist).

Figure 3.2. 'Bailarina' by Adrián Portugal from the series 'Retratos de peruanos ejemplares', 2005 (by permission of the artist).

and is a constant source of conflict and complaints among residents, but the situation also demonstrates the form Lima and Callao has taken the growth of since the 1940s. The urbanisation of Lima-Callao has been chaotic, informal, and marked by socio-spatial inequality and segregation. Its current shape and size are, in great part, the result of the autonomous agency of its inhabitants. In fact, about 60 per cent of Lima-Callao housing is the result of *autoconstrucción* [self-build] and it is estimated that some four million people live in illegal settlements, with ongoing processes of formalisation (Metzger et al., 2014). The people living in informal settlements in Lima are usually depicted as recent migrants from rural areas in the highlands, who moved to Lima pursuing the promise of a better life. Some political and cultural actors share an epic narrative of that process, with a language that reflects the physical and cultural conquest of the centre by the marginalised and oppressed. But recent research shows that new settlements such as Pachacutec are the result of learned modes of *autogestión* [self-management] and occupation of land, led not by recent migrants, but by new generations of people born in Lima and Callao, with no other means of accessing housing. They are vulnerable members of the precariat, but kow how to use resources to find a place for themselves in the city and to fight for it. Adrián Portugal's Inca Pachacutec, carried by a dense mass of mostly young supporters from Ciudadela Pachacutec, contributes to this renewed vision about informal Lima. They are not recent migrants; they are young *limeños* determined to fight for a place to live on their own terms.

A big and dense crowd of mostly young supporters also surrounds the cumbia dancer. Cumbia is the most popular music genre in Peru. A recent survey (Instituto de Opinión Pública, 2017) on musical tastes indicates that 40 per cent of the population favours this genre over others. It finds that cumbia followers are mostly under 40, from the less privileged groups in society, and with secondary or technical education. The survey shows that cumbia has also gained audiences among people of higher income and education levels. This could reflect the post-conflict cultural process, described by Fiorella Montero-Diaz (2016, p. 191; see also her chapter in this volume), in which people from the white upper classes of Lima want to 'integrate with the broader Peruvian population' through the consumption of certain genres of music, including cumbia, previously looked down on in a racist fashion.

In cumbia concerts, young female dancers are normally on the margins of the band, acting as adornments. Portugal's portrait makes the dancer the focal point: she is not at the side of the frame; instead the image captures her giving her all to the dance, with detail that takes us from the make-up and dressing process to the energy and sweat of a passionate performance. This image expands the contemporary visual repertoire of Peru's racially fragmented and sexually conservative society. The combination of violent racism and machismo defines an ambiguous relationship with the body of mestizo women, imagined as at once sexually uncontrollable and subordinate, available for pleasure, but denied recognition or social respect, as argued by Marisol de la Cadena (2000) and Mary Weismantel (2001), among others, and as documented and analysed by Peruvian narrators of Lima and provinces in the 20th century (Barrig, 1981). In this image the photographer is an accomplice of the dancer; he fully embraces her own presentation, in its beauty, strength and vulnerability.

When asked, Adrián Portugal said that he could accept an interpretation of his photographs as being anti-racist, but that is not his starting point. The reality of racism is indirectly addressed by presenting the anti-racist stance of the protagonists of his images, embedded in their struggles for citizenship rights, or occupying a space in the city and the country that they had to take almost by force. In both images the tension between the strength and the vulnerability of the protagonists is evident. The personal investment in an effective appearance in front of an audience is also revealed. Unlike the conventional portraits of heroes in history books – typically posing alone against a solemn background – which Portugal contrasts with his exemplary Peruvians, these young heroes are surrounded by a multitude that they belong to, although some still question and reject their presence, which affects their lives in a significant way.

Race and anti-racism in Argentina

After the restoration of democracy in 1983, Argentina continued to implement the neoliberal economic policies started by the dictatorship and developed other political and cultural reforms of the type being applied in Latin America following the Brady plan.[15] These included the promotion of multiculturalism and the guaranteeing of rights for ethnic minorities. In the three decades that followed, progressive policies and discourses have alternated – or coexisted – with racist ones. Argentina is a signatory of the 1965 UN International Convention on the Elimination of All Forms of Racial Discrimination. In 1988, law 23,592 defined racial discrimination as a criminal offence and as an aggravating circumstance in legal indictments and in 1995, the National Institute Against Discrimination and Xenofobia was established (Sutton, 2008). In 2000 Argentina signed the 169 ILO Convention on Indigenous and Tribal Peoples, and in 2003 President Néstor Kirchner passed migration law 25,871 which, according to Alejandro Grimson (2017, p. 124), represented a significant step in 'the struggle against xenophobia, racism and prejudice', although it was repealed by President Mauricio Macri soon after he came to power in 2015.

Grimson (2005, p. 28) explains that by the 1990s when the failure of neoliberal policies became evident, 'ethnicity had a new role to play in the re-imagining of Argentina'. Until then, the accepted narrative was that Argentina was a predominantly white country that had circumvented *mestizaje* due to the

---

15 The Brady plan was designed by the US Treasury in 1989 as a way of solving Latin America's debt crisis.

disappearance of both indigenous peoples and Afrodescendants in different historical circumstances (Sutton, 2008). Exaggeration of the numbers of immigrants from Bolivia, Paraguay and Peru, together with official attacks on the presence of recent migrants, linking them to precarious jobs and criminality, became a resource to rationalise the failures of neoliberalism in Argentina. After the severity of the crisis of 2001–2 these arguments were no longer plausible, and the Néstor and Cristina Kirchner regimes campaigned against them (Sutton, 2008). But racist arguments that blame the poor for poverty, precarity and crime have continued and have become contentious. Media representations, local authorities and social media frequently juxtapose 'migrants from neighbouring countries', as they are usually referred to by the press, with the Argentinian poor, racially marked as *negros*, and represent them all as dangerous, uneducated parasites on the state. Thus, a *negro* could be any person deemed non-white or not European enough. This creates a paradox and a tension in the racist politics of visibility and invisibility of the poor and 'non-white' people in Argentina. Widespread narratives about the nation invisibilise the Afroargentinian population, but the everyday use of the term *negro*, which conflates class and non-whiteness, makes the non-white poor hyper-visible (Adamovsky et al., 2016, p. 3; Peñaloza, 2007). The fact that anti-racism in Argentina found official support at different moments in recent years, becoming part of the official political discourse, backed by transnational organisations, has fuelled vibrant oppositional manifestations to policies that racialise segments of the population. La Marcha de la Gorra is an expression of that opposition.

Colectivo Manifiesto

Colectivo Manifiesto is a group of 12 male and female photographers in the city of Córdoba, who have worked as a collective since 2013.[16] Their main commitment is to produce coverage for events that the mainstream media ignores or silences, but that responds to the concerns and demands of diverse social movements. Some of their work involves interventions in public spaces where these movements undertake activities. According to Manifiesto's website, the creation of the collective responded to its members' similar aesthetic and political perspectives, and to their shared experience of supporting and participating in the same 'student protests, in the struggles for land and housing, in the festive celebrations in our neighbourhoods, in resistance to the extractivist multinationals', and documenting police brutality. 'We come from different fields such as literature, social communication, design, cinema, architecture and, of course, photography.' They characterise their organisation as 'independent and horizontal'. They are committed to producing quality images that are challenging as well as meaningful, breaking 'the artist's solitude

16   See https://colectivomanifiesto.com.ar.

and becoming a collective and rebellious voice'. They want to use photography as a tool to make visible alternative social and political narratives that contribute to the 'dream that another world is possible'. They position their work outside the mainstream and the centre, Buenos Aires, and locate the origins of the group in the streets of Córdoba, amidst struggles resisting or confronting power. Everyone's positionality and subjectivity preceded the collective; it is what enabled its formation, despite their diverse trajectories and occupation.

La Marcha de la Gorra

Since 2014, Colectivo Manifiesto has actively participated in the Marcha de la Gorra, a street protest that has taken place every November in central Córdoba since 2007. Over the years, the march has increased in size and visibility, attracting thousands of students, social organisations and citizens, who gather in repudiation of a provincial legal framework that regulated, among other things, police procedures.[17] The Código de Faltas [code of infractions] lists forms of behaviour considered offensive, even though these do not figure as crimes in the penal code. The code has existed since 1980 and has different versions in different provinces, but they all allow the preventative detention of individuals by the police. In Córdoba, the code was embraced by Governor José Manuel de la Sota (1999–2007, 2011–15), as the main support for his security policies. The article of the code targeted by the Marcha de la Gorra allowed preventative detention for the infraction of *merodeo* [loitering]. The vagueness of the definition of this offending behaviour produced a broad spectrum of arbitrary police practices, including harassment, arrests and physical punishment, which mostly targeted young men, considered potentially dangerous due to their appearance, including dress style, skin colour and type of hair (Bonvillani, 2016). Disguised as a vaguely phrased preventative legal instrument, this repressive technique affected mostly poor, young male adults (Lerchundi and Bonvillani, 2014, p. 45).[18] The Código de Faltas was repealed and replaced in 2015 by the Código de Convivencia Ciudadana [code of citizen coexistence]. Loitering in urban areas might be considered suspicious, but it is no longer an offence. However, a new infraction vaguely described as 'suspicious behaviour' allows for similar arbitrary detentions, mostly affecting the same young demographic.[19] In legal terms, a few articles of the old and new provincial codes violate the guarantees established by the national constitution

17 In 2017 the Marcha de la Gorra was held for the first time in Buenos Aires, two weeks later than the 11th Marcha de la Gorra in Córdoba, under the slogan 'Cuando la gorra crece, nuestros derechos desaparecen' [When the cap grows, our rights disappear]. The march was repeated in other cities with provincial versions of the same code of infractions.

18 Reports vary over the years but figures indicate that above 70 per cent of detainees are males between 16 and 30 years of age; of them, 50 per cent were charged with loitering.

19 Similar procedures are used in the UK, the USA and France, targeting mostly young men of distinct racial groups.

and the international treaties ratified by Argentina (Guiñazú, 2008; Job, 2011; Bolatti et al., 2013), including the International Convention Against Racism, which has constitutional status.

The Colectivo de Jóvenes por Nuestros Derechos [youth collective for our rights] is the main organiser of this march. It has become a political and cultural manifestation typical of the current communicative style of youth politics in Latin America – performative, celebratory, rich in visual displays, which include the body used as canvas, and featuring varied artistic expressions, such as dances, *batucadas, murgas*, theatre, choirs and graffiti (Reguillo, 2000). *La gorra* [the cap] works as a double metonym. It represents the young people who wear it, which makes them subject to suspicion, but it is also a derogatory nickname for the police.[20] Alongside the young people who feel vulnerable to arbitrary detentions, participants of the march include members of social, political and student organisations, and victims of police abuse or their relatives; many double up on the roles of militants and victims of the police. Young participants have asked for the repeal of both codes, denouncing the serious consequences that the detentions have on their life experiences, and claimed their right to circulate in the city.

In 2014 Manifiesto produced portraits of participants of the Marcha de la Gorra against a white background. They invited participants to step aside from the march to pose for the improvised studio they had installed on the sidewalk. In the days following the march of 2015, Manifiesto displayed the previous year's portraits, both in public spaces and in social media. In a conversation with Triquell in 2014, members of Manifiesto mentioned that they wanted to play with Richard Avedon's portraits of the American West (1985), using a white cloth background as a means of decontextualisation, but making the context from which they came very evident by the use of ad hoc t-shirts, banners and other paraphernalia. Further visual productions from the march have continued this focus on the faces and bodies of those participating in the march, taking them away from the collective to demonstrate each individual's commitment to the cause (a clear example is the impressive collaborative video produced in advance of the march of 2017 with images from the previous year projected onto symbolic walls in Córdoba).[21]

When Manifiesto published a Facebook album containing those images, they triggered an interesting political micro event. An anonymous user shared them on an anti-left Facebook page called 'Me lo contó un zurdo' [I was told by a lefty] making a deliberately equivocal use of Manifiesto's images and

---

20 The mottos 'My cap is none of your business' and 'Why your cap and not mine?' have figured in different versions of the march, alluding to the antagonism between the wearers of both caps.

21 See the video at https://www.facebook.com/latintacba/videos/1960758790864915/?hc_ref =ART96e8c1MATEjI7OLozIc9ccn9iv-NGMu4Aq4rHc_XgE8rJG6DjTTVu4JbKorjGyB8 andpnref=story (accessed 28 Nov. 2018).

starkly disputing their meaning.[22] Taking advantage of the decontextualised format of the images, they inserted texts that reproduced a multi-layered set of assumptions and representations that can be decoded in the context of sharp criticisms of populism, and the supposed abuse of the welfare system by 'the poor', a category loaded with racist connotations. A young female, who in the eyes of the author of this intervention probably does not fit the physical stereotype of a *villera* [shantytown dweller], is described as a middle-class progressive girl dressed as a poor person. However, in the same image, and in crass language, other stereotypes emerge. She is the violent mother of an unwanted child and a hypocrite who probably lives on state benefits but will not admit it. A young male's portrait shows him wearing a hoodie and a cap, and the texts around him curiously combine a robber's threats and the kind of justifications for criminal behaviour, such as blaming society for his fate, that are commonly contributed to the left. All the texts are saturated with spelling errors and stereotypical accents and *villero* expressions. The violent language used in this intervention is precisely situated in the context of 2015, reflecting the middle-class discourse against social welfare policies such as universal payments per child, the assumption being that women from the *villas* would have children as a strategy to receive this benefit. It accuses the left of being naïve and complicit with criminals who abuse the state and of being unable to grant security to ordinary citizens.

This contentious use of Manifiesto's portraits brings us close to the relationship between stigma, discrimination and physical appearance. The photographs shared on a social media platform and presented without any kind of textual anchoring, facilitated their manipulation, deepening the distance between producers and spectators, but at the same time, they produced a political event exposing social relations to the public, mediated by these photographs that, once in the public domain, can be moved in unforeseen directions (Azoulay, 2010). Besides being used as a way to support the march and denounce racism, they were appropriated to engage in a debate about the 'real nature' of the people portrayed, with contents that reaffirmed negative stereotypes about young men and women who live in the poorer areas of Córdoba.

Agustina Triquell interviewed Manifiesto members Marcos and Mar shortly before the second intervention. They stressed their stance of working with photography as a tool for change and political action. They shared images of the 2014 march, portraying social activists and university students, young victims of the Código de Faltas, and dwellers in the areas where the code is severely enforced. There was no room for an equivocal interpretation of the circumstance in which those images were taken. The march appeared as the theme, with the demonstrators in a metonymic relationship to it. During the interview, they shared their idea of using these images for an urban intervention,

22 In 2017 the page showed 3,700 followers and, on average, posts received comments or likes from close to 100 people.

Figure 3.3. The two portraits by Colectivo Manifiesto, as altered by anonymous Facebook users.

while framing them with a text that would leave no room for ambiguities. The message on the public street should be as clear as possible. The choice was a text written in the plural first person: *'El miedo que te venden lo pagamos nosotros'* [we have to pay for the fear they sell to you]. A few days before and during the march of 2015, six different images reproduced around ten times each, were carefully displayed in different spots in the city, mainly downtown, on bus stops and walls, in different sizes and formats (panels of 3 x 2 metres or 0.8 x 0.6 metres). The framing aimed at establishing a dialogue between passers-by and the photographs on the walls. The installation transformed the city into a palimpsest where a complex set of gaze exchanges could take place: high definition images of young people staring straight at the camera, the eyes of the spectators, and the gaze of the person behind the camera.

The visual economy that links the agents described above with you, the reader, now regarding the images, later entered the context of the Anthropology Museum in Córdoba, where it encountered yet another audience and was framed as an intervention that openly questioned racism in Argentina. In 2016, Ludmila da Silva Catela, the museum director, invited Manifiesto to exhibit their images as part of the bicentenary celebrations of the 1816 Declaration of Independence from Spain. The collective faced the challenge of considering how to enter into dialogue with the weight of an anthropological tradition in the use of photography, anthropometry and the visual recording of 'the other'. Although the previous title *'El miedo que te venden lo pagamos nosotros'* was centrally displayed in the main exhibition area, the museum exhibit title was 'Black on white, 200 years of racism'.

In this new public space, Manifiesto used a different strategy to convey their message. Photographs of the participants in the march were displayed in different formats and sizes in the museum's central corridors. Some of those facing the central stairs of the building could be seen from anywhere. Members of the collective added their own portraits to the exhibit, and some photos were next to texts from the protagonists. In alliance with the collective, the museum engaged in an intervention that made evident the politics of the visibility and invisibility of Argentina's African heritage, with a parallel display of their own historical material in the exhibition rooms. Thus, the whole museum highlighted the discussion about the construction of blackness in Argentina that associates dark skin with poverty and, more recently, with immigration from other Latin American countries. The exhibition received important local press attention and, according to Da Silva Catela, the museum received large numbers of visits organised by teachers who attached great importance to the open discussion of the historical and contemporary issues that the exhibition had brought together.

On being attentive and anti-racism

Achille Mbembe (2016) states that as part of its unstable nature, racism generates thoughts of fear and confusion, becoming an endless source of suffering and catastrophe. To Mbembe, the critique of racism entails ethical and political dimensions that are conducive to the actions of caring and healing. These actions should transcend the politics of difference and should be embraced by a universal community, which defies the idea of race and its denial of commonality. Mbembe's stance allows for a reflection on the role that the photographers of Manifiesto play in defying prejudice and resisting the racialisation of poverty and marginality in Argentina, even if they, the photographers, are not considered 'Black'. And it helps us in thinking about the role that Supay Fotos may be playing in producing images of Peruvians which break away from visual repertoires emphasising racial difference over a shared universal humanity, becoming part of a process of healing the wounds inflicted by racism on Peruvian society.

Manifiesto and Supay have different projects. Their contexts are different, as well as their aesthetic language, their purpose and practice. However, both groups combine photojournalism with unique projects of documentary photography that serve similar pedagogical and political purposes. They want us to be part of the play of gazes that takes place in their photos, they compose narratives to guide our reflection on the issues that matter to them because they matter to others, even if those issues are not part of the official political agenda. Both use the internet to provide free access to their images and narratives.

By preparing their images through careful editing, they generously share their gaze and their experience of documenting actions and issues, enriching the visual repertoire attached to struggles in favour of rights to dignified housing, access to land and water and protection of the environment, and against police brutality and racism. Through this they extend the political dimension of these struggles and grievances to the level of representation (Memou, 2013). Following Masschelein (2010), theirs is a pedagogy that involves paying attention. Attention is what allows us to share their experience. And – going back to Mbembe – one of the meanings of being attentive is to care.

Bibliography

Adamovsky, E., S. Caggiano, N. Fernández Bravo, M.L. Ghidoli, M.C. Martino, E. Lamborghini and L. Geler (2016) 'Reflexiones de los autores y las editoras sobre el debate', *Corpus*, 6 (2): 1–31.

Azoulay, A. (2010) 'Getting rid of the distinction between the Aesthetic and the Political', *Theory, Culture and Society*, 27 (7–8): 239–62.

— (2015) *Civil Imagination: A Political Ontology of Photography* (London: Verso).

Barrig, M. (1981) 'Pitucas y marocas en la narrativa peruana', *Hueso Húmero*, 9: 73–89.

Benklers, Y. (2006) *The Wealth of Networks: How Social Production Transforms Markets and Freedom* (New Haven, CT: Yale University Press).

Bonnett, A. (2000) *Anti-racism* (London: Routledge).

Bonvillani, A. (2013) 'Cuerpos en marcha: emocionalidad política en las formas festivas de la protesta juvenil', *Nómadas*, 39: 91–103.

— (2016) 'Habitar la marcha: notas etnográficas sobre una experiencia de protesta juvenil', *Universitas Psychologica*, 14 (5): 1599–612.

Caggiano, S. (2012) *El sentido común visual. Disputas en torno a género, 'raza' y clase en imágenes de circulación pública* (Buenos Aires: Miño y Dávila).

Carreras, C. (2010) *Laberinto de miradas* (Barcelona: Jordi Labanda).

Cortés Roca, P. (2011) *El tiempo de la máquina. Nación y modernidad* (Buenos Aires: Colihue Imagen).

De la Cadena, M. (2000) *Indigenous Mestizos: The Politics of Race and Culture in Cuzco, Peru, 1919–1991* (Durham, NC: Duke University Press).

Didi-Huberman, G. (2008) *Images in Spite of All: Four Photographs from Auschwitz* (Chicago, IL: University of Chicago Press).

Drinot, P. (2011) 'The meaning of Alan García: sovereignty and governmentality in neoliberal Peru', *Journal of Latin American Cultural Studies*, 20 (2): 179–95.

Edwards, E. (2015) 'Anthropology and photography: a long history of knowledge and affect', *Photographies*, 8 (3): 235–52.

Fairey, T. (2017) 'These photos were my life: understanding the impact of participatory photography projects', *Community Development Journal*, https://doi.org/10.1093/cdj/bsx010.

Freixa Font, P., M. Redondo Arolas and J. Córdova Morán (2015) 'Retrato ciudadano: una metodología para promover la visibilidad, la identidad y el debate desde la práctica fotográfica colectiva', paper given at Congreso Iberoamericano de Comunicación, Cultura y Cooperación, Madrid.

Glasius, M. and G. Pleyers (2013) 'The global moment of 2011: democracy, social justice and dignity', *Development and Change*, 44 (3): 547–67.

Gonzales Granados, P. (2016) 'Hacia una antropología compartida. Reflexiones, experiencias y propuestas acerca de la fotografía participativa en investigación antropológica', *Revista de Antropología Social*, 25 (1): 61–84.

Goodale, M. and N. Postero (eds.) (2013) *Neoliberalism Interrupted: Social Change and Contested Governance in Contemporary Latin America* (Stanford, CA: Stanford University Press).

Grimson, A. (2005) 'Ethnic (in)visibility in neoliberal Argentina', *NACLA Report on the Americas*, 38 (4): 25–9.

— (2017) 'Argentina's anti-immigrant about-face', *NACLA Report on the Americas*, 49 (2): 123–6.

Hale, C. (2002) 'Does multiculturalism menace? Governance, cultural rights and the politics of identity in Guatemala', *Journal of Latin American Studies*, 34 (3): 485–524.

Hershberg, E. and F. Rosen (2006) 'Turning the tide?', in E. Hershberg and F. Rosen (eds.), *Latin America After Neoliberalism: Turning the Tide in the 21st Century?* (New York: The New Press), pp. 1–25.

Instituto de Opinión Pública (2017) *Radiografía social de los gustos musicales en el Perú* (Lima: Instituto de Opinión Pública).

Jelin, E., P. Vila and A. D'Amico (1987) *Podría ser yo: los sectores populares urbanos en imagen y palabra* (Buenos Aires: CEDES).

Job, S. (2011) 'Apuntes para una comprensión posible del Código de Faltas', in L. Crisafulli and I. León Barreto (eds.), *¿¡Cuánta falta!? Código de faltas, control social y derechos humano* (Córdoba: INECIP), pp. 23–6.

Lerchundi, M. and A. Bonvillani (2014) 'Jóvenes y código de faltas: una experiencia de detención', *Justicia Juris*, 10 (1): 43–52.

Lindstrom, N. (1998) *The Social Conscience of Latin American Writing* (Austin, TX: University of Texas Press).

Marzo, J.L. (2006) *Fotografía y activismo. Textos y prácticas* (Barcelona: Gustavo Gili).

Masschelein, J. (2010) 'E-ducating the gaze: the idea of a poor pedagogy', *Ethics and Education*, 5 (1): 43–53.

Mbembe, A. (2016) *Crítica de la razón negra* (Buenos Aires: Futuro Anterior).

Memou, A. (2013) *Photography and Social Movements: From the Globalisation of the Movement (1968) to the Movement Against Globalisation (2001)* (Manchester: Manchester University Press).

Metzger, P., P. Gluski, J. Robert and A. Sierra (2014) *Atlas problématique d'une métropole vulnérable: inegalités urbaines a Lima et Callao* (Marseille, Paris: IRD, PRODIG).

Montero-Diaz, F. (2016) 'Singing the war: reconfiguring white upper-class identity through fusion music in post-war Lima', *Ethnomusicology Forum*, 25 (2): 191–209.

Oliart, P. (1998) 'Alberto Fujimori: "The man Peru needed"?', in S. Stern (ed.), *Shining and Other Paths: War and Society in Peru, 1980–1992* (Durham, NC: Duke University Press), pp. 411–24.

— (2008) 'Indigenous women's organizations and the political discourses of indigenous rights and gender equity in Peru', *Latin American and Caribbean Ethnic Studies*, 3 (3): 291–308.

— (2014) 'Fusion rock bands and the "New Peru" on stage', in P. Vila (ed.), *Music and Youth Culture in Latin America: Identity Construction Processes from New York to Buenos Aires* (Oxford: Oxford University Press), pp. 174–203.

Pinney, C. (2016) 'Crisis and visual critique', *Visual Anthropology Review*, 32 (1): 73–8.

Poivert, M. (2002) *La photographie contemporaine* (Paris: Flamarion).

Reguillo, R. (2000) *Emergencia de culturas juveniles. Estrategias del desencanto* (Editorial Norma: Bogotá).

Ritchin, F. (2013) *Bending the Frame: Photojournalism, Documentary and the Citizen* (New York: Aperture).

Rosenberg, F. (2016) *After Human Rights: Literature, Visual Arts and Film in Latin America 1990–2010)* (Pittsburgh, PN: University of Pittsburgh Press).

Rosler, M. (2007) *Imágenes públicas: la función política de la imagen* (Barcelona: Gustavo Gili).

Rowe, W. and V. Schelling (1991) *Memory and Modernity: Popular Culture in Latin America* (London: Verso).

Sassen, S. (2013) 'Does the city have speech?', *Public Culture*, 25 (2): 209–21.

Scheper Hughes, J. and A. Dalla Dea (2012) 'Introduction. Authenticity and resistance', *Latin American Perspectives*, 39 (183): 5–10.

Smith, S.M. (1999) *American Archives: Gender, Race and Class in Visual Culture* (Princeton, NJ: Princeton University Press).

Sommer, D. (ed.) (2006) *Cultural Agency in the Americas* (Durham, NC and London: Duke University Press).

Sutton, B. (2008) 'Democratic citizenship, human rights and anti-racist politics in Argentina', *Latin American Perspectives*, 35 (163): 106–21.

Tagg, J. (2003) *El peso de la representación* (Barcelona: Gili).

Vich, V. (2014) *Desculturizar la cultura. La gestión cultural como forma de acción política* (Buenos Aires: Siglo XXI).

Weismantel, M. (2001) *Cholas and Pishtacos: Stories of Race and Sex in the Andes* (Chicago, IL: University of Chicago Press).

4. Subverting racist imagery for anti-racist intent: Indigenous filmmaking from Latin America and the resignification of the archive

Charlotte Gleghorn

Aberrant readings in motion

In a 1983 text analysing the semiotics of racism in the cinema, Stam and Spence argue: 'Racism is not permanently inscribed in celluloid or in the human mind; it forms part of a constantly changing dialectical process within which, we must never forget, we are far from powerless' (p. 20). Stam and Spence employ the term 'aberrant readings' to describe those spectatorial 'readings which go against the grain of the discourse' (p. 18), appropriating this semiotic method of decoding explicitly for visual cultures. In this early article on filmic racism published in *Screen*, Stam and Spence call attention to the unpredictable nature of spectator responses; in particular, they highlight that even if a film putatively overturns racist stereotypes and their attendant filmic conventions, audience reactions are always cross-hatched by cultural expectations, class, gender and national bias, not to mention concerns pertaining to discourses of the historical moment. In racist aberrant readings 'an anti-racist film ... subjected to the ethnocentric prejudices of a particular critic or interpretative community, can be read in a racist fashion' (p. 19).

This discussion of aberrant readings presents a theoretical point of entry to examine the reverse movement; how spectatorial interferences may also act as what Stam and Spence term a 'counter-pressure to colonialist representations' (p. 19). In particular, this chapter explores how anti-racist aberrant readings of a racist repertoire are brought to life in a sample of recent Indigenous films from Latin America through engagement with the archive, critical spectatorship and extreme reflexivity. In the works analysed below, the friction produced between different modes of framing and interpreting indigeneity is dramatised through a metered unfurling of the relationship between director, subject and audience, enabling powerful anti-racist cinematic interventions on and off screen.

C. Gleghorn, 'Subverting racist imagery for anti-racist intent: Indigenous filmmaking from Latin America and the resignification of the archive', in P. Wade, J. Scorer and I. Aguiló (eds.), *Cultures of Anti-Racism in Latin America and the Caribbean* (London: Institute of Latin American Studies, 2019), pp. 73–99. License: CC-BY-NC-ND 4.0.

Cinema in Latin America has always participated in shaping discourses of race, yet scholarship addressing the boom in Indigenous filmmaking from the region seldom makes explicit reference to racism, but rather to *indigenismo* and cultural *mestizaje*. This critical blind spot is largely in keeping with what Peter Wade (2018, p. 93) has dubbed a 'powerful conceptual divide' between analyses of Afrodescendant and Indigenous experiences of colonial hierarchies.[1] As has been argued elsewhere, Indigenous movements tend to mobilise a lexicon of discrimination and culture, while Afrodescendant discourses articulate a critique of race more forcefully (Hooker, 2009). Scholarly approaches to a large degree have replicated this structure. This concealing of 'race' (though not of its racist machinations) has eclipsed the fact that 'the category Indian was an integral part of the colonial encounters within which the discourse of race emerged' (Wade, 1997, p. 37). Despite the limited traction of race in approaches to Indigenous cinema in Latin America, several projects across the region – where access to film technologies, like other material needs, is mapped onto racial hierarchies – attest to how film is seen as a powerful instrument to 'unpick' racialising portrayals and model critical Indigenous forms of spectatorship which might ameliorate the lived effects of racism. For filmic tropes, as Shohat and Stam (1994, p. 137) observed, though 'quasi-fictive', 'exercise real effectivity in the world'.

Recent examples of collaborative Indigenous filmmaking in the work of the Colombian collective Zhigoneshi Centro de Comunicaciones and the Brazilian Vídeo nas Aldeias reveal clearly the shifting dialectical processes of cinematic racism described in the discussion of aberrant reading. *Nabusímake: memorias de una independencia* [Nabusímake, memories of an independence] (Amado Villafaña and Zhigoneshi Colectivo de Comunicaciones, 2010), *Sey arimaku o la otra oscuridad* [Sey Arimaku: the other darkness] (Pablo Mora, 2012), *Sangradouro* (Divino Tserewahú and Vídeo nas Aldeias, 2006) and *O Mestre e o Divino* [The Master and Divino] (Tiago Campos Torres, 2013) all offer Indigenous film politics which work through textual, cartographic, visual, verbal and filmic archives as a means to envision an active and dynamic indigeneity on screen. The salvaging of sequences from an earlier audio-/visual repertoire – governed by anachronistic, though by no means forgotten, tropes of race – is employed in varied ways in order to initiate discussions across generations, activate affective ties and imagine cultural futures. By insisting on the afterlives of these racialising archives of indigeneity, this chapter argues

1 For this reason, some scholars are uncomfortable relating the term race with Indigenous cinema. In the words of Pablo Mora, 'la palabra raza es … una invención de origen colonial de clasificación y subordinación de las poblaciones no europeas que sirvió para legitimar la conquista y la colonización española en América. Por eso me niego a hablar de cine y raza y prefiero hablar de cine étnico' [the word race is a colonial invention used to classify and subordinate non-European populations which served to legitimise the conquest and Spanish settlement in America. This is why I refuse to speak of cinema and race and prefer to talk of ethnic cinema] (Mora Calderón, 2016).

that these films perform the act of 'aberrant reading' in order to reveal how Indigenous self-determination in film is produced in counterpoint to, and in conversation with, these earlier audio-/visual paradigms.

The analysis pivots around three iterations of audiovisual sovereignty and the films' disturbance of archives of archetypal indigeneity. The first example, *Nabusímake*, centres on the resignification of photographs and film excerpts, and suggests that the wresting of archives long guarded from Indigenous reinterpretation presents a forceful political act. The second film, *Sey arimaku*, reinterprets stereotypical notions of indigeneity through a contrapuntal method which illustrates the dialogic (de)construction of race through filmmaking. Finally, the parallel film trajectories presented in *Sangradouro* and *O Mestre e o Divino* playfully and humorously displace audiovisual discourses which remain invested in the pristine native. The selection of films, though sharing some characteristics with the wider tendency to reflexivity in Indigenous filmmaking and documentary, demonstrates an acute and refined awareness of the legacy of asymmetrical power relations with regard to Indigenous access to film technology. The ways in which the works scrutinise non-Indigenous filmmakers and gatekeepers, putting them on the spot and making them the 'object' of the filmic gaze and voice, orchestrate powerful critiques of the racialising mechanisms which underpinned the archive and archetype of filmic indigeneity. Moreover, both *Sey arimaku* and *O Mestre e o Divino* nest sequences from earlier films by the same communities which afford them a deeper engagement with the process of audiovisual sovereignty. When viewed together, the range of examples attests to how the mise-en-scène of reviewing practices crafts an Indigenous film politics which models aberrant readings as an idealised form of anti-racist spectatorship, confronting rather than eluding racialising vision. The relevance of these works and their dramatisation of aberrant readings is here illuminated through the concept of visual sovereignty.

Aberrant readings and visual sovereignty

Recent critical efforts to recover Indigenous contributions to film and photography heretofore criticised for their distortion of Indigenous lives and modernity resonate with this armament of aberrant readings. Like cinema, 'photography too was a handmaiden of empire' (Spitta, 2013, p. 167) and, building on a tradition of 18th-century *casta* paintings used to serialise phenotypes of racial mixture, would be instrumentalised for scientific ends to measure race in anthropometric portraiture (Poole and Zamorano Villarreal, 2012).[2] The groundbreaking work by Deborah Poole (1997) on the Andean visual economy in the 19th century illuminated the processes by which photographs would participate in the circulation of notions of race internationally. Also in the Andean context, recent work on the Peruvian photographer Martín

[2] For detailed and recent appraisals of *casta* paintings, see Katzew (2004) and Carrera (2003).

Chambi and the Cuzco School of photography has examined the monumental portrayals of indigeneity which foreground the abstract and other-worldly (Spitta, 2013), pointing to a more playful interpretation of monumental sites through photography which draws attention to divergent political and affective projects (Scorer, 2017). Spitta (2013, p. 170) argues, however, that approaches to these photographic works remain largely unable to 'evade the ready-made ethnographic narratives that dominate our epistemology'.

The films discussed here invoke such prior narratives, which asserted Indigenous stasis and tradition through a technology premised on an Anglo-European gaze and version of modernity. In early 20th-century film and photography, Indigenous experiences of technologies such as the gramophone, the watch and the camera, were often erased in order to favour tropes of the Noble Savage or the Vanishing Indian (Tobing Rony, 1996; Hearne, 2006). According to Fatimah Tobing Rony (1996, p. 102), efforts to revive through film purportedly obsolete Indigenous cultural practices were analogous to taxidermy: 'Since indigenous peoples were assumed to be already dying if not dead, the ethnographic "taxidermist" turned to artifice, seeking an image more true to the posited original'. This desire for authenticity, investing the Native with a range of mythologies ranging from the telluric through to the barbaric or the dying, with every degree of *other* in between, would leave an indelible mark on Indigenous representation in moving images. Many film and television productions continue to barter in the phantasmagorical 'pristine native', actively concealing or manipulating evidence of the technologies which Indigenous communities use in order to bolster preconceptions of a pre-modern and naïve state of being. This refusal of contemporaneity, disavowal of change or relegation of indigeneity to the past represents the 'denial of coevalness' which for a long time characterised anthropological enquiry (Fabian, 1983). Making Indigenous presence felt today in terms which acknowledge cultural continuity and resist reification is thus an urgent task for many filmmakers.[3]

One of the key ways to challenge the normative understanding of these productions as exclusively manipulative of Indigenous experience has been to carefully unearth the decisive influence Indigenous advisors, script writers, actors, and in some cases camera-wielders, had on a wide range of films. Michelle H. Raheja's 2007 study of Robert Flaherty's *Nanook of the North* (1922) – for Tobing Rony (1996, p. 88) a case of 'cinematic taxidermy' *par excellence* – highlights how, despite the film's problematic staging of a pristine, pre-modern and naïve Inuit reality, there are coded messages in the film which, with access to different epistemological frameworks, might offer a different interpretation. In her analysis of the famous scene when the childlike Nanook first sees a gramophone, Raheja draws on Tobing Rony's earlier interpretation

3 Photography in particular has been susceptible to these charges of petrification since the very aura of the medium promoted a sense of capturing a particular moment in time, which further emphasised the stasis of indigeneity (Poole, 2005, p. 164).

of a sequence when actor Allariak is depicted smiling directly at the camera. Tobing Rony (1996, p. 111)writes 'the enigma of Nanook's smile allows the audience to project its own cultural presuppositions: from the point of view of an outsider he is childlike, from the Inuit point of view he may be seen as laughing at the camera'. Raheja takes this observation further, suggesting that Nanook's laughter during the gramophone scene is precisely a knowing mocking of Flaherty's attempts to manipulate reality. In Raheja's words (2007, p. 1160), 'Nanook's response [to the gramophone] might register one thing to his non-Inuit audience and another to members of an Inuit community who recognize the cultural code of his smile'. This account of a differentiated engagement with a film that has contributed to the entrenched idea of indigeneity as out-of-sync with modernity is a clear example of the polarised readings film may generate. Raheja's approach, which acknowledges degrees of Indigenous complicity in well-worn filmic tropes of indigeneity, also owes much to the affective ties *Nanook of the North* has built with contemporary Inuit communities since its making. Today, members of the Inuit community connect with their ancestors on film, through handed-down stories, photographs, and the influence of this early filmmaking experience on the community, evidenced through the continuing engagement with the technology of photography and film production in the area. As Catherine Russell (1999, p. 113) has underlined, 'the apparent persistence of *Nanook* in Inuit culture as a site of re-viewing, remaking, and rereading suggests that while the salvage paradigm is an ethnographic allegory of colonialism, it may also preserve a utopian form of memory of some historic value to native communities'. Indigenous engagement with *Nanook*, then, as with Westerns about manifest destiny, is far from straightforward.[4]

Raheja (2007, p. 1162) considers this reinterpretation of older films on Indigenous terms as a form of visual sovereignty, unveiling sites of knowledge production which would otherwise be eclipsed by western interpretations. These efforts to reinstate Indigenous agency in complex histories of entanglement once again reiterate how looking, or more appropriately, watching, is an activity which can be read with and against the grain. Aberrant readings, to adapt the work of Alia Al-Saji (2014, p. 136) on the phenomenology of racialising vision, 'can become the location for violent and objectifying misrepresentation, but also for critical attunement and affective openness'. If in *Nanook* and other examples proffered by Raheja this act of sovereignty is performed through the reception and reinterpretation of films, in the works analysed here audiovisual

---

4   Cree director Neil Diamond, for instance, explores why as a young boy he was fascinated by the Indians of Hollywood Westerns in the feature documentary *Reel Injun* (Neil Diamond, Catherine Bainbridge and Jeremiah Hayes, 2009). The film opens with a revealing voiceover: 'Growing up on the reservation, the only show in town was movie night in the church basement. Raised on cowboys and Indians, we cheered for the cowboys, never realizing we were the Indians.'

sovereignty is staged in the objectification of watching as a diegetic and reflexive act.

The Brazilian organisation Vídeo nas Aldeias has been using photography and film as instruments to document, discuss and alleviate the more nefarious changes Indigenous communities have been experiencing in the country from its beginnings in 1987 (Aufderheide, 2008). An independent NGO since 2000, Vídeo nas Aldeias boasts a healthy list of productions, many of which harness the vestiges of a racist archive to prompt discussion at community level. Zezinho Yube's striking film *Já me transformei em imagem* [I've already become an image] (Zezinho Yube and Vídeo nas Aldeias, 2008) draws on both Native and non-Native archives in order to craft a narrative that revolves around five historical periods – pre-contact, rubber raids, enslavement, the land rights era and, finally, the present of filmmaking – in his Huni Kui community in Acre state in northern Brazil. Archival footage and oral testimony attest to the impact of colonial intervention and the *seringueiros*, the rubber tappers, in the area, while the film presents a welcome opportunity to reconsider how the audiovisual record may be recontextualised. The film revisits the painful moments when Yube's people were renamed Kaxinawá by the white man, forced off their land by rubber tappers and enslaved and marked as property, but equally emphasises the enduring resilience and cultural vitality of his community. The songs, dances and testimonies that feature are therefore testament to Huni Kui efforts to use audiovisual technology in order to safeguard cultural knowledge and generate transgenerational dialogue, as well as to reassess the exploitation of natural resources related to Huni Kui territories.

Já me transformei em imagem explicitly reveals its concern to engage directly with the spectator in the prologue to the film, when one of the elder authorities of the community interpellates the audience, asking them to listen up and pay attention to what he will say. His authority is conveyed visually and aurally in this direct address and is further accentuated as he begins to tell us about the pre-contact time of the Huni Kui. During this sequence, the low camera angle establishes his authority in relation to the other members of the community and the spectator. His recognition of change, however, in his discussion of the hunting tools the Huni Kui use today demonstrates that this collective history and identity is always under negotiation and moreover, that Indigenous communities are always adapting and transforming, contrary to popular myth.

This reflexivity, often in the form of a direct address such as the one described above, or in sequences showing the community filming or watching films collectively, performs an important function in authorising the work for Indigenous filmmakers. According to Faye Ginsburg (1994, p. 370), 'Such reflexivity is not a Brechtian innovation; rather it authorizes the reconfiguring of traditional practices for video as "true" and properly done'. Furthermore, given the acute awareness of cultural appropriation and loss of voice and knowledge in filmmaking among Indigenous communities, the overt emphasis

Figure 4.1. Hunikui authority addressing the spectator in the prologue to Já me transformei em imagem *(2008). Courtesy of Zezinho Yube and Vídeo nas Aldeias.*

on Indigenous point of view and authorship in these videos reclaims the medium for the community's own purpose and self-fashioning. Though this reflexivity is not new in documentary praxis, the opening invitation of *Já me transformei* ascribes authority to the Huni Kui elder (and later the filmmaker when we hear his voiceover) and crucially reverses the economy of the gaze associated with outmoded ethnographic film. Here, the observed of the past become the observers looking and speaking back at the spectator.

The acknowledgment of point of view and the constructedness of representation are now recurrent devices in contemporary Indigenous filmmaking, determined to unveil the site of epistemic privilege. This reflexivity not only serves to deconstruct the economy of the gaze and voice in filmmaking, but also suggests how the recycling of racialised tropes and archives of indigeneity in fact reiterates the purposeful anti-racist commitment of the documentaries. *Nabusímake, Sey arimaku o la otra oscuridad, Sangradouro* and *O Mestre e o Divino*, while from different communities and operating in different national contexts, share disputed and violent missionary pasts: *Nabusímake* and *Sey arimaku* engage with the history of the Capuchin mission established in the Sierra Nevada de Santa Marta in the north of Colombia; while *Sangradouro* and *O Mestre e o Divino* harness the legacy of a Salesian mission and one missionary in particular, Adalbert Heide, in Xavante territory in Mato Grosso state, Brazil.

In addition, *Sey arimaku* and *O Mestre e o Divino*, doubly reflexive for their encasing of other reflexive films within their structure, offer a framework to consider how Indigenous perspectives on film and the image are entwined with this earlier racist repertoire, and today dramatise the decodification of the archive as a means to model a critical anti-racist spectatorship.

Nabusímake: memorias de una independencia

The Colombian documentary film *Nabusímake* centres on the history of the place of the same name, and in 37 minutes develops a method of historical research drawing from Indigenous and non-Indigenous sources of knowledge. With excellent digital cinematography, the sources come from oral and written testimonies of community members, the *mamos* [the spiritual guardians of the communities], the press and pre-existent film sources. The documentary was produced collectively by Zhigoneshi Colectivo de Comunicaciones, with funding from the Colombian Ministerio de Cultura, in the context of the 2010 bicentenary of independence commemorations.[5] Zhigoneshi comprises members from all four Indigenous communities who live in the Sierra Nevada de Santa Marta and who have strong historical connections: the Wiwa, Arhuaco, Kogui and Kankuamo. The collective has made a number of films, with members of the group specialising in different facets of the production process – sound, lighting, camera – but the member who has the most consolidated work to date is Amado Villafaña, the director of *Nabusímake*. In piecing an alternative version of Nabusímake's past together, the video poetically entwines the history of the occupation of the Arhuaco sacred site with the audiovisual and political history of Colombia.

The Capuchin Mission school, el Orfelinato las Tres Avemarías, ultimately approved in 1916 by state authorities and established the following year in Nabusímake (or San Sebastián de Rábago, the missionaries' name for the settlement), like many other colonialist schooling projects, sought to assimilate Indigenous peoples into the fabric of the (mestizo) nation state. Religious authorities had been in the region since the mid 18th century but it was not until the early 20th century that tensions between the *colonos* [settlers], *misioneros* [missionaries] and Arhuacos seemed to intensify and worsen (Muñoz, 2017). As the film makes clear, in 1916, a delegation of Arhuaco leaders travelled to Bogotá to petition President José Vicente Concha (1914–18) for the establishment of a school in the area devoted to the teaching of mathematics and Spanish, subjects seen as necessary and beneficial to the community's development priorities, particularly in the context of disputed

---

5   A truncated version of *Nabusímake* can be viewed online here: http://uno.memoriasdelalibertad. org/#videos (accessed 4 March 2019). The other films produced as part of this 'Memorias de la libertad' *bicentenario* programme are: *Jiisa weçe: raíz del conocimiento* (Cineminga, 2010) and *Mi finK* (Grupo Fundación Villa Rica and Soporte Klan, 2010).

and exploitative commercial trade relations in the area (p. 391). However, the state had previously authorised the founding of a mission school in San Sebastián de Rábago in 1914, and upon the request of the Arhuaco leaders in 1916 masked their true intentions in acquiescing to the delegation's demands. Thus, from 1917 the Capuchin mission instructed young men and women from the Arhuaco community in the region in leaving behind their language, clothes and other social and cultural customs termed *salvaje* [savage]. Including the chewing of *áyu* or coca leaf, all were deemed incompatible with the Colombian project of nationhood. The Orphanage, contrary to its name, actively orphaned children by attempting to strip them of Arhuaco culture. Though Arhuaco records – oral and written[6] – document and remember this period with 'emociones cruzadas de malestar y admiración' [mixed feelings of unease and admiration] (Mora, 2009, p. 34), this indoctrination continued until 1982, when the Consejo Indígena Arhuaco organised and finally managed to expel the Capuchins from the site, culminating in the rebirth of the place as Nabusímake the following year.

From the outset, *Nabusímake* establishes its relationship to historical reconstruction. A short fragment of black and white church bells ushers in the director, Amado Villafaña, who in Arhuaco language addresses the camera directly, and who is shot from a low angle against the backdrop of a limpid blue sky, in a 'rotundo gesto de anfitrión' [emphatic gesture as host] (Mora, 2015, p. 90). He states: 'Aquí estamos en Nabusímake. Aquí nos dejaron desde el principio de la creación. Ahora hemos venido a recoger información sobre los padres capuchinos' [Here we are in Nabusímake. This is where they left us since the beginning of time. We have come to collect information about the Capuchin priests]. A series of versatile transitions between archival footage of a religious procession in 1962, and the colour rendition of this same celebration from 2008, cements this fluid relationship between the past and the present. In this way, the film initiates a journey accompanying the director and his children, Gunzareymun and Ángel, as they collate the history of Nabusímake from the arrival of the Capuchin missionaries to the ultimate ousting of the church authorities in 1982. In acknowledging the enmeshed histories of Arhuaco organisation and forced conversion through an exploration of embodied and recorded memories of the mission, the documentary powerfully illustrates the negotiated status of the archive in reconstructing memory for the community.

The establishment of the mission would coincide roughly with the first attempts of Colombian entrepreneurs to create a national cinema. However, it is worth noting that early filmic records concerning the territory's Afrodescendant and Indigenous communities from the late 1920s and early 1930s were designed to appeal commercially and were made by filmmaker-

6 One of the key sources employed in the film and in work on Arhuaco activism more generally is the testimony written by the Arhuaco, Vicencio Torres Márquez, *Los indígenas arhuacos y la 'vida de la civilización'*.

explorers (Mateus Mora, 2013, pp. 60–4). Later, the mission would collaborate in producing its own – exuberantly racist – feature film, *El valle de los arhuacos* (Vidal Antonio Rozo, 1964), which Angélica Mateus Mora (2013, p. 71) has dubbed a form of 'cine de evangelización' [evangelising cinema]. *El valle de los arhuacos*, which is also cited in *Nabusímake*, foregrounds racialised depictions of the Arhuaco as dirty, corrupt, drunk, murderous, superstitious and ultimately, as destined to 'desaparecer como indio' [disappear as Indians] (ibid., p. 84). *Nabusímake* revisits this production as an intertext in a compelling scene following the visit of the director and his children to Bogotá to view the film where it is housed in the Fundación Patrimonio Fílmico archive. There, the camera witnesses the confused reaction of the receptionist who receives Amado Villafaña, the crew and Ángel and Gunzareymun, as they explain their interest in viewing the film. Once inside, *Nabusímake* stages a lesson in how to interpret *El valle* critically, through the deconstruction that Amado Villafaña offers of the filmic representation of the Arhuacos. With the silhouette of the Villafaña family and Amado's *tutosoma* hat in the foreground, and the screened film in the background, the dissonance between the family's viewing practices in the present and the projected narrative could not be made more clear. When Ángel asks after the screening if things were really like that back then, Amado proclaims that everything they saw was a complete lie. Thus, the right to decipher and interpret otherwise these racist archives is pitted as an overtly political and pedagogical act. This reviewing of racist archives might even be termed a kind of audiovisual repatriation. In Dobbin's (2013, p. 129) terms, this gesture is not so much a repatriation of concrete material items to source communities 'but rather [of] elements of history, memory, and identity that are associated with the images'.

The archives that underpin the documentary are housed in different kinds of repositories – some personal, some state, some communitarian and some in the vibrant voice of testimony – with differentiated possibilities for access and interpretation. Early on in the documentary, as Amado Villafaña and his children look out over the settlement of Nabusímake with a photograph of Villafaña's father in hand,[7] the director tells Gunzareymun and Ángel about a collection of photographs which he came across when speaking with Manuel Chaparro, a former *cabildo* [traditional authority] of the Arhuaco community. These photographs, though this is not made explicit in the film, were taken by a Swedish ethnographer, Gustav Bolinder, during two separate trips he made to the area in 1914–15 and 1920–1 (Mora, 2015; Muñoz, 2017). As Catalina Muñoz (2017, p. 377) carefully documents, these photographs do not have widespread circulation in the community today, though enlargements of four of them were selected for display outside the community meeting house. The others remain in the private collection of Manuel Chaparro.

7 The director's father, Juan Bautista Villafaña, was the designated interpreter among the Arhuaco delegation that petitioned the president for a school in 1916.

The director connects the cruel mistreatment community members associate with the mission with the photos he saw, swiftly corroborated in the film by the testimony of Damiana Crespo, a former student at the school, who speaks of the most common abuses witnessed during her time as a pupil. Ángel then asks his sister: 'Después de ver las fotos, ¿cómo sería esa época? Imaginemos….' [After seeing the photos, what do you think it was like back then? Let's imagine…]. Cross-cutting between shots of Ángel's face and a restaging of the grievances suffered under Capuchin rule – animating the aforementioned photographic collection – this sequence dramatises the children's imagination in sepia tones. Several of the photos are re-enacted in sequence, combining different episodes of Arhuaco subjugation under the missionary authorities spatio-temporally. The re-enactment is employed as a way to represent the violence of the mission from an Arhuaco perspective based on accounts of the time and the oral and archival sources available, but it also performs a mediating role between the different generations involved in the making of the video.[8] Each photograph, belonging to a wider collection of images with text in the case of Bolinder's work, or set to motion in their re-activation in *Nabusímake*, draws attention to how photographic imagery, when removed from the containing discourse of the archive of collection, can afford new interpretations which can be made to cast new narratives. Moreover, the 'Indigenous repurposing' of such images often serves to rebuild community and family filiations (Hearne, 2006, p. 308). In this example, the photograph of the children's paternal grandfather presents a springboard to reconsider the role of photography in documenting the family's and – by extension – the community's past.

The specific photo the director recalls from the Bolinder collection – one of a girl tied to a pole, which is staged in the dramatised sepia scene in the film – is in fact from the collection of photographs published following the 1914–15 expedition (Muñoz, 2017, p. 389). These images appear to pre-date the foundation of the mission school in Nabusímake; according to Bolinder's own captions included in the publication, the grievances documented are attributable to the Arhuaco community (Bolinder, 1915, cited in Muñoz, 2017). In fact, Bolinder's first trip to the area appears to have been precisely on the heels of the Vanishing Indian. According to Muñoz (2017, p. 385),

> In his early pictures, Bolinder construed the Arhuaco as an isolated, authentic and uncontaminated indigenous group. Local archival sources show that, at the time of Bolinder's expedition, the Arhuaco engaged in different forms of interaction with their non-indigenous neighbours including trade, labour relations and land transactions. Bolinder carefully silenced this part of Arhuaco life in order to show his audience an autochthonous and exotic indigenous community, on the margins of capitalism.

---

8 See Córdova (2014) for another approach to re-enactment in recent Latin American Indigenous film.

Figures 4.2 and 4.3. Bolinder photo and re-enactment in Nabusímake *(2010). Courtesy of Pablo Mora, Amado Villafaña and Zhigoneshi Colectivo de Comunicaciones.*

This description corresponds wholesale with the salvage ethnography tradition, in vogue at the time. In their remediation, however, the photographs – the originals are intercalated with the dramatisation – are afforded a new role that interrupts the original purpose of the photographs with a politicised Arhuaco interpretation. The recasting of the Bolinder image as an authentication of the Capuchin order's cruelty demonstrates the ways in which the Arhuaco protagonists and filmmakers reassert control over the telling of ethnographic fictions. In the temporal and spatial splicing of Capuchin violence, *Nabusímake* offers an Arhuaco version of the past and simultaneously lays out a path to historical consciousness as the documentary represents a learning journey for the director's children.

Of course, for many the revisiting of moments of catechism, forced conversion, stolen children and punished tongues remains too painful. While some people may have affective ties to archival images – not least the director and his children – others may prefer to avoid rehearsing the abuses of the past. As Pablo Mora (2009, p. 34), the executive producer of several films made by the Zhigoneshi Collective and close collaborator of Amado Villafaña's in particular, writes as a preamble to a sample of the Bolinder photographs published in the community magazine:

> ¿Qué sentido tiene hoy, veintisiete años después de que la misión capuchina saliera de la región, reintroducir el espectáculo de viejos abusos? No sobra describir con palabras escuetas que se trata de una jovencita amarrada, un grupo de niños en formación disciplinar, un *mamo* al que le están cortando el pelo y otro amarrado por la espalda, conducido por un mestizo sonriente. La contemplación de estas imágenes dolorosas nos hiere y no es suficiente decir que eran otras épocas –a casi cien años de distancia– y otras costumbres educativas hoy en desuso, como esta de evangelización compulsiva.
>
> [What use is it today, 27 years after the Capuchin mission has left the area, to reintroduce the spectacle of past abuses? Is it not enough to describe with a few well-chosen words that they show a girl tied to a post, a group of children organised in military file, an Arhuaco elder whose hair is being cut, and another elder with his hands tied behind his back, all orchestrated by a smiling mestizo. The contemplation of these painful images hurts us and it is not enough to say that those were other times – almost 100 years ago – and that other educational customs were used, which are no longer used today, such as forced catechism.]

As Mora's discussion intimates here, the community was split over whether to dramatise these photographs at the time and would eventually use actors in the assemblage of staged photographs (Mora, 2015, p. 89). In the end, and despite the tensions this re-enactment caused, the sequence was filmed and included in the final documentary. This use of the Bolinder photographs in *Nabusímake* might therefore be seen to chime with Hulleah J. Tsinhanjinnie's (2003, p. 41) concept of photographic sovereignty:

> It was a beautiful day when … I first encountered photographic sovereignty … when I decided that I would take responsibility to reinterpret images of Native peoples. My mind was ready, primed with stories of resistance and resilience, stories of survival. My views of these images are Aboriginally based … not a scientific godly order but philosophically Native.

The animation of ethnographic stasis in the film is crucial to understanding how the archive encloses the potential for the future, serving a politicised historical memory, activated through aberrant fictions of the photographs. In other words, 'As much as and more than a thing of the past [...], the archive should call into question the coming of the future' (Derrida and Prenowitz, 1995, p. 26).

Sey arimaku o la otra oscuridad

Sey arimaku o la otra oscuridad returns to the re-enactment of the Bolinder photographs in order to reveal more of the context around the images' appearance in the community. The sequences show the four enlarged Bolinder photographs which Zhigoneshi exhibited outside the community meeting house to document reactions to these images. The dramatised photograph sequence here features in colour and from different angles to the final edited sepia sequence in *Nabusímake*. Mora suggests to Villafaña in the voiceover that they view the *Nabusímake* re-enactment scene once more, this time within *Sey arimaku*. The sequence's reappearance in *Sey arimaku* therefore offers a behind-the-scenes insight into the negotiations that the production of *Nabusímake* demanded, demonstrating a quite different story to the appearance of the archive within the earlier documentary. This sequenced approach to the filmic oeuvre of the collective illuminates how the archive continually transforms in meaning through politicised reinterpretations.

Sey arimaku is a feature-length documentary charting the relationship between Pablo Mora and Amado Villafaña. In its most straightforward terms, *Sey arimaku* might be termed a making-of film on the production and première of the collective's feature documentary *Resistencia en la línea negra* [resistance on the black line] (Amado Villafaña Chaparro, Saúl Gil and Silvestre Gil Sarabata, 2011), at the same time as it is a powerful, multilayered and multivocal meditation on the relationship between an Arhuaco filmmaker and an anthropologist filmmaker. In fact, the title, *Sey arimaku*, subtly reflects the identity of the film's lead protagonist. In an interview conducted in 2011 during the Native American Film and Video Festival held at the National Museum of the American Indian in New York, Amado Villafaña explains that in the Arhuaco language his name is 'Sey arimaku: la palabra "sey" significa antes de haber la luz, "arimaku" es una actividad definida antes de haber la luz. Sey arimaku es actividad definida antes de haber la luz' [*Sey arimaku*: the word 'sey' means before there was light, and 'arimaku' is a specific activity. *Sey arimaku* is a specific activity that happened before there was light] (Villafaña, cited in Gleghorn, 2011). The film only briefly acknowledges this highly explicit reference to the title in the caption that appears under Amado Villafaña's name towards the beginning. The cosmological value of darkness and shadow, however, is exploited throughout the production for its symbolism and in the commentary provided by Villafaña and other members of Zhigoneshi on the interpretation and use of filmic and photographic technology among the Arhuaco.

The off-screen voiceover (alternating between Pablo Mora and Amado Villafaña) reinterprets film excerpts from the two directors' earlier productions, offering commentary on the negotiations which took place behind the scenes and documenting the evolving relationship between the filmmakers, from their beginnings working together, to the completion of the full-length feature documentary, *Resistencia*, their most ambitious project to date. The film's structure charts the relationship between Mora and Villafaña episodically, by turns humorous and serious, from their tentative first encounter in 2006, to the première of *Resistencia en la línea negra* in Bogotá in 2011, a mise-en-abyme framing device which bookends the entire documentary. This added layer of reflexivity conveys both Villafaña's and Mora's approaches to visualising indigeneity, elements which are not readily discernible in the reflexive documentaries they discuss, including *Nabusímake*.

This recourse to an off-screen voiceover, with the directors verbally interpreting 'against the grain', draws attention to the way that *Sey arimaku*, more than a treatment of the violence committed against Indigenous communities, ecological disruption and cosmological imbalance in the Sierra Nevada, ruminates on the ways in which filmmaking materialises a negotiated vision. In *Sey arimaku*, the voiceover interpretation and reflexive sequences reveal diverse perspectives integral to the cross-cultural collaboration, while affording the opportunity to critique mythologies of technology's incompatibility with indigeneity. Early on in the 60-minute documentary a sequence contextualises *Sey arimaku* as a film about 'cómo los indígenas arhuacos cogen una cámara y qué hacen con ella' [how the Indigenous Arhuacos grab a camera and what they do with it]. In footage from 2007, Mora explains that at the request of the Organización Gonawindúa Tayrona, one of the foremost Indigenous organisations from the Sierra Nevada de Santa Marta, he set out to document how this group of Arhuacos is using film. The voiceover that immediately ensues, however, conveys how this sequence represents the first time that Mora actually became the object of Villafaña's gaze: 'estábamos igualados', says Mora, 'cada uno con su cámara' [we were on an equal footing, each with his own camera].

This alternating of footage and voices from both Mora's and Villafaña's perspectives represents the central preoccupation of the film: how these two filmmakers, with different cultural frameworks, use audiovisual media and how they document their own interpersonal relationship in so doing. The spectator witnesses what Mora's voiceover frames as Villafaña's unskilled manipulation of the camera: first a 'selfie' sequence with the camera turned back on filmmaker Amado as he rides a mule; then a jerky sequence as Villafaña, camera in hand, journeys through the rugged mountain terrain. Mora's voiceover jokingly asks if this is a 'subjetivo de la mula': a subjective shot from the perspective of the mule, which Villafaña is riding. This uncomfortable mocking of the Arhuaco filmmaker's competence is immediately neutralised by Mora's assertion that Villafaña's composition of frame is comparable to that of a professional. Following this commentary on Villafaña's camera skills, the sequence segues into another scene; this time it is Villafaña who mocks Mora's (in)ability to film on the uneven and unfamiliar *páramo* terrain. Villafaña asks 'y ese desenfoque, ¿qué? ¿La cámara tenía problemas?' [and this blurriness, what's that about? Was there a problem with the camera?] To which Mora replies, 'no, ¡el que tenía problemas era el camarógrafo!' [no, the problem was with the filmmaker himself!]. Sequences such as these, eliciting both laughter and provoking candid revelations, are interwoven throughout *Sey arimaku* with additional footage shot by other members of the Zhigoneshi collective, alongside scenes from the première of *Resistencia en la línea negra* in the Centro Ático at the Universidad Javeriana in Bogotá. By way of the reflexive voiceover, the two filmmakers breathe life into the praxis of audiovisual sovereignty, offering potent commentary on how film technology might be interpreted according to a different matrix. This is equally true of the sequence when two members of the community sacrifice a sheep by cutting its throat on camera. According to Mora's voiceover here, Villafaña did not want this to be captured at first, in a gesture of self-censorship attesting to the construction of such acts as emblematic of the savage Indian. These sequences, which could be considered performed vignettes of tropes of indigeneity, represent the first of a series of moments in *Sey arimaku* that interrogate how the spectre of the primitive and savage Indian, incompatible with film technology, surfaces to this day.

During a pivotal moment in the city scenes, a Bogotano camera technician gives Villafaña a thorough dressing down about his treatment of the camera: he attributes the damage to the camera to the 'selva', assuming that Villafaña, as an Indigenous man, must live in the forest and is therefore not accustomed to using such technology, nor equipped to protect it from the presumed humidity of the environment. This projection of Indigenous persons onto selvatic regions is commonplace and simultaneously functions to mark the urban metropole as a non-Indigenous space. This kind of discrimination is felt acutely by Indigenous peoples in cities across the region (Wade, 1997, p. 38) and serves to highlight the enduring racialisation experienced in relation to film.

In a sequence entitled 'El malestar de la tecnología' [technology's unease], Felipe Ortiz, another Arhuaco member of the Zhigoneshi collective, becomes exasperated as he tries to find a firm footing for his tripod atop uneven ground and shrubby thicket. This sequence, interrupted by the chirpy sound of his mobile phone ringtone, then cuts to a testimony of how Ortiz understands audio technology according to Arhuaco principles. He explains that if he wears, as is customary, the *tutosoma* – the white hat representing the sacred snowy mountain tops in the Sierra Nevada – he is unable to use standard headphones, as the earpieces will no longer reach his ears. Therefore, he concludes 'si yo quiero hacer una entrevista buena, tener un buen sonido, parece que yo tengo que deshacerme de algo […] Deberían existir unos audífonos propios' [If I want to do a good interview, with quality sound, it appears I have to get rid of something... We should have our *own* headphones] (Felipe Ortiz, cited in *Sey arimaku*). This short but illuminating example of the relationship between the sacred significance of the hat Arhuaco men use and the use of headphones in filmmaking alerts the spectator, and the director of the film Pablo Mora, to the intricate negotiation of the technology according to cosmological principles. Of course, the headphones could be used round the back of the head instead of on top, but the crucial point here is that Ortiz first interprets the two aspects as mutually exclusive – one has to stop being an Arhuaco man in order to be a filmmaker. Elsewhere in Zhigoneshi's oeuvre and indeed later in *Sey arimaku* this reconceptualisation of filmic technology surfaces again, reiterating the knowing incorporation of equipment and techniques into Arhuaco interpretive frameworks. The *tutosoma* scene, which offers the spectator one reason as to why some Arhuaco may have perceived film technology as alien to their culture, resonates with enduring preconceptions regarding the stasis and tradition of Indigenous cultures in contrast with the dynamism and modernity of audiovisual technology. For as long as Indigenous persons have participated actively in the fabrication of their own image, there have been detractors who claim that film corrupts the cultural authenticity of Native groups (see Faris, 1992). Yet in the sequences in *Sey arimaku* the trope of the pre-modern Indian is in fact turned on its head. Ortiz's knowing negotiation of the meaning of technology according to Arhuaco principles – later corroborated in *Sey arimaku* with more testimonies regarding the sacred origin of light and shadow (cosmological harbingers of the use of filmmaking in the community) – demonstrates how Indigenous epistemologies are in fact transforming the medium of film, and not vice versa.[9] In this respect, the film rehearses prejudices pertaining to the pre-modern archives of indigeneity in order to demonstrate how racialised subjects transform meanings through aberrant readings.

Sey arimaku concludes following the official ending of the projection within the film of *Resistencia en la línea negra* with an interesting coda in which Pablo Mora and Amado Villafaña re-stage an old photograph of a Frenchman

---

9   This idea has been forcefully argued by Terence Turner (1992) in relation to early video experiments with Kayapó communities.

Figures 4.4 and 4.5. Juxtaposing the past of the archive and the future of interpretation in Sey arimaku *(2012). Courtesy of Pablo Mora Calderón.*

marquis and Amado's father from 1932. Villafaña verbally deconstructs the pose and content of the photograph, which leads Mora to wonder how people would interpret their own rendition of this photographic scene in 20 years. Would Mora remain the manipulative white man? Would Villafaña be the wise shaman? This invitation to consider how their own photographic portraiture will age demonstrates how the film urges us to reconsider the changing value attached to images and films as they traverse time and space. Like the re-enactment of the Bolinder photos, the staged photo with which the film closes illuminates the evolving archival traces of these images, for it uses mise-en-scène as the vehicle by which to encounter the past, the present and the future in one condensed staged shot. In this sense, *Sey arimaku* offers an aberrant reading of aberrant practices, one which crafts an anti-racist purpose in its insistence on active interpretation and refusal of longstanding tropes and myths of the cinematic Indian.

O Mestre e o Divino

If *Sey arimaku* orchestrates aberrant readings as conscious interaction and audiovisual friction between archives of archetypal indigeneity, *O Mestre e o Divino* crystallises the enduring effects of mythologies of the cinematic Indian through careful juxtaposition. The film stages an encounter between three different filmmakers: Tiago Campos and Divino Tserewahú, who have made earlier films collaboratively, in addition to Adalbert Heide, a Salesian missionary. *O Mestre e o Divino*, fêted in international festivals and awarded three prizes at the prestigious Brasília film festival in 2013, studies the evolving relationship between a German missionary, Adalbert Heide, passionate about his Super 8 recordings of the Xavante, and Divino Tserewahú, altar-boy-cum-director, who was introduced to the recordings of his own community from a young age. Tserewahú has embraced film ever since. Their association is fully documented in the 85-minute feature documentary by Tiago Campos, Vídeo nas Aldeias' long-term collaborator.

Campos began working with the Xavante filmmaker in 2006 when he delivered editing workshops for Indigenous filmmakers as part of the Vídeo nas Aldeias training programme. Tserewahú began to work with film and with Vídeo nas Aldeias alongside his brother Jeremias in the 1990s. When his brother took up a job with the FUNAI, the state indigenist institution, Divino Tserewahú would assume the position as community filmmaker for Vídeo nas Aldeias and in the mid 1990s, he would have his first major experience working with the organisation on the production of the television series, *Programa do Índio* (Carelli, 1998). Since then, Tserewahú has produced seven films, three of which were realised with Tiago Campos: *Pi'onhitsi. Mulheres xavante sem nome* [unnamed Xavante women] (2009), *Sangradouro* (2009) and Campos's feature-length documentary, *O Mestre e o Divino* (2013). From Mato Grosso state, Divino Tserewahú's work focuses particularly on the ritual elements of Xavante culture and on the legacy of the Salesian mission and school founded in the area. *Sangradouro* explores the contradictions generated in his community since contact with the Salesian missionaries in 1947, juxtaposing archival footage from missionary and other sources with sequences of the contemporary community. In so doing, *Sangradouro* demonstrates the negotiated status of film among this Xavante community, resignifying the value and meaning of the racist discourses underpinning the missionary productions.

Scenes of community viewings of archival film are commonplace in the work of Vídeo nas Aldeias, and draw attention to the potential for subversive spectatorship from the outset. In the opening scenes of *Sangradouro*, for instance, the sequences of archival film that are cut into the narrative are crucially subverted through Divino Tserewahú's voiceover. The disembodied 'voice-of-God' narration is here in Xavante language, contrasting with the newsreader-style voice in Portuguese we hear over the introductory touristic sequences of Rio de Janeiro. The morphing of the archival image of the village into the village in contemporary times emphasises the continuity, not extinction, of the community, and if this visual motif were not enough to channel the theme of resilience the film takes a humorous turn as our gaze lands in the reservation to the song 'Eye of the Tiger', by Survivor. In other words, Tserewahú's voiceover provides a counter-interpretation, reads against the grain, culminating in the amusing significance of the rock anthem.

These humorous moments, also exploited in the candid discussions of technology explored above in relation to *Sey arimaku*, counteract the dominant representational paradigms which have documented Indigenous persons through the 'seriousness of racial exploitation' (Schiwy, 2016, p. 226). Though *Sangradouro* and *O Mestre* unapologetically confront enduring racist assumptions regarding cultural authenticity and the contamination of Indigenous purity in the careful montage of archival and contemporary footage, these moments of laughter shape spectators' responses to the works in terms far more complex than mere pity or outrage at exploitation narratives. In Freya Schiwy's recent work (2016) on humour in Indigenous videos from Latin America she suggests that 'the comic mode in video helps younger videomakers negotiate the tensions and challenges to the status of elders that their access to audiovisual technology brings about' (p. 238). This comic mode likewise dramatises how Indigenous audiences in community settings perform aberrant readings and connect in myriad ways to the often racist representations projected on the improvised outdoor cinema screens.

The screened diegetic audience in the film, far from being passive spectators, are actively engaged in the constitution of their present through filmmaking. In the conceit of a mise-en-abyme the spectators of *O Mestre e o Divino* are able to observe how Indigenous filmmakers and audiences alike self-consciously interpret the well-worn tropes of indigeneity enacted on screen. This screened community audience includes the young Xavante filmmaker Divino Tserewahú. This filmic study of the consumption of condescending and whitewashed versions of the Noble Savage deconstructs the community viewing experience as one of active reflection and participation. This is revealed in the documentary through excerpts of the Xuxa show (performing 'Vamos brincar de indio', or: how to be more Native than the Native), Hollywood Westerns, Karl May Indianer films from Germany and crucially also an earlier 1991 documentary, *Tsa'amri: The White Man Who Became an Indian* (Eike Schmitz, 1991), about Aadelbert Heide, the Salesian priest who 'went native' with the Xavante. Thorny questions regarding the authenticity of Xavante cultural reproduction and the suitability of film to record Xavante culture are frequently staged in testimonial sparring in *O Mestre e o Divino,* positioning Heide as the self-styled guardian of Indigenous authenticity and Divino Tserewahú as an Indian who has sold out to western commercial charms. As Robert Stam (2015, p. 264) eloquently summarises, 'In a kind of phantasmatic indigeneity, the older European filmmaker, in a regime of cinematic tutelage, imagines himself as "protecting" the image of the Xavante, and seems obviously threatened by the indigenous upstart who might end his imagistic and cognitive monopoly'. This threat is quite literally staged on screen as the Xavante filmmaker negates the version Heide has presented on camera as to how and why he began to use film.

Notwithstanding these conflicts, including one particularly uncomfortable moment when Heide berates Divino – or Winnetou as he calls him – for not knowing how to make Xavante headdresses ('não faz nada de Xavante', Heide says – you don't do anything properly Xavante), the film also depicts a

Figure 4.6. Still of Tsa'amri redeployed in O Mestre e o Divino *(Tiago Campos Tôrres, 2013)*.

touching relationship between Tserewahú and Heide, or Tsa'Amri as he was nicknamed among the Xavante community. As Laura Graham (2014, p. 91) writes on *O Mestre*, 'the film focuses on the complex relationship between the two men, with Divino acknowledging the Salesian influences that, for better or worse, have shaped him and his community'. Heide's fascination with the fictitious Apache Indian Winnetou, created by German author Karl May (1842–1912) at the end of the 19th century, informs his own account of his arrival to the Xavante community.[10] In fact, the scenes borrowed from both Heide's Super 8 films of the Xavante and of the films he would show in his community screenings (martial arts, *Winnetou*, action and Westerns) display a marked preference for romantic images of the landscape and desire for a fantasy of Indigenous authenticity. With the exception of images of Heide himself 'going native' in the films, Heide's filmic narratives distance themselves from the reflexivity which has become commonplace in contemporary Indigenous filmmaking, instead buying wholesale into the romantic fabrication of the Indigenous pastoral.

In Divino Tserewahú's films, by contrast, there is an emphasis on the negotiations of the community in the preservation of ceremony: he seeks to resuscitate rituals long abandoned, as in the case of the film *Pi'onhitsi*.

10 A recent film, *Searching for Winnetou* (2018), directed by the Ojibwe author and playwright Drew Hayden Taylor, explores the cultural appropriation and fascination of Germans with Indigenous culture.

Mulheres xavante sem nome from 2009, and to record them, preserving and transforming cultural traditions through film technologies. Tserewahú equally depicts Xavante travelling to the supermarket in the city, listening to non-Xavante music, and negotiating actively the role of film in the community. In *O Mestre e o Divino* we witness both filmmakers 'censor' to some extent the scenes of community life they record, with clothing and technology once again representing a stain on the presumed purity of Indigenous cultural traditions. However, rather than aligning with a sense of permanence and harmony with nature, Tserewahú's films place emphasis on the conscious processes of political resilience, adaptation and cross-generational cultural transfer.

The battle of the gaze witnessed in *O Mestre e o Divino* through the friction produced in the contrasting archival representations assembled is, of course, all staged by the editing and script of Tiago Campos. His familiarity with Divino Tserewahú and Aadelbert Heide granted a degree of intimacy and sensitivity to the film, for he was able to coax the two filmmakers into interesting scenarios which present their views in counterpoint. Where *Sey arimaku* employs voiceover by Pablo Mora and Amado Villafaña alongside images produced by Zhigoneshi to discuss filmic collaboration and stage contested narratives of indigeneity among the Arhuaco, Tiago Campos's documentary orchestrates an encounter between different aesthetic repertoires. These may intersect with and influence each other but nonetheless remain quite independent political projects. Campos's overt mediation of the dialogues that structure the film – captured in sequences where the spectator witnesses him insisting on questions – attest to his own investment in using film to document and promote Indigenous cultural practices. The overarching discourse presented in *O Mestre e o Divino* is one of active negotiation and dissonant views regarding the ways in which film may or may not be appropriate for a Xavante, in step with the hyper-reflexivity of Vídeo nas Aldeias films more generally. The on-screen Xavante audiences and competing tropes of indigeneity insist upon the enduring effects of the racialised present even as the film distils a form of spectatorship which upends the effects of these cinematic mythologies of the Noble Savage.

Conclusion

Stam and Spence's (1983, p. 12) critique of race and spectatorship highlights how the grammar of film might dupe the audience into forms of racist identification with filmic protagonists and narratives (1983, p. 12). The instrumentalisation of racialising scripts discussed here does not re-legitimise, however, the by now decoded and debunked biological discourses of race (Wade, 2008, p. 184). Over three decades since the publication of Stam and Spence's article, it is possible to see how recent film practice and criticism have sought to recover the varied attachments Indigenous audiences and filmmakers may have to a racist archive, thus resisting the idea that the spectator is 'unwittingly sutured into a colonialist perspective' (1983, p. 12). While Stam and Spence wrote of the relationship between the film's audience and its audiovisual discourse, the works discussed here employ diegetic examples of spectatorship and anti-racist vision. Like the individuals and collectives involved in their making, these films affirm the need to stage an audiovisual 'duel' between the repertoire betrothed by colonialism and the proposals generated by those who have been racialised by instruments of power. In this way, the different dramatisations of aberrant readings – intercepting the archive, reflecting upon audiovisual technology and its use, and the humorous juxtaposition of divergent scripts of indigeneity – underline the enduring effects of racism. In so doing, anti-racist film practice suggests that racist archives might serve alternative purposes in showing to participants and audiences alike how to move beyond racialising scripts of coloniality. The emphasis here on recasting the racist precepts of cinema in Latin America urges us to consider why discussions of racism have largely disappeared from film criticism on indigeneity in the region.

The work of Zhigoneshi and Vídeo nas Aldeias recycles the debris of the colonial and ethnographic archive, alongside mythologies of the cinematic Native, dramatising the struggle over representational regimes. There are, of course, other films which to varying degrees employ the photographic, textual and filmic archive to create a sort of productive friction in the narrative of memory and survival, one which fully exploits what Faye Ginsburg (2006, pp. 200–1) has termed the 'contradictory potentialities' of film. But what the documentaries discussed here demonstrate so clearly is that the filmic apparatus is constantly being remade according to different epistemological frameworks, through a logic of collaborative audiovisual reciprocity. This audiovisual reciprocity – the juxtaposition of different gazes, voices and archives on a potentially equal footing (*igualados*, as Mora said) – affords the different filmmakers and dramatised spectators the opportunity to illustrate their awareness of the racialising discourses of film and interrupt robust and racialised 'habits of seeing' (Al-Saji, 2014, p. 136). This interruption is further extended through the scenarios in which the works are screened – the projected acts of decoding the archive in urban centres and international film festivals disturb entrenched racialised demographics which displace indigeneity from the cities and its imbrication in national and international dynamics. In this way, they confront spectators by conjuring and juxtaposing shifting understandings of Indigenous identities. These four films stray from prescribed scenarios for indigeneity on screen, documenting in moving images the process of audiovisual repatriation and sovereignty which seeks to reinterpret racist portrayals. In their insistence on uprooting comfortable interpretations of archives which index indigeneity through colonial eyes, *Nabusímake, Sey arimaku, Sangradouro* and *O Mestre e o Divino* denounce the effectivity of these racialised portrayals and overturn their substantive meaning for anti-racist ends.

Bibliography

Al-Saji, A. (2014) 'A phenomenology of hesitation: interrupting racializing habits of seeing', in E. S. Lee (ed.), *Living Alterities: Phenomenology, Embodiment, and Race* (Albany, NY: State University of New York), pp. 133–72.

Aufderheide, P. (2008) '"You see the world of the other and you look at your own": the evolution of the video in the Villages Project', *Journal of Film and Video*, 60 (2): 26–34.

Carelli, V. (1998) 'Crônica de uma oficina de vídeo', available at http://www.videonasaldeias.org.br/2009/biblioteca.php?c=24 (accessed 28 Nov. 2017).

Carrera, M.M. (2003) *Imaging Identity in New Spain: Race, Lineage, and the Colonial Body in Portraiture and Casta Paintings* (Austin, TX: University of Texas Press).

Córdova A. (2014) 'Reenact, reimagine: performative indigenous documentaries of Bolivia and Brazil', in V. Navarro and J.C. Rodríguez (eds.), *New Documentaries in Latin America* (New York: Palgrave Macmillan), pp. 123–44.

Derrida, J. and E. Prenowitz (1995) 'Archive fever: a Freudian impression', *Diacritics*, 25 (2): 9–63.

Dobbin, K. (2013) '"Exposing yourself a second time": visual repatriation in Scandinavian Sápmi', *Visual Communication Quarterly*, 20 (3): 128–43.

Fabian, J. (1983) *Time and the Other: How Anthropology Makes Its Object* (New York: Columbia University Press).

Faris, J. (1992) 'Anthropological transparency, film, representation and politics', in P. Crawford and D. Turton (eds.), *Film as Ethnography* (Manchester: University of Manchester Press), pp. 171–82.

Ginsburg, F. (1994) 'Embedded aesthetics: creating a discursive space for indigenous media', *Cultural Anthropology*, 9 (3): 365–82.

— (2006) 'Rethinking the "voice of god" in indigenous Australia: secrecy, exposure, and the efficacy of media', in B. Meyer and A. Moors (eds.), *Religion, Media and the Public Sphere* (Bloomington, IL: Indiana University Press), pp. 188–204.

Gleghorn, C. (2011) 'Interview with Amado Villafaña', Native American Film and Video Festival, National Museum of the American Indian, New York. Unpublished.

Graham, Z. (2014) '"Since you are filming, I will tell the truth": a reflection on the cultural activism and collaborative filmmaking of *Video Nas Aldeias*', *Visual Anthropology Review*, 30: 89–91.

Hearne, J. (2006) 'Telling and retelling in the "Ink of Light": documentary cinema, oral narratives, and indigenous identities', *Screen*, 47 (3): 307–26.

Hooker, J. (2009) *Race and the Politics of Solidarity* (Oxford: Oxford University Press).

Katzew, I. (2004) *Casta Paintings: Images of Race in Eighteenth-Century Mexico* (New Haven, CT: Yale University Press).

Mateus Mora, A. (2013) *El indígena en el cine y el audiovisual colombianos: imágenes y conflictos* (Medellín: La Carreta Editores).

Mora Calderón, P. (2009) 'Reapariciones del pasado', *Zhigoneshi*, 10: 33–4.

— (ed.) (2015) *Poéticas de la resistencia: el video indígena en Colombia* (Bogotá: Cinemateca Distrital and IDARTES).

— (2016) 'Cine y raza: video indígena en Colombia', transcript of the Cátedra Cinematogáfica delivered 2 Aug. 2016 at the Cinemateca Distrital Bogotá, available at http://catedracinemateca.blogspot.co.uk/2016/09/cine-y-raza-video-indigena-en-colombia.html (accessed 28 Jan. 2018).

Muñoz, C. (2017) 'Moving pictures: memory and photography among the Arhuaco of the Sierra Nevada de Santa Marta, Colombia', *History and Anthropology*, 28 (3): 375–97.

Poole, D. (1997) *Vision, Race and Modernity: A Visual Economy of the Andean Image World* (Princeton, NJ: Princeton University Press).

— (2005) 'An excess of description: ethnography, race, and visual technologies', *Annual Review of Anthropology*, 34: 159–79.

Poole, D. and G. Zamorano (eds.) (2012) *De frente al perfil. Retratos raciales de Frederick Starr* (Zamora: El Colegio de Michoacán).

Raheja, M.H. (2007) 'Reading Nanook's smile: visual sovereignty, indigenous revisions of ethnography and *Atarnajuat* (The Fast Runner)', *American Quarterly*, 59 (4): 1159–85.

Russell, C. (1999) *Experimental Ethnography: The Work of Film in the Age of Video* (Durham, NC: Duke University Press).

Schiwy, F. (2016) 'Who's laughing now? Indigenous media and the politics of humor', in J. Poblete and J. Suárez, *Humor in Latin American Cinema* (New York: Palgrave Macmillan), pp. 223–46.

Scorer, J. (2017) 'Photography and Latin American ruins', *Journal of Latin American Cultural Studies*, 26 (2): 141–64.

Shohat, E. and R. Stam (1994) *Unthinking Eurocentrism: Multiculturalism and the Media* (London and New York: Routledge).

Spitta, S. (2013) 'Monumentally Indian: the photography of Edward Curtis and the Cuzco School of Photography', *Comparative American Studies*, 11 (2): 166–84.

Stam, R. (2015) *Keywords in Subversive Film/Media Aesthetics* (Oxford: John Wiley and Sons).

Stam, R. and L. Spence (1983), 'Colonialism, racism and representation', *Screen*, 24 (2): 2–20.

Tobing Rony, F. (1996) *The Third Eye: Race, Cinema, and Ethnographic Spectacle* (Durham, NC: Duke University Press).

Torres Márquez, V. (1978) *Los indígenas arhuacos y la 'vida de la civilización'* (Bogotá: Librería y Editorial América Latina).

Tsinhanjinnie, H.J. (2003) 'When is a photograph worth a thousand words?', in C. Pinney and N. Peterson (eds.), *Photography's Other Histories* (Durham, NC: Duke University Press), pp. 40–52.

Turner, T. (1992) 'Defiant images: the Kayapo appropriation of video', *Anthropology Today*, 8 (6): 5–16.

Wade, P. (1997) *Race and Ethnicity in Latin America* (London: Pluto Press).

— (2008) 'Race in Latin America', in D. Poole (ed.), *Companion to Latin American Anthropology* (Oxford: Blackwell), pp. 177–92.

— (2018) 'Afro-Indigenous interactions, relations, and comparisons', in A. de la Fuente and G.R. Andrews (eds.), *Afro-Latin American Studies: An Introduction* (Cambridge: Cambridge University Press), pp. 92–129.

Filmography

El valle de los arhuacos [The valley of the Arhuacos] (1964) Vidal Antonio Rozo. Empresa Cinematográfica Colombiana Calima (Calima, Colombia).

Já me transformei em imagem [I've already become an image] (2008) Zezinho Yube and Vídeo nas Aldeias (Olinda, Pernambuco, Brazil).

Jiisa weçe: raíz del conocimiento [Jiisa weçe: the roots of knowledge] (2010) Fundación Cineminga (New York, New York, United States of America)

Mi finK (2010) Grupo Fundación Villa Rica and Soporte Klan. Fundación Subliminal and Ministerio de Cultura de Colombia (Bogotá, Colombia).

Nabusímake: memorias de una independencia [Nabusímake, memories of an independence] (2010) Amado Villafaña and Zhigoneshi Colectivo de Comunicaciones (Sierra Nevada de Santa Marta, Colombia).

Nanook of the North (1922) Robert Flaherty. Pathé Exchange (Buffalo, New York, United States of America).

O Mestre e o Divino [The Master and Divino] (2013) Tiago Campos Torres and Video nas Aldeias (Olinda, Pernambuco, Brazil)

Pi'onhitsi. Mulheres xavante sem nome [*Pi'onhitsi*: Xavante women with no name] (2009) Divino Tserewahú and Tiago Campos Torres. Video nas Aldeias (Olinda, Pernambuco, Brazil).

Reel Injun (2009) Neil Diamond, Catherine Bainbridge and Jeremiah Hayes. Rezolution Pictures, National Film Board of Canada (Montréal, Québec, Canada).

Resistencia en la línea negra [Resistance on the black line] (2011) Amado Villafaña Chaparro, Saúl Gil and Silvestre Gil Sarabata. Colectivo Zhigoneshi (Sierra Nevada de Santa Marta, Colombia).

Sey arimaku o la otra oscuridad [*Sey arimaku*: the other darkness] (2006) Pablo Mora and Colectivo Zhigoneshi (Sierra Nevada de Santa Marta, Colombia).

Tsa'amri: The White Man Who Became an Indian (1991) Eike Schmitz. Atlantis-Film (Berlin, Germany).

Tsõ'rehipãri, Sangradouro (2006) Divino Tserewahú and Tiago Campos Torres. Video nas Aldeias (Olinda, Pernambuco, Brazil).

5. Cultural agency and anti-racism in Caribbean conceptual art

Fabienne Viala

Caribbean societies have been shaped by the slave trade, the plantation system and by structural racism. The prevailing social order in the post-plantation societies of the Caribbean has been established on the basis of what Charles Mills (1997, p. 11) defined as a racial contract, the general purpose of which is 'the differential privileging of the whites as a group with respect to the non-whites as a group, the exploitation of their bodies, land, and resources, and the denial of socioeconomic opportunities to them. All whites are beneficiaries of the Contract, though some whites are not signatories to it'.

While the past continues to haunt the present and to reproduce racial hierarchies, it is extremely conflictive to bring out questions of accountability, responsibility, reparations and reconciliation in the civil debates of Caribbean societies, whether those debates are political or memorial. Identity politics prevails in such ways that wounded attachments 'form the basis for infelicitous formulations of identity rooted in injury' (Brown, 1995, p. xii). Claiming equal rights on the basis of the wounds inflicted by the historical past has become the only way to contest the homogeneous deracialised representations of belonging imposed by the postcolonial national administrations, while in reality racial hierarchies continue to control agency and impact on the wellbeing of those who do not fit in the dominant racial group. Each Caribbean country has built its own official narrative of race in the nation, whether it is based on idealised miscegenation in Puerto Rico and Trinidad and Tobago, on the myth of a raceless Cuban *hombre nuevo*, or on assimilation and Frenchness in Guadeloupe and Martinique. Because those postcolonial narratives are race blind and leave in the shadow the ghosts of the past, alliances are formed in the periphery of mainstream national politics around racial categories. Those local- and ethnic-oriented factions, whether they take the shape of local political parties or of citizen-led societies, have been multiplying in Caribbean societies like constellations of fragmented and competing post-national identity claims based on race. This particular kind of identity politics does not facilitate anti-racism, it actually reinforces the boundaries between racial and ethnic groups, and obscures the possibilities of setting up transitional measures that would

F. Viala, 'Cultural agency and anti-racism in Caribbean conceptual art', in P. Wade, J. Scorer and I. Aguiló (eds.), *Cultures of Anti-Racism in Latin America and the Caribbean* (London: Institute of Latin American Studies, 2019), pp. 101–23. License: CC-BY-NC-ND 4.0.

allow for starting a collective process of justice making, from the historical traumas of the past to their ongoing violence in the present.

Contemporary art, as a conceptual mode of relationship with its public, has become in the last 20 years a privileged platform for contesting the everyday racism that shapes the life and the future of Caribbean generations on the island-nations, and in the diaspora. While literature has been the major tool for developing a sense of collective belonging and racial awareness in the Caribbean region, ever since the abolition of slavery across the whole region, visual and performative art have relied on embodied and affective idioms that do not require specific linguistic competences or any educational background to touch their audience. If we keep in mind that language and education are two factors that have constantly limited the possibilities of pan-Caribbean dialogue and inter-Caribbean connections, and that literature belongs to an elite culture (with the exception of Cuba), it is not surprising that contemporary artists of the region, often self-taught, have found in visual and performative creative imagination a fruitful medium to engage the Caribbean wider audience with the issues of racial discrimination that continue to haunt their present. Conceptual artists of the region have been proposing new multidirectional strategies that help relocate the struggle against racism in a global debate against exploitation, drawing on tropes that do not necessarily reproduce the narration of the transatlantic slave trade but bring it into dialogue with other historical wounds. I will focus here on three different artistic approaches that magnify the potential of agency and embodiment as conceptual languages to bring the past into the present, establish new modes of visual and sensory transactions with their audience, and facilitate the possibilities of starting a process of transitional, reparatory and restorative justice.

François Piquet, a white French artist who has been living and working in Guadeloupe for the last 20 years, questions the haunting legacies of slavery in the French Caribbean *départements* from the perspective of the implicated subject, neither victim nor perpetrator, but fully engaged in a process of accountability and reconciliation. Piquet belongs to a minority in the realm of contemporary Caribbean art, where black identity politics prevails, insofar as his phenotype identifies him as one of the beneficiaries, though not signatory, of Mills' racial contract. This ambivalent position allows him to contest all forms of memorialisation driven by competitive memory and to relocate his artistic agency within the racialised complexity of the world he inhabits.

Jeannette Ehlers is a mixed-race Caribbean woman, based in Denmark, who performs the past in the present by trusting the body as a valuable and skilled archive. Marked by the traumatic history of slavery passed on to her by older generations, Ehlers experiments with performative techniques to create empowering and participatory artworks that act out non-formalised, hidden and unthought pains. Re-enactment becomes a way to strike back our intimate ghosts, while recontextualising the crimes of slavery in the contemporary hierarchies and discrimination that rule our world.

Ano is a black Guadeloupian artist who lived and worked most of his life in Guadeloupe before moving to Montréal a decade ago, where he is now an established artist of the diaspora. Ano's eclectic artworks make tangible the fact that racial hierarchies have been expressions of politics of the body since the plantation. While the artist considers that today's world-system is blind and deaf to the colonial conditions in which people continue to be enslaved, he finds in conceptual art the interdisciplinary resources to shape a new visual politics in which non-rational and emotional language empowers the spectator with a new way of seeing, and establishes the conditions for starting to build collaboratively a new social order.

Piquet, Elhers and Ano share the view that the legacies of slavery continue to shape the structures of power in the world they inhabit. But they also have in common the refusal of victimhood, which they see as unproductive in their quest for restorative justice. So to avoid falling into the old rut of endlessly representing and repeating trauma, the three artists have invested the field of creative interpretation with the power to invite audiences to take part in a wider debate about the legacies of human bondage, exploitation, dependency, inequality and alienation. The artistic aesthetics of Piquet, Elhers and Ano seek to reconcile the recognition of past traumas with restorative and cathartic processes designed to overcome traumatic memory. In the artworks and performances considered in this chapter, this aesthetic relies on the use of an embodied metonymy: infamous objects and practices known for the role they have played in human bondage and mass murder, such as cremation, whipping and punishment collars, become the very channel that facilitates agency, self-reflection and creation in the artitsts' exhibitions and performances. From their own particular locus of enunciation, whether it is Guadeloupe, Denmark or Québec, Piquet, Ano and Elhers question the tropes that continue to feed racist discourses and they site their origins in the history of the plantation. While Piquet and Ano, who have collaborated several times in joint exhibitions in Guadeloupe, approach the body as a space in need of mental decolonisation, Ehlers approaches the legacies of slavery from the perspective of gender and feminism.

Each of the three parts of this chapter focuses on one particular exhibition/performance and analyses how each artist's work conceptualises race consciousness by creating artistic channels to embody reparative justice. The criteria for choosing these three artists were twofold. First, Piquet, Ano and Ehlers are internationally recognised artists who represent Caribbean conceptual art from complementary perspectives: a white male artist, settled in the Caribbean, who chose to engage with the history of slavery as his own; a black Caribbean male artist whose recent relocation to Canada repositioned his Caribbean gaze as a critical weapon against a profit-making globalised economy; and a mix-raced female artist, born and based in Europe, whose creativity is fuelled by her Caribbean ancestry and by a heritage of violence. All three emblematise the new artistic directions that Caribbean art has recently been taking in fighting racism and negotiating traumatic pasts.

Second, all three artists invalidate the two major stereotypes that are currently responsible for preventing reparative justice from happening legally: the idea that slavery and racism against non-white people belong to the past; and the notion that slavery and racism concern only black people. The works of the three artists relocate both slavery and racism in the here and now. Ano demonstrates how much the world we inhabit today is constructed on the basis of the globalised profit-making system created for the purpose of transatlantic slave-trading, which invented racism against black African bodies as a justification for the profitable economy that emerged. Piquet and Ehlers show how much the pain and trauma of the past continue to be encoded in our social-bodies, whatever the colour of our skin. All three believe in the power of art as a thought-provoking machine to fight back the ghosts of the past in order to champion justice.

François Piquet's 'Réparations': art and justice in Guadeloupe

François Piquet was born in mainland France and has been living and working in Guadeloupe for the last 20 years. When he arrived on the French Caribbean island to make a new life with his family, he knew very little about its colonial past and even less about the history of slavery. Like most of the French people, who are educated at school with a history curriculum that totally ignores the French Republic's enslaving past, Piquet had little or no understanding that in post-plantation Guadeloupe – this *département d'outremer* – society would be structured along entrenched racial lines, directly inherited from the slaving system. In contemporary Guadeloupe, agency – defined as one's power to freely choose, execute and control one's own volitional actions (Jeannerod, 2003) – is bound to the colour of one's skin. Career orientation, sexual behaviour and social status depend on one's belonging to whiteness or blackness, according to a subtle template of shades and blood combinations.

As a *zorey* (the name given to white Caucasian people in Guadeloupe) and a *metro* (short for *métropolitain*, someone from mainland France), Piquet's choice to become an artist in Guadeloupe, to make Guadeloupe's history his own, and to embrace conceptual art as *the* platform to condemn the haunting legacies of the past in the postcolonial present, is remarkable and rare enough to be mentioned here. His artistic practice is inscribed in a reparative justice manifesto, rooted in truth-telling and reconciliation, no matter how taboo the disturbing and protean reality of racism might be. Piquet's exhibition 'Réparations' was shown as part of Guadeloupe's Fonds d'Art Contemporain in Saint Claude, 2016. This chapter looks at three series of sculptures and drawings, examining how the works embody a symbolic strategy of repair, informed by transitional justice and a multidirectional interpretation of traumatic memory (Rothberg, 2013).

In a Caribbean country where the legacy of slavery and structural racism continues to impact on people's mental, social and economic wellbeing, Piquet's approach to collective remembrance goes beyond the limited epistemology of wound culture, and beyond the Manichean aesthetics of identity politics. 'Réparations' paves the way for a reconciliatory dialogue between the descendants of the victims of slavery and the great-grandchildren of the perpetrators of slavery crimes, but also between citizens of the world sharing a sense of attachment and implication to other traumatic histories outside the Caribbean region. Piquet's work facilitates an artistic transaction of embodied empathy, in the line of Jill Bennett's theory (2005) of empathic vision. They bring together audiences who feel concerned that a collective body – to which they belong in some way – has been responsible for unpunished acts of violence, which the artist fully acknowledges and represents as soul murders, following Gabriele Schwab's definition (2010, p.14): 'crimes that kill what is most essential to a person while leaving his/her body alive'. The argument put forward in this chapter is that Piquet's work contributes to the advancement of the struggle against racism through a poetics of implication: that is a thought-provoking encounter between art and justice in which feelings of empathy, concern and accountability are motivated neither by guilt nor by shame, and in which the wrong-doing is acknowledged as unacceptable and neither denied nor placed at a distance from the audience.

Transitional justice can be defined as a set of measures, judicial or not, that intend to redress the legacies of human rights abuses. The aim is to recognise the dignity of the victims as human beings and citizens; to redress and acknowledge the violations; and to prevent them from happening again. Whether they are individual, collective, material or symbolic, reparations are one among many transitional justice measures, like criminal prosecutions, truth-finding commissions and legal reforms (mostly of the military, police and judicial system).[1]

Transitional justice refers to post-conflict contexts and to the ways in which countries emerging from periods of repression address systematic human rights violations, but the transatlantic slave trade and its legacy present an especially complicated case. The slave trade amounted to genocide on a grand scale, that continued for four centuries, and which was legal according to European law at the time. And although there are no direct survivors, there are many generations of descendants.

---

1   International Centre for Transitional Justice, https://www.ictj.org/about/transitional-justice (accessed 15 March 2019).

No transitional justice measures were ever taken in the Caribbean. After abolition, social and economic adjustments were made by the white colonial powers so that they could continue to profit from the exploitation of non-white bodies, either by apprenticing formerly enslaved people, or by using Indian 'coolie' indentured workers (Heuman, 2014), and slavery was never condemned as a human rights crime. No criminal prosecutions against white racist institutions took place; on the contrary, slave owners in Europe received financial reparations for the slaves they had lost (Hall, 2014). Neither restorative commissions nor reparative actions were proposed, despite the fact that victims and perpetrators had to continue to live together on the same island. It was a time prior to the Second World War and the Nazi genocide, before the institutional frameworks of transitional justice initiated by the Nuremberg Trials existed.

In 2013, CARICOM[2] put forward a legal claim for reparations for slavery against the former European countries that had made incalculable profits from slavery. None of the European countries involved in slavery has acknowledged any legal or economic responsibility for the underdevelopment of the Caribbean and for its most obvious legacy, racism, which continues to condition agency in the Caribbean and in other white-dominant societies. In France, the 2001 Taubira Law declared slavery to be a crime against humanity, but the law has not to date been applied to make any symbolic or material compensation. European states are sorry that slavery happened, but agree that contemporary generations cannot be blamed for what happened in the past.

Against such a denial of accountability, CARICOM drew on transitional justice approaches to write a ten-point plan in 2014 which combines backward- and forward-looking transitional justice arguments. The backward-looking approach is based on the fundamental right of the victim to be compensated for the damage caused: because slavery is a crime against humanity, the heirs of enslaved people should receive compensation for what was suffered by their ancestors. The forward-looking approach is to propose development programmes to redress the situation of inequality in which black people are living as a direct consequence of slavery and of the plantation system (Corlett, 2010). The plan demands formal public apologies from the European states enriched by slavery, the cancellation of the monetary debt of the Caribbean countries, and programmes to develop cultural institutions and memorials, healthcare, psychological counselling, education, technology, literacy and

---

2 In 1973, Barbados, Jamaica, Guyana and Trinidad formed CARICOM (Caribbean Community) as a Commonwealth market zone with privileged economic, educational and cultural links. It now includes all the Anglophone Caribbean islands, Haiti and Surinam. CARICOM's mission is to develop and protect the exchanges between the Caribbean nations in the context of their strong dependence on global capitalism and Northern America and Europe since the collapse of the Berlin wall.

collaborations with Africa, including repatriation to Ethiopia for those who demand it (mostly Rastafarians).

Piquet's work, as much as it resonates with the aforementioned specific context of transitional justice, contributes to the debate by using an artistic language that brings the audience closer to the subject matter, emotionally and psychically, while disengaging from legal and moral discourses. When asked about his work, Piquet makes clear that the sculptures and drawings in 'Réparations' are not part of any kind of material, individual or collective reparatory demand:

> My motivation for this project is rooted in the overwhelming responsibility I feel to acknowledge that this is where I am. I cannot pretend I am not here. Most of the time, the one who repairs is not the one who caused the damage. I take care of the world in which I live by repairing today's damages as they were caused and informed in the past. I do it the best I possibly can and from where I stand. Instead of claiming reparations, I want to do and make reparations. (Interview with François Piquet, February 2018, my translation)

While Piquet dissociates his work from the claims for moral and memorial reparations, his approach in fact blends many reparative and restorative strategies into an artistic statement of accountability, the key to which is overcoming denial, guilt and shame, and to making room for starting the reconciliation process.

In the context of Holocaust studies, Soshana Felman (2002, p. 153) argues that art brings traumatic pasts closer while law creates an inevitable distance that does not facilitate the psychic comprehension of traumatic history:

> Law is a language of abbreviation, of limitation and of totalization. Art is a language of infinity and of the irreducibility of fragments, a language of embodiment, of incarnation, and of embodied incantation or endless rhythmic repetition. Because it is by definition a discipline of limits, law distances the Holocaust; art brings it closer.

In line with Felman's position, Piquet's work proposes an artistic mode of expression for comprehending traumatic events that continue to nurture inequalities in the present. As this painful past is not his own, the artist uses art as a medium to express, share and engage his feeling of implication in the history of slavery, in which he is neither a victim nor a perpetrator. This echoes Michael Rothberg's definition (2013, p. 40) of the implicated subject as someone who 'does not fall under the direct form of participation associated with traumatic events, such as victimization or perpetration'. The implicated modes of relation encompass 'bystanders, beneficiaries, latecomers of the post-memory generation and others connected "prosthetically" to pasts they did not experience'. Piquet feels that he is ethically implicated in the realms of the white-dominant culture that perpetrated slavery, without being himself a perpetrator. As a white man, citizen, father and artist living in Guadeloupe,

Figure 5.1. Moun Brilé by François Piquet, 'Réparations', Fonds d'Arts Contemporains, Guadeloupe, 2016 (by permission of the artist).

he cannot ignore the fact that racism is the template that structurally informs agency in his country. Therefore, through his art he aims to ignite feelings of indignation against racism and all forms of crime born from and justified by racist ideologies, leaving us with the urgent need to unite against human rights violations in the present, out of our emotional empathy and connection with crimes committed in the past. In 'Réparations', Piquet experiments with agency as an embodied power for repairing, mending, adapting or adjusting damaged materials to give them new life as 'repaired' objects. Through the invention and making of sculptures, he questions what it can mean to do reparations, with his own body force, instead of claiming them on the basis of moral principles.

'Moun brilé ou la fabrique du noir' [Burnt People or The Making of Blackness], is a series of ten calcined wood sculptures with anthropoid shapes (see fig. 5.1). The artist collected a wide range of different local woods on the island – Péyi, Acacia, Kénet, Épini, Kaymitié, Mapou, Cythère and Résinié. As the wood pieces collected were dead, he carved them to remove any rotten deposits and to shape them into large heads, looking up to the sky with mouths wide open. He then burnt the wood, turning it pitch black, like charcoal. He varnished the burnt wood sculptures, to 'fix their négritude' as the artist puts it, and planted white teeth in their open mouths.

For Piquet, creating large-scale pieces to make reparations comes with polyvalent agency. The creative process starts with collecting the primary material for his sculptures, so as to constitute a memorial archive. Piquet's archive combines symbolic materials, that belong to the natural flora of the island, or that show a connection with the history of slavery: wood, leather and iron were used to make rum barrels, shackles and whips, and to elaborate all the instruments of control over the production of goods on the island, whether sugar, indigo, tobacco or human beings. Agency then takes the form of the artist's work to transform the collected materials into artistic objects, in a way that requires some particular physical skill, as in the case of burning huge and heavy pieces of wood. For the teeth, Piquet used two types of coral, which he cut into the shape of teeth and mounted on screws in the wooden jaws of the sculpture, like dental implants. He completed the work with dental prostheses.

All stages of the creation of the work were filmed or photographed by the artist, so as to testify to the process of making, and rendering it explicit to the audience. Neither the films nor the pictures are the final or central focus of 'Réparations', but their presence in the exhibition nevertheless offers a complementary archive that records the implicated agency of the artist while constructing each piece in *Moun brilés*. Watching the artist making the sculptures allows the audience to articulate emotional and embodied connections with the wounded, as they are being constructed by Piquet.

The use of fire to burn what stands for human beings conjures resonances of cremation and genocidal practices, while the blackness and white teeth recall the commodification of enslaved people into cheap labour, according to which teeth were the promise of good health and hence the proof of a good financial investment for the slave owner. While the shouting mouths of the sculptures recall Césaire's 'great negro cry'[3] (1970), their non-figurative shape allows for multiple emotional readings and for the convergence of empathic visions beyond the specific context from which the artist is speaking. Piquet calls for different histories of violence, such as transatlantic slavery or the Jewish genocide, without making one more prominent than the other and without making explicit reference to any single event. In fact, while the blackness of the wood could be read as a direct reference to the context of slavery in Guadeloupe, the same exhibition set outside the Caribbean could speak to racial and genocidal crimes where cremation was used. At the same time, cremation and teeth implantation reverses the process of human destruction that happened in the Nazi camps into a process of artistic creation, leading to the rebirth of the wounded into artworks. The artist inscribes juxtaposed histories of violence in the materiality of the artwork without equating them with one another. Instead, he fixes the reference to those traumatic histories into the very material he carves, burns and varnishes, and in the process of making the sculpture. Piquet avoids the trap of pitting traumatic histories against each other in the service of identity politics, instead bringing out their close relationships to each other, creating an empathic connection with the spectator, which Bennett (2005, p. 7) called a 'direct engagement with sensation':

> The affective responses engendered by artworks are not born out of
> emotional identification or sympathy; rather they emerge from a

3 'Pousser d'une telle raideur le grand cri nègre que les assises du monde en seront ébranlées' ['Shouting the great negro cry so persistently that the foundations of the world will tremble'], my translation.

> direct engagement with sensation as it is registered in the work. In this regard, trauma-related art is best understood as transactive rather than communicative. It often touches us but it does not necessarily communicate the secret of personal experience.

Indeed, following Bennett's quote, Piquet's *Moun brilés* do not praise identification with the victims, nor rehabilitation of the perpetrators. The energy behind the artworks rather points at evoking a sense of responsibility and accountability in spectators of all backgrounds and origins; the audience does not need to identify with the wounded as belonging to one specific community of victims. By the simple fact of their presence, and by their sensorial response to the sculptures they see, they are entrusted with the artist's implication into histories of wound making. 'Réparations' is an overall acknowledgement of the wound of slavery and a space to mourn those who suffered it, a call for contemporary generations to feel responsible for the crimes of the past, without any essentialist or identity diktat, and a recognition that racism, as it continues to rule Caribbean society and the white-dominant world, is based on delusional beliefs of ownership that continue to hurt and kill people.

In this regard, the act of 'making' becomes key to the active reparations Piquet is enacting. In the catalogue of the exhibition, Piquet reminds his audience that white men invented blackness as a concept to exploit and control the Arawak, the African and the Indian people and, by the same token, they invented whiteness. Structural racism was born as a man-made construction that did not need to be true to become and remain a reality. Likewise, Piquet's reparations demonstrate that art can make, as in manipulate, whatever is needed to repair the misconceptions that have for so long damaged the relational transactions of mankind. Most of those reparations, while symbolic in their meaning, are so real that they are inscribed in the materiality of the artworks. Piquet therefore creates the conditions for the awakening of a new reality, a world ruled by the dynamic of repairing.

In the second series of sculptures entitled *Ce qui peut être sauvé/ What Can Be Saved*, Piquet restored, surgeon-like, the dead pieces of wood he collected, but this time, instead of burning them, he kept what was still alive. The pieces of wood became parts of other man-size sculptures, mended with clay and iron to allow those 'repaired' bodies to stand upright on the floor without crutches. The final sculptures of *What Can Be Saved* look like people with broken, amputated or half-cut members, survivors of dirty wars, cruel repression and systematic violence. But they do stand on their feet, proudly, in resonance with the pride contained in the great negro cry of the *Moun brilés* sculptures. As much as he creates a space for staging the wound and the trauma, Piquet also restores the dignity of the wounded body, beyond the shame and guilt of victimisation, triggering a sense of shared responsibility in the mending process.

This does not mean that the artist claims that everything can be repaired. On the contrary, 'Réparations' leaves us with a sense that repairing is a fragile act that can also be delusional. This is explored in the series of eight drawings called *Réparations simulacres/ Fake reparations*. The genesis of these drawings is as thought-provoking as the one that led to the *Moun brilés* series. In 2014, Piquet's daughter found half a human skull while playing on the beach at Raisins Clairs, near the village of Saint-François. The unearthing of skulls and bones is not unusual in Guadeloupe, where the slave graveyards have never been formally mapped, nor protected or restored as sites of mourning for the people of Guadeloupe, despite the fact that 90 per cent of the population are slave descendants. For the last 17 decades since slavery was abolished, hotels, houses and blocks of flats have been built without any prior archaeological excavation. Raisins Clairs has been scientifically identified as a plantation graveyard and Piquet had the skull appraised. Unfortunately, as it was incomplete, it was impossible to identify it as belonging to a specific time period: it was as likely to be the skull of someone buried after abolition in 1848 as that of an African enslaved person.[4]

Piquet felt the responsibility to 'make' something out of his finding, like with the rest of his archive, but he refused to use the skull in the service of a specific identity claim. Instead, he took it as a model for a series of eight charcoal drawings in the style of still-life sketches. In *Fake Reparations*, the skull is remade into multiple functional objects, from an ashtray to a piggy bank, from a Mickey Mouse mask to a carnival mask, from a plate to a floating buoy, and even as a stand to hold a Legion of Honour medal. Out of respect for these human remains, Piquet chose to draw the skull instead of using it as a rough artistic material. In each drawing, the skull becomes a trivial object, ironically mended, pointing at Piquet's critique of the many ways in which colonial and postcolonial discourses, since the abolition of slavery, have dealt with the trauma of slavery so as to maintain control over identity and people's sense of belonging. The political and social after-effects of the establishment of Guadeloupe as a French *département* in 1946 have made identity conflicts worse than ever. The trauma of slavery has become the touchstone of wound culture doctrines which equate one's identity to (a very narrow reading of) African victimisation on one side, and to racist white supremacist views on the other side, preventing society from moving on to reach a level of discourse in which reconciliation and dialogue would be possible. Such pathogenic forms of remembrance, by reinforcing delusional divisions between black and white, prepare the ground for anti-racism and continue to damage the relationships between Guadeloupians, whatever their family history. Piquet's answer to Schwab's question (2010, p. 2) – 'how do we deal with a haunting past while simultaneously acting in the present with its ongoing violence?' – is to deal with it by making art. Piquet refuses to passively accept the unequal structures of power at large in the *département* but at the same time he stays away from

4   Archaeologists have been able to identify skulls of enslaved people thanks to the shape of their teeth, filed into sharp ends as a tribal custom in West Africa.

political discourses that revolve around identity politics and in which, as a *zorey*, he would not find any suitable platform to be heard. Making art for Piquet means using his own body and agency to produce artistic objects with meaning.

Jeannette Ehlers' *Whip It Good*: embodied metonymy and re-enactment

Jeanette Ehlers is a Danish-Trinidadian artist based in Copenhagen. Her interdisciplinary portfolio includes video installations, films and performances, in which she questions the legacies of slavery in white-dominant societies, and the continuing re-enactments of colonial violence in the present. As a mixed-race female artist with African-Caribbean ancestry, Ehlers's artistic language aims at acting out the encrypted memory of her black heritage in formats that make it decipherable and meaningful in the present. Denmark, where Ehlers was educated from a young age, had Caribbean colonies. Her Trinidadian father played an important role in the shaping of her Caribbean identity to the point that he has been the protagonist of some of her video installations. Ehlers uses her Caribbean-Atlantic history as the trigger for most of her artworks, such as the video *Black Bullets*, winner of the main prize at the Caribbean Festival of the Image in 2015 held at the Mémorial Acte museum in Guadeloupe.

Conceptual art for Ehlers is restorative in the sense that it gathers together the painful experiences of a traumatic past she has never fully known but which she has lived, as those experiences have been passed on to her by previous generations. The effects of this are amplified, given that slavery's imprint of racism is to be felt in the present day. But while recovering something of the emotion that was present in the initial trauma of slavery, Ehlers' performances trigger multidirectional networks of meaning so powerful that they debunk any temptation to turn the trauma into an identity fetish. She explores the body as a powerful agent of post-memory, defined by Marianne Hirsch (1996, p. 659) as a form of memory that connects to its object 'not through recollection but through an imaginative investment and creation'.

The performance *Whip It Good: Spinning from History's Filthy Mind* revolves around a white canvas, in front of which Ehlers, dressed in white and wearing white make-up on her face and on her bare arms and legs, holds a whip, which she rubs in charcoal and relentlessly whips the canvas with (see fig. 5.2). She eventually passes the whip to the audience for them to finish the work on the canvas.[5] *Whip It Good* was first commissioned in 2013 by the Art Labour Archive in Berlin, and eventually toured in Florida (2014) and in London, at the Royal Academy of Arts and at Autograph (2015). Each time, the reaction of the audience, when asked to whip the canvas, was key to the performance, precisely because it interactively engaged with the act of whipping as a complex

5   http://www.jeannetteehlers.dk/m4v/video21.htm (accessed 15 March 2019).

Figure 5.2. Whip It Good *was first commissioned by Art Labour Archives and Ballhaus Naunynstrasse, Berlin, 2013. (Photo, by permission: Nicolaj Recke, Brundyn Gallery, Cape Town, South Africa, 2015.)*

and brutal act carrying multiple layers of traumatic referencing. Ehlers herself was struck by the fact that that not only the willingness of the spectators to take the whip, but also the whipping gesture of those who accepted the invitation, varied considerably depending on whether they were a woman, a man, a white or a black person.

Leaving aside the fact that whipping is something that just a few people have personally experienced in contemporary times, and which requires some physical ability not all may have, the fact that some spectators refused to engage fully with a brutal gesture associated with domination and humiliation, while others were ready to do so, reveals that one's body acts out traumatic gestures differently, not only according to one's personal story, but also to which story one wants to tell about oneself publicly. Ehlers herself acknowledges that she has a complex relationship with the whip, not because she has experienced being whipped or has ever whipped anybody, but because her ancestors from her father's side were enslaved Africans in Trinidad and Tobago. While performing the unspoken, her body mobilises a sensorial language, which creates the conditions for a reconciliatory debate to happen between different, latent, but always embodied, perspectives on violence and domination, blurring the limits between collective and individual memory. Ehlers' performance plays on the degree to which bystanders, all with their own personal and intimate stories, are comfortable participating in such an event, and hence she redefines accountability as a site of empowerment and liberation.

Whip It Good explores the relationship between agency and re-enactment, and particularly the extent to which memory works as an inherited archive unconsciously stored in the body and retrieved by the kinetic return to gestures of the past. While the whip works as a metonymy of slavery, the act of whipping lends itself to multiple interpretations that powerfully combine empowerment with re-enactment.

The first knot of meaning triggered by Ehlers' performance resides in the act of whipping as a re-enacted gesture, which empowers the black woman to strike back. The act of white men whipping enslaved women belongs to the historical vignettes one has in mind when thinking about the history of slavery from a gender perspective. So much so that this image can be defined as a primal scene of slavery in the collective imagination: one among many punishing methods, connoting phallic domination, that allowed overseers and masters to control the female bodies over which they ruled, or which they owned, in the psychopathological and delusional system of slavery.

In this vein, *Whip It Good* positions itself in a dialogue with the works of other black feminist artists who symbolically reverse the dynamics of power in their artworks by handing the whip to the enslaved woman, as in Kara Walker's 2012 *Palmetto Libretto; Sketch for an American Comic Opera with Fort Sumter*. In this four-panel pastel and graphite drawing series, Walker reimagined the key episode that was the catalyst for the American civil war – the Confederate attack on Fort Sumter, South Carolina. Walker's drawings turn the history of slavery in the United States of America into four ironic, brutal and powerful vignettes, which portray slavery and racism as the original sins of the American nation. The scene happens on the edge of Charleston bay, with Fort Sumter in flames in the background. The drawings at each end of the frame work as symmetrically inverted vignettes, and metaphors of the north and south: while the drawing on the far left represents a naked black enslaved woman standing up and whipping a naked white man lying on the floor with his hands tied. Meanwhile, the drawing on the far right represents a white man, dressed in white, whipping a naked black woman. While the woman's nudity points at her ongoing commodification by male- and white-dominant American society, and signals rape as the usual practice of control, agency is rendered more complex as the black woman powerfully holding the whip converses visually with a third female character in the middle image. This occupies two panels: a white woman in the water, trying to save a naked black man from drowning; she holds him firmly with one arm while waving a piece of white cloth with the other hand, as a sign of surrender and help-seeking. The white flag in the air recalls the two whips brandished by the other figures, male and female, at each end of the artwork. Walker pairs black and white, female and male, naked and clothed, in a visual charade that re-enacts a historical episode so as to turn it into an enigmatic and ironic mythology of violence, targeting the very foundation of American civil rights.

Walker's and Ehlers' works are encoded in black and white and they seem to be in dialogue as they reverse the codes of white/male supremacy to empower the woman to claim back her agency. By doing so, they turn whipping into a metonymy and slavery into a foundational trauma continuing into the present. The title *Whip It Good* suggests that anger can lead to relief, recalling Audre Lorde's view in *Sister Outsider* that anger is useful for developing knowledge and should be deployed creatively (Lorde, 1984). Ehlers' position in the debate of black liberation is that art can be assigned a cathartic and imaginative task, that of re-making memory so as to invent new possibilities for her contemporaries as they participate in a debate about justice and freedom. While the genesis of this discussion is to be found in the past, its actual meaning happens in the present, confirmed by the participatory and ephemeral dimension of the performance.

In *Whip It Good*, the whip is turned into a paint-brush in a non-neutral space, the art gallery. The Berlin production took place in a classical art setting, and Ehlers was surrounded by white marble Apollos and Venuses while whipping her canvas. This leads to the second knot of meaning in her *Whip It Good*. While the performance is to a certain extent the re-enactment of a collective and historical initial trauma, it is at the same time a metaphoric displacement of the history of slavery in the realm of art, questioning the meaning of artistic agency, from a black female perspective, while the art world is ruled by European and masculinist canons. The value of art – what makes it 'good' – is also addressed, as the title suggests that the canvas should be whipped with a proper skill and natural ability. This opens the way for multiple stories of empowerment. The whip becomes the key for performing agency, with whichever meaning the person controlling the whip wants to give it. Ehlers' re-enactment triggers resistance and liberation as much as execution and control, eventually inviting anyone to 'feel good after whipping it', whatever 'it' might mean for each individual. As they leave their trace on the canvas, lash after lash, the emotions that inhabit the whipping agent acquire value. Art-making becomes a force for tackling preconceived standards of beauty, whether they conform to the blueprint set by the European canon dating back to times of slavery (ideological value), or they are designated by the market economy that decides arbitrarily what each artwork is worth and the price that should be paid to own it (financial value). Ehlers' approach resonates with André Lepecki's (2016, p. 21) definition of re-enactment as 'a will to perform chronopolitical acts informed by an ethics of returning, by a dance of reflection, by affective transmission, all essential in resisting the neoliberal impetus to never look back'.

The creative force of *Whip It Good* is cathartic and participatory. It bets that looking back in anger might be the best way to draw out the ghosts and become an agent of one's life. The final canvas is the result of collective whippings and it encapsulates the memory of each performance. Each canvas looks different as it records the many different ways in which the participants used the whip, with different strength, style and frequency. The quantity of charcoal on the whip, the strength and swiftness of the lashes, the intervals of time between each lash are empirical elements which have an impact on the way the canvas looks at the end, to the point of sometimes being completely torn apart. *Whip It Good* performs the story of the artwork in the making. It ultimately talks about art, and of its role, power and function in the public space. Ehlers' conceptual art speaks the language of collective accountability, arguing for freedom and liberation through gestures that might not seem easy to perform, as they offer the possibility of acting out hidden affects that are unformed, or still to be defined. It demonstrates that the collective dialogue around past traumas that continue to haunt the present, like the unsolved traumas of slavery fuelling racism and racial discrimination in the present, can only happen at the level of creative interpretation, which avoids the trap of reproducing the past and repeating the trauma. Ehlers's metonymic re-enactment echoes Robert Blackson's (2007, p. 30) view that, 'drawing personal motivation from either your past or historical references is the conventional element necessary to construct a re-enactment. The degree to which performers empower themselves through layers of authenticity is secondary to their willingness to allow personal interpretation rather than verisimilitude to influence their actions'.

The subtitle 'Spinning from History's Filthy Mind', borrowed from Krista Franklin's poem 'Black Bullets', questions the extent to which we are ready to face and do something in the present with the haunting pains of our past. The canvas stands for a totalising metaphor that encompasses the many painful pasts which each and every one of us unconsciously carries with us in life, in spite of ourselves. Ehlers brings what Christopher Bollas (1987) defined as unthought knowledge to the realm of participatory art; by the same token, she creates an empowering mode of emotional exchange, beyond the rationality of language, between those who have been 'shaped by traumatic events that can be neither fully understood nor re-created' (Hirsh, 1996, p. 569).

Ano's 'Egoportraits': decolonial ways of seeing

Ano, born Eddy Firmin, is a Guadeloupian artist, who has been living and working in Montréal for the last ten years. His preferred modes of expression range from ceramic sculpture, furniture collage and drawing, to video installations and performance. Such an eclectic style, nurtured by experimental and interdisciplinary techniques, participates in a will to decolonise the arts from the modern/European canons, which classify aesthetics and art practices into rigid norms, criteria and disciplines. Ano approaches conceptual art as a transcultural and emotional language of inexhaustible possible combinations, and with the power to break from the European colonial and postcolonial myths of modernity and decolonisation. By fusing different visual techniques, the artist seeks to embody the continuity of slavery, from the sugar era in the plantations to the consumption of luxury goods in today's global market economy. Ano's artistic world mirrors the world-system as he sees it today, that is as a world in which 'non-European people are still living under crude European/Euro-American exploitation and domination' (Grosfoguel, 2011, p. 13).

In the 2017 exhibition 'Egoportrait ou l'errance des oiseaux/ Egoportrait or the Wandering of the Birds', at the Gallery Dominique Bouffard in Montréal, Ano reminded us that we are contemporary human specimens who have inherited a world which was shaped by slavery and its epistemological implications. The sculptures, drawings, installations and filmed performances allow us to see that slavery has taken new forms but is still entwined with domination and exploitation today. Among Ano's influences, we find the Latin American theorists of decolonial thinking. The artist believes, like Ramón Grosfoguel (2011, p. 10), that the logic behind today's colonial situations are ruled by coloniality, as opposed to colonialism: situations of 'cultural, political, sexual and economic oppression of subordinate racialized/ethnic groups by dominant racial/ethnic groups with or without the existence of colonial administrations'. Following Enrique Dussel (1994), Walter Mignolo (2000) and Anibal Quijano (2000), Grosfoguel demonstrates that race and racism are the organising principles that structure the multiple hierarchies of the world-system. The mythology of decolonisation obscures the fact that the colonial past continues to shape current racial hierarchies at a global level, despite the eradication of the colonial administrations. Ano gives artistic shape to Grosfoguel's view (p.24) that today's world-system privileges 'the culture, the knowledge and the epistemology produced by the West inferiorizing the rest'.

In the *egoportraits* (which in Canadian French means selfies) displayed in the exhibition, the artist uses his own face and body as an unlimited archive informed by the historical legacy of slavery, lending itself to multiple reproductions and transformations.[6] In this new relational mode between the exposed body of the artist and the viewing bodies of the audience, the duplication of the artist's image into sculpted and video portraits serves as a language to communicate with the spectator; it relies on visual language and its power to embody the continuity of the past in the present. Ano's own image becomes the allegory of mankind and the primary material to conceptualise how the majority of today's men and women are still enslaved by a profit-driven set of hierarchies.

As a Caribbean black man who is not a direct victim of slavery, but who is marked by its history as a descendant of enslaved people, Ano experiments with self-representations as visual channels to unveil the ways in which he perceives that slave-like conditions continue to be the dominant relational mode in

---

6   http://eddyfirmin.wixsite.com/ano-art/un-pti-peu-alors (accessed 19 March 2019).

today's world. Ano's 'Egoportrait' allows him to speak from the subaltern side of the colonial difference inscribed in his black ancestry:

> While my artworks are about the pride I feel as the descendant of a people who survived slavery in the Caribbean, they also express my never-ending and horrified astonishment at seeing the history of slavery repeat itself with a violence always more concealed and secret. My artworks are most of the time self-portraits questioning the schemes and templates that have been informing my inner self. My 'I' of contemporary slavery echoes my ancestral I/my historical self of the slavery plantations. From the yoke of enslavement to the yoke of trendy brands, history repeats itself as a selfie from one slavery to the other. (Interview in AICA 2017, my translation)

One particular kind of self-portrait is the series of five ceramic busts that the artist made with sophisticated mouldings of his own head, face and skull. He then painted each of the busts to transform them into visual riddles that embody the many forms of human trafficking and consumerist dependency which continue to control the lives of people who are still, metaphorically speaking, enslaved.

One bust represents Ano with his eyes closed and his skull disproportionately stretched. The full bust is painted in black. The brand and logo of Adidas are written on the skull while a golden ribbon covers his closed eyes like a mask.

On another bust, Ano's sculpted avatar wears a bright red helmet, in the style of native American caps, while the brand Campbell Soup is painted on his white face, leaving the spectator with the ironical spectacle of a man tinned like a soup, while the words 'fucking soup' are written on his upper lip.

In the same vein, the third bust shows Ano's face painted in white with his head covered by a cobalt blue helmet showing a lily; this emblem stands for Québec's independence, while recalling at the same time the French monarchy which established slavery as a modern mode of mercantilism in the Caribbean.

For the fourth bust, the artist decorated the top part of the figurehead with elegant pink and black letterings recalling the Chanel logo. This time, the sculpted persona wears big bunny ears, echoing the rabbit character of Guadeloupian folklore. In the folktales of *Compère Lapin*, which means Rabbit companion, we follow the adventures of animal characters with archetypal human personalities, affects, vices, skills and appetites. Rabbit is the cunning one, always able to make up stories that give him the advantage over the others, skilled in fooling and tricking his adversaries so he always comes out on top in any situation, even those in which he was initially the more vulnerable. Rabbit is a French Caribbean version of the Anancy spider trickster of the African-Caribbean folktale, and of the Br'er Rabbit of the American South. He embodies the creativity of the enslaved man to escape the control of the colonial power and to perform his volitional actions no matter how difficult the situation might seem. The bust of Ano as Rabbit is a direct reference to the skills of survival and resistance that the artist inherited from his enslaved ancestors and which he utilises in the realm of art. As a subaltern specimen of today's world-system, the black descendant of enslaved people continues to develop his creative skills for escapism, rebellion and irony, of which the crafted series of busts are a demonstration.

The last bust represents Ano fully painted in black with short hair, no beard, and his neck enchained in a golden slavery yoke. The top part of the head is painted with the Vuitton logo in bright green lettering. This egoportrait tells us that the 'I' of the slave seems to have persisted through time to become another enslaved ego, bound to networks of commodification, branding and global industry, in which profits and benefits continue to go to the descendants of the ones who enslaved those who were not Europeans. In Ano's perspective, the world-system is ruled by routes of global trade in which non-European bodies continue to have less value and to be more vulnerable to harm and pain than others.

Sculpted portraits belong to a classical tradition where mimesis, by representing the head and face of a person in the most realistic manner, aimed at praising the authority of the person represented. Busts of European men who colonised the global south have always been part of the colonial aesthetic, as signs of the coloniality of power of European institutions. Ano ironically diverts the function of the bust from its colonial symbolic to present five busts of the same black man, in different postures of enslavement and resistance. While the eyes, the mouth or the neck seem to be under the control of the luxury brands to which the figurehead is bound, the helmets of resistance signal the impossibility of getting rid of the agency of the self. Ano's self-portraits propose a new egopolitics in which race is not erased in the universal representation of the self designed by European philosophy. On the contrary, race becomes the locus from which the subject initiates and executes his agency. For Grosfoguel (2009, p. 14), Western philosophy created a myth of a disembodied and neutral subject, to support what he calls the ego-politics of knowledge:

> In Western philosophy and sciences, the subject that speaks is always hidden, concealed, erased from the analysis. The ego-politics of knowledge has always privileged the myth of a non-situated ego. Ethnic/racial/gender/sexual epistemic location and the subject that speaks are always decoupled. By delinking ethnic/racial/gender/sexual epistemic location from the subject that speaks, western philosophy and sciences are able to produce a myth about *Truthful Universal* knowledge that conceals who is speaking, as well as obscuring the geo-political and body-political epistemic location in the structures of colonial power/knowledge from which the subject speaks.

Ano's self-portraits relocate the subject in the locus of enunciation. They give him the shape of a black man of Caribbean origin, living in Montréal as an expatriate within a Northern American and French-speaking world, where the history of slavery is almost totally invisible and unknown.

Instead of giving titles to his self-portraits, Ano marks each of them with one letter of an alphabet he created made of 18 pictographs that the artist imagined as sensual modes for representing specific emotions. The use of this emotional alphabet allows him to partly escape the coloniality of power. Just as enslaved people escaped the control of the European hegemony by creating their own language, culture and modes of relation, Ano sees art as an empowering mode of expression which enables him to bypass the rationality of linguistic rules. Hence he is reluctant to label his artworks with a didactic title to guide the spectator's understanding; instead, he invites those who look at his works to enter an emotional mode of relation, signalled by a pictographic encoding which is foreign to them. In his view, the latter empowers the spectators to become agents of their own way of seeing, without being blinded by the criteria of classification and understanding that rule European rationality. In this series of ceramic self-portraits, slavery appears as a visual leitmotiv, inscribed in the artworks to stimulate interpretation and critical thinking from the spectator. As a key point of origin of the racial and colonial European epistemology which constructed the racial hierarchies among the humans of today, slavery takes the shape of visual encoded signs inviting the spectators to become agents of their own gaze by looking critically at the works displayed in the exhibition space. As a way of seeing differently, the conceptual inscription of slavery facilitates agency and triggers the possibility for the spectators to make sensory interpretations that will eventually decolonise their mind through their active gaze, along the lines of bell hooks's (1995) definition of black representation as a new way of seeing.

Ano also produced a video self-portrait that interestingly resonates with the participatory and metonymic strategy of Ehlers, as much as with the multidirectional implication of Piquet's artistic manifesto. For this performance, which took place in the streets of Montreal and was shown on film during the exhibition, the artist imagined and built a technological device which is a modern replica of the iron neck collar, an instrument of punishment and humiliation during the slavery era. While the neck is held in a collar yoke, iron bars on each side of it trap each hand within shackles. It is extremely painful to wear an iron collar and overseers and slave traders relied on the fact that no one could resist such pain. Ano built a lighter version of the collar with four selfie telescopic perches, at the end of which he put a smartphone. This high-tech collar forces the body to wear an uncomfortable instrument that restricts the movements of the upper body, while allowing the person wearing it to see his/her body in positions that are normally not accessible to human sight: with Ano's selfie collar, anyone can have a simultaneous and multidirectional view of his head, skull and face, from four different angles, front, sides and back. In other words, the multidirectional irony that Ano experimented with in the ceramic busts becomes an available embodied practice when wearing the selfie collar, offering new possibilities of self-introspection.

Over two months, Ano walked the streets of Montréal inviting passers-by to try the device on. Many of those who accepted had no idea that it was inspired by the torture instrument of the collar used by slave owners to control the bodies of those they enslaved. Most of the public were ignorant of the history of slavery in the Caribbean and knew little about the island of Guadeloupe. Like Ehlers, who turned the whip into an instrument of agency and control in her power, Ano turned the collar into a tool for self-analysis and intimate personal inquiry, beyond identity politics. Given that the smartphones record the movements of the head and the face while wearing the selfie collar, the device allows for a multiplication of self-representation and points at a new kind of visual narcissism to experiment with self-investigation and critical thinking. It questions the role and the power of images, the relationship we hold with ourselves as representations, and ownership over our own bodies.

Conclusion

Piquet, Ehlers and Ano share the view that art is a conceptual language with restorative potential. Their artistic practice relies on the participatory energy of their audience, whether spectators become implicated viewers or actors of their creations. Their artworks avoid didacticism and are deprived of any figurative representation of slavery. In 'Moun brilés', 'Whip It Good' and 'Egoportrait', we are reminded that racial domination was born with modern/European/patriarchal/heterosexual epistemology and conquest and exploitation of the rest of the world. Both the coloniality of power, in the case of Piquet and Ano, and the coloniality of gender, in the case of Ehlers, are conceived as common heritages that played a foundational and crucial role in shaping the world-system we inhabit now, and which continues to classify human life according to racial hierarchies.

Empathy, re-enactment and irony are different strategies used by each of the three artists to stimulate the interest of the bystanders and invite them to play a part in the reparative process and find a positive way forward. This resonates with restorative justice processes that bring into communication those harmed by crime and those responsible for the harm, so as to enable everyone offended by a particular situation to participate in repairing the damage done. Piquet, Ehlers and Ano embody different Caribbean perspectives informed by their gendered and geographical locus of enunciation in a racially determined environment. Cremation, whipping and bondage are transformed and reinvented into metonymic facilitators of a wider scenario in which the audience takes part in a process of accountability for wounds inflected today by templates of oppression invented in the past.

Bibliography

AICA (2017) Association Internationale des Critiques d'Art, online journal, https://aica-sc.net/2017/03/06/eddy-firmin-dit-ano-egoportrait-ou-lerrance-des-oiseaux/

Bennett, J. (2005) *Empathic Vision: Affect, Trauma and Contemporary Art* (Stanford, CA: Stanford University Press).

Blackson, R. (2007) 'Once more ... with feeling: reenactment in contemporary art and culture', *Art Journal*, 66 (1): 28–40.

Bollas, C. (1987) *The Shadow of the Object: Psychoanalysis of the Unthought Known* (New York: Columbia University Press).

Brown. W. (1995) *States of Injury: Power and Freedom in Late Modernity* (Princeton, NJ: Princeton University Press).

Césaire, A. (1970) *Les armes miraculeuses* (Paris: Gallimard Poésie).

Corlett, A.J. (2010) *Heirs of Oppression: Racism and Reparations* (Lanham: Rowman & Littlefield).

Dussel, E. (1994) *1492: El encubrimiento del otro: hacia el origen del mito de la modernidad* (La Paz, Bolivia: Plural Editores).

Felman, S. (2002) *The Juridical Unconscious: Trials and Traumas in the Twentieth Century* (Cambridge Mass.: Harvard University Press).

Grosfoguel, R. (2009) 'A decolonial approach to political economy: transmodernity, decolonial thinking and global coloniality', *Kult* 6: 10–38, http://postkolonial.dk/kult-6-special-issue-latin-america/

— (2011) 'Decolonizing post-colonial studies and paradigms of political economy: transmodernity, decolonial thinking and global coloniality', *Transmodernity: Journal of Peripheral Cultural Production of the Luso-Hispanic World*, 1 (1): 1–38.

Hall, C. (2014) *Legacies of British Slave-ownership: Colonial Britain and the Formation of Victorian Britain* (Cambridge: Cambridge University Press).

Heuman, G. (2014) *The Caribbean. A Brief History* (London: Bloomsbury Academic).

Hirsch, M. (1996) 'Past lives: postmemories in exile', *Poetics Today*, 17 (4): 659–86.

hooks, b. (1995) *Art on My Mind: Visual Politics* (New York: New Press).

Jeannerod, M. (2003) 'The mechanisms of self-recognition in humans', *Behavioural Brain Research* 142 (1–2): 1–15.

Lorde, A. (1984) *Sister Outsider* (New York: Ten Speed Press).

Mignolo, W. (2000) *Local Histories/Global Designs: Essays on the Coloniality of Power, Subaltern Knowledges and Border Thinking* (Princeton, NJ: Princeton University Press).

Mills, C. (1997) *The Racial Contract* (Ithaca, NY: Cornell University Press).

Lepecki, A. (2016) *Singularities: Dance in the Age of Performance* (New York: Routledge).

Quijano, A. (2000) 'Coloniality of power, ethnocentricism, and Latin America', *Nepantla* 1 (3): 533–80.

Rothberg, M. (2013) 'Multidirectional memory and the implicated subject: on Sebald and Kentridge', in L. Plate and A. Smelik (eds.), *Performing Memory in Art and Popular Culture* (New York: Routledge), pp. 39–58.

Schwab, G. (2010) *Haunting Legacies: Violent Histories and Transgenerational Traumas* (New York: Columbia University Press).

6. Anti-racism in the classroom and beyond: teacher perspectives from Rio de Janeiro

Gudrun Klein

Until lions have their own storytellers, tales of hunting will always glorify the hunter

Statement by Pai Paulo in the 2007 carnival song of the Orùnmilá Centre[1]

In Brazil, the 1990s and early 2000s were marked by various public policy reforms that were meant to tackle persistent and significant racial and social disparities, and were closely tied to the agenda of the Brazilian Worker's Party. These reforms contributed to turning issues of race and racism into part of the national agenda. In 2003, former president Luiz Inácio Lula da Silva (Worker's Party) introduced law 10.639/03, which made it compulsory to teach African and Afrobrazilian history and culture in every public and private primary and secondary school throughout the country. A few years later, in 2008, law 11.645/08 altered the original version, adding indigenous history and culture to it.[2] These laws were part of a greater body of affirmative action meant to tackle Brazil's significant racial inequality.

Representatives of the black and indigenous movements had fought for the implementation of these laws for many years. They understand them as a tool to combat racism, whose existence has long been downplayed or even denied in Brazilian society, and the legacy of the myth of 'racial democracy',[3]

1   Initially, the Orùnmilá Cultural Centre was founded as a Candomblé *terreiro* [house of worship] by the Candomblé priest Pai Paulo and the Candomblé priestess Mãe Neide. It now also functions as a cultural centre, containing a library with a collection covering themes of race, black culture, education, and African and Afrobrazilian history. The centre provides space for workshops and seminars, cultural dance and music performances, political debates and policy advocacy (cf. Da Costa, 2014).

2   Despite the law having been altered in 2008, many scholars still refer to its unaltered version (law 10.639/03), which did not include indigenous history or culture. With regard to the implementation of this law, most studies focus solely on Afrobrazilians and fail to take the experiences of indigenous people into account. The same can be said about most educators and social activists in this field. This chapter refers to version 11.645/08, unless used in an ethnographic context in which the original version was cited specifically.

3   The myth of Brazil being a racial democracy took root and flourished in the decades between the World Wars, when whitening politics were gradually replaced by the belief that blackness

G. Klein, 'Anti-racism in the classroom and beyond: teacher perspectives from Rio de Janeiro', in P. Wade, J. Scorer and I. Aguiló (eds.), *Cultures of Anti-Racism in Latin America and the Caribbean* (London: Institute of Latin American Studies, 2019), pp. 125–45. License: CC-BY-NC-ND 4.0.

as well as a tool for the reparation of injustices caused by the country's colonial history, slavery and its *branqueamento* [whitening][4] politics of the 19th and 20th centuries (Hofbauer, 1995).

The turn from denying the existence of racism to the implementation of affirmative action did not happen overnight. After the end of the military dictatorship in 1985, Brazil experienced a process of democratisation in which black activists reorganised and increasingly gained influence in politics as well as in national debates about race. Since 'racial democracy' was an ideology of non-racialism and therefore frequently interpreted as anti-racist, the importance of making race and racial inequality visible has become a vital part of the black movement's agenda. After a long period of extensive grassroots campaigning carried out by black activists, the 1990s saw increasing numbers of people in Brazilian society recognising racism and starting to put pressure on the state to extend real democratic citizenship and human rights to its black population (Telles, 2004, p. 53).

As Telles (2004) observes, anti-racist work and the achievements of the black movement in Brazil drew on grass-roots mobilisation, but were also significantly strengthened by the influential support of international allies and global civil society actors who denounced the government for its lack of effort to counter racial exclusion and inequality. A crucial event was the Third UN World Conference on Racism in Durban in 2001, which brought unprecedented global media attention to issues of race in Brazil. Shortly after that, the introduction of affirmative action policies followed, such as law 10.639/03, which provided a new legal framework for black activists to combat racism.

The goal of this particular anti-racist curricular reform was to stimulate the entire population to re-evaluate the role Africans, Afrodescendants and indigenous people played in the history of the country (Pereira, 2011, p. 40). The aim was to valorise black and indigenous culture and facilitate the black and indigenous populations' active participation in public life. The document *National Guidelines for the Teaching of Ethnic and Race Relations*

---

and race mixture were less significant than the environment and culture of a person, turning racial mixture into a strength rather than a weakness (Dávila, 2003, p. 8). This narrative erased the history of racial exclusion, oppression and resistance between different racial groups in the country (Soeterik, 2013, p. 9) by propagating the belief that all citizens were racially diverse and differentiated treatment of ethnic groups was therefore impossible. Damatta (1987) defines racial democracy as the founding myth of Brazilian race relations.

4   After the abolition of slavery in 1888, Africans and Afrobrazilians continued to be regarded as inferior but also a permanent presence. Over the course of half a century, a policy of assimilation was followed, attempting to anchor Brazil exclusively in its European heritage (Akkari, 2012, p. 165). The country's ideological goal of whitening the black and indigenous population was imagined to be achievable by extensive European immigration.

and of Afro-Brazilian and African History and Culture (DCNERER),[5] which was drafted by the Ministry of Education and the Office for the Promotion of Racial Equality,[6] was released in conjunction with the first version of the law to clarify its background, purpose and goals.[7] Topics such as the history of Africans and Africa, the struggle of black and indigenous people in Brazil, Afrobrazilian and indigenous culture, and the formation of the nation from an indigenous and Afrodescendant point of view were meant to be incorporated into the curriculum (Palácio do Planalto, 2008). Furthermore, the document acknowledged the black movement's efforts that had led to the introduction of the law (Prefeitura de São Paulo, 2004).

However, various obstacles still exist with regard to the implementation of the law. More than a decade after the first version of educational law 10.639/03 was signed, Brazilian educators and scholars (Ferreira, 2008; Júnior and Silva 2013, among others) as well as black and indigenous activists frequently state that '*a lei não pegou!*' [the law has not caught on]. Schools' rhetoric often continues to reproduce the discourses of racial democracy and colour-blind meritocracy. It rarely includes reflections on historical processes or on the (re-)construction of race in debates about social inequality, but often reproduces and normalises deprecatory and stereotypical representations of Afrobrazilians and indigenous people. The image of the uncivilised, inferior and primitive indigenous or black person is still rooted in many people's ideas about indigeneity and blackness (Oliveira, 2005, 2012; Warren and Sue, 2011; Da Costa, 2014). This is symptomatic of Latin American countries; like Brazil, various other countries have a rather sophisticated legislative corpus protecting the rights of historically marginalised groups. However, the gap between legislation and effective implementation is vast.

How policy is created is crucially important, but what is often overlooked is the way policy reforms are experienced and implemented at the micro level (Paschel, 2016, p. 228). The sole existence of a law does not guarantee its implementation, or as Flyvbjerg (1998, p. 325) states: 'Whereas constitution writing and institutional reform may often be essential to democratic development, the idea that such reform alters practice is a hypothesis, not an axiom.' Gomes (2001, p. 89) adds that laws are never neutral. No matter how progressive a law might be, its legitimation is dependent on social dynamics, political debates and daily practices. Furthermore, the social and educational reality that a law addresses is always marked by complexity and confrontation

---

5   Diretrizes Curriculares Nacionais para a Educação das Relações Etnico-Raciais e para o Ensino de História e Cultura Afro-Brasileira e Africana (Prefeitura de São Paulo, 2004).
6   Secretária de Políticas de Promoção da Igualdade Racial (SEPPIR).
7   When the law was altered in 2008 to include the teaching of indigenous history and culture, the document DCNERER was not adapted and remains in its original form, omitting indigenous people to this day.

as well as contradiction, and is never isolated from social and racial relations. Looking at the everyday practices of those who are active in individual institutions contributes to our understanding of the dynamics of social change (Gillborn, 1994, p. 147). This chapter approaches the irregular and complex implementation process of law 11.645/08 through the examination of spaces where an anti-racist agenda is being advanced and ethnic-racial education is flourishing – even if such spaces might still be few and far between.

Gomes and Jesus (2013) demonstrate that initiatives of regional education offices paired with actions of school leaders are crucial for the implementation of pedagogical practices that comply with law 11.645/08. Nevertheless, in schools where practices that question ethnic-racial relations are found, they can be attributed predominantly to the efforts of individual teachers rather than the school as a whole (p. 28). The question then arises as to who these individuals are who further the agenda of the curricular reform on the ground – be it in education offices or in schools. Frequently, efforts to implement law 11.645/08 are carried out by actors with ties to social movement organisations and who play multiple roles, acting as teachers, education officials and academics.

This chapter provides ethnographic insight into various experiences that led a group of teachers with whom I worked during 12 months of fieldwork in a suburb of Rio de Janeiro,[8] to take on both the role of advocates for and practitioners of the law, and also the role of anti-racist activists more broadly. What can we learn from those of their experiences – which transformed their understanding of history and racial relations in Brazil – that can function in similar ways in another context, and thus help us understand the effectiveness of affirmative action in the field of education?

I first touch upon the structural environment in which advocates of the law operate and the power structures they manoeuvre through. Second, I explore how personal trajectories influence the teachers' understanding of racial identity and the role appearance plays in this process. I will argue here that the commitment to anti-racist education is strongly connected to personal beliefs and experiences; in particular, to the complex and often ambiguous process of assuming one's racial identity and accepting the implications that come with it. Third, I discuss instances of discrimination experienced by some of the white teachers and how the expression of these can complicate their position as 'allies' in anti-racism.

---

[8] In 2015–16, I carried out 12 months of ethnographic fieldwork in educational institutions where individuals act as advocates of law 11.645/08. I attended a public school run by the state of Rio de Janeiro, a public school run by the state of Brazil and a teacher education course held at the Universidade Federal Rural do Rio de Janeiro, UFRRJ [Federal Rural University of Rio de Janeiro]. I followed teachers, school leaders, students and their families inside and outside school to assess the understanding these people had of law 11.645/08.

Power and authority

Even though some school leaders and education officials do not show awareness of law 11.645/08, or treat it with indifference or neglect, it can be regarded as a tool giving legal authority to those who wish to transform the current education system. In an interview, Luiz, a lecturer at the UFRRJ, who previously worked as a state school teacher and identifies as *negro* [black],[9] remembers his early teaching practice and how it has changed since the law passed in 2003:

> Being in school and in touch with various people of the [black] movement, I started to do activist work and talk about racial issues in school as early as 1994, and I did this together with a few like-minded people I found inside school. I started to have this discussion in school and all of this was before law 10.639, before 2003. We worked on a few projects ... When law 10.639 emerged, it was like they put a weapon in our hands. Now we could really demand for it to be complied with. This is when our work really began!

Simply knowing or talking about the existence of a law does not automatically entail its implementation. As there is no legal document that defines the amount or content of activities the secretariats or schools should carry out, their efforts vary considerably. In 2008, five years after the first version of the law was enacted, the Secretaria de Estado de Educação do Rio de Janeiro (SEEDUC) [State Secretariat of Education of Rio de Janeiro] created the Comitê Estadual Étnico-Racial [State Ethnic-Racial Committee] as a response to the law. Nevertheless, as Soeterik (2013) observes with regard to secretariats concerned with the implementation of law 11.645/08 created by the education ministry, barriers have been caused by highly fragile institutional structures and a lack of financial resources for specific activities.

A former employee of a municipal education secretariat in a suburb of Rio de Janeiro, Úrsula, explained in an interview that the implementation of measures to promulgate the law depends very much on the individual will of the regional secretariat's staff, which in turn depends on the political structures in the respective municipality.

---

9   In pursuit of the greater cohesion of black people and their struggle for recognition and the critique of the myth of 'racial democracy', the black movement promoted the political and symbolic category *negro*, which does not only refer to skin colour or race but also to an identification with the struggle for the recognition of Afrobrazilian and African history and culture. Whereas some dark-skinned people refer to themselves and other dark-skinned people as *moreno* [mixed, brown] and avoid calling them *preto* [black], the category *negro* is often used as a statement to demonstrate pride about one's Afrobrazilian appearance and physical markers. However, Sheriff (2001) states that the preferred use of mixed race and lighter skinned terms in comparison to black ones often responds to cultural censorship and courtesy more than reflecting the opinion of the speaker. The term is also widely used in academic contexts for statistical purposes, since it allows the grouping together of the census categories *pardo* [brown] and *preto*, and it is increasingly used in governmental and other official contexts.

Úrsula identifies as a white woman and is very passionate about the implementation of the law. She had been working as a teacher in private and municipal primary school education for 15 years before she joined the municipal education secretariat in 2013. When she started to work there, she suggested specific activities with regard to the implementation of law 11.645/08. However, the lack of a designated person who would be able to allocate funding made it difficult for Úrsula to carry out any of the activities she had planned. When she managed to put together a teacher training workshop with a guest from a *quilombo*[10] and an indigenous activist, which involved hardly any costs, she was convinced that she had found a way to work around the obvious obstacles. Nevertheless, when she presented her initiative to the sub-secretary for approval, she was told that no teachers in the municipality could be taken out of the classroom to undergo this particular type of training.

Hence, even before implementation efforts reach the school level, they have to overcome obstacles encountered in regional education offices, such as the absence of anyone assuming responsibility, lack of funding, or even direct obstruction. Once initiatives are publicly announced and advertised, frequently they meet opposition from the school leadership, the student body or parents.

Úrsula told me that the educational secretariat she worked for had avoided promoting the law until a lawyer from the Ministério Público do Estado do Rio de Janeiro [prosecutor's office of the state of Rio de Janeiro] arrived asking to see evidence of its implementation within the municipality and threatened to take the case to the prosecutor's office.

The lawyer told Úrsula that if nothing was being done with regard to the implementation of the law, she must denounce the regional secretariat at the public prosecutor's office. Úrsula saw an opportunity in this encounter and decided to tell the lawyer that the secretariat was in fact working on ethnic-racial issues. Had she admitted that the secretariat was not complying with the law, a long bureaucratic process with an uncertain outcome would have followed. Instead, Úrsula chose to use this encounter to achieve instant changes: she told her superior that the lawyer threatened consequences if the secretariat did not start to incentivise schools to implement the law. Úrsula's strategy proved to be effective: after the lawyer's visit she was finally able to obtain funding for some of the projects she had wanted to bring to life, such as to offer courses on the implementation of the law for the staff of the secretariat itself.

In 2013, which marked ten years since the implementation of the first version of the law, an event to commemorate its anniversary was planned by the municipal education secretariat. To promote it, 10,000 flyers were printed, but according to Úrsula, hardly any were distributed. And despite her superior having the budget to print the flyers, Úrsula claimed that there were no funds for a car to pick up speakers for her events or to visit schools in the municipality.

---

10   *Quilombos* are settlements notionally founded by *maroons* [escaped enslaved African and black people].

To her, it felt like empty excuses, and in the end, due to political restructuring in the secretariat, the event never even took place.

Thus the excuse Úrsula gave the lawyer – that changes in staff hamper the effective implementation of projects – was not untrue and is a significant factor in the levels of frustration of those trying to initiate projects. Municipal elections take place every four years, which means that most of the staff of the education secretariat (and other public offices) are replaced. As a consequence, it becomes almost impossible to continue most of the new projects and work in progress. At the same time, the decentralised organisation of the secretariat into various sub-divisions working individually impedes the efficient development of common projects:

> Each sub-secretary, there was one for human resources, administration, one that took care of the people, for pedagogy, nutrition … Each one would do whatever they want. There is no centralised work. It's just craziness! Nobody knows what the other one is doing – very crazy. When the new government arrives they just do what they want, it doesn't matter what we have started. […] Whoever works for the councillor will get a position, or from the mayor. Not many people are competent; there is no public competition, all the jobs are allocated by personal ties. In order to get into the secretariat of education you have to have [know] someone. Everything is about political relationships, like a councillor whom you supported in his campaign, and then he puts you there. […] Every four years there are municipal elections, every councillor acts as the *padrinho* [patron saint] of a school, it isn't official, it isn't legal. There is legislation about this, about the influence of the political sphere though, about the electorate. They know the school, that's where they get the votes, where they show their work, have events in school, take care of the school.

Úrsula stresses the fact that questioning authority/power within this context is not something to be done casually:

> [The] rain comes into the secretariat, there are rats, the drain just runs through, it's horrible. It's horrible, I complain but then people tell me talk less, you have a child to raise, it's a very tense situation, so I shut up. […] I don't like this *jogo político partidário* [political party game], and especially here [in this particular municipality] it is complicated. Beyond being not ethical, it is also something dangerous. Things work with violence. They are criminals. […] I think this is how it works in other municipalities as well.

The lack of funding, ever-changing staff and the absence of a person in charge are accompanied by the fear of challenging those in power and the threat of unpredictable consequences. Similarly to Úrsula's education secretariat, in the majority of educational institutions those who actively work on the implementation of the law are in the minority and act out of their own volition. In fact, activities developed by actors from civil society – within civil society but also within the official political and the pedagogical arena – have been the main motor behind the implementation of the law (Soeterik, 2013, p. 125; Pereira, 2003, p. 28).

Discourses about race

The mere existence of legislative measures is not sufficient to further an anti-racist agenda. Rather, their execution and the way they are being executed depend on individual actions, which are informed by personal beliefs and experiences. What sets people apart who understand themselves as anti-racist and are often understood by others as such? The following section presents the individual contexts and experiences of those who follow an anti-racist agenda and advocate for the law's implementation; these experiences are often connected to the way they approach questions of race and racism.

While working at the municipal education secretariat, Úrsula was enrolled in a teacher education course at the UFRRJ that was dedicated to the implementation of law 10.639/03 and attended by teachers from schools all over the city and suburbs of Rio de Janeiro. At the beginning of term, on an oppressively hot and humid day, she invited me to a meeting of a research group on anti-racism and the implementation of law 10.639/03 she and a few other students had joined. During the meeting, which was held at the home of one of the participants, I heard a particular narrative which would be repeated many times during teacher education classes at the UFRRJ. Everyone was asked to explain their reasons for studying law 10.639/03 and their motives for joining the meeting. What all participants, independent of the colour of their skin, disclosed was that they had not learned about or understood institutional and systemic racism until they were adults. They grew up in a society in which many people deny discrimination based on race while idealising European aesthetics, culture and knowledge production. Burdick observes that 'racial exclusion speaks in two voices: it values whiteness and at the same time says that colour is not important' (Pinho, 2009). People often deny that racial discrimination exists and conclude that social inequality is a class problem. Those who advocate overtly for racial identifications in the name of anti-racism may even be accused of fomenting racism (Wade, 2010, p. 43; Da Costa, 2014, p. 1).

Lilian, a young history teacher, comes from an interracial family, which she described as having a white mother and a *negro* father. She had only recently decided to stop straightening her hair chemically and instead let her naturally curly hair grow back. Therefore, she was wearing a coloured hairband made into a turban, which covered the hair that was still in transformation: as the chemical treatment damages the hair up to its root, it is necessary to let it grow out to allow the natural curls to grow back. All the women I talked to who were going through this process of transformation during my fieldwork either braided artificial hair into their outgrowing hair or wore turbans to cover it until it reached a length they felt comfortable with. Wearing a coloured turban made out of fabric influenced by African prints as well as braiding hair can be read as aesthetically claiming one's *negra* identity, as both practices result in a look that diverges from white European norms of female beauty. Gomes (2006) describes the construction of the *negra/negro* identity as a process that does not only come from within a person, but is also created in relation to the outside world and how one's body is perceived by others. Bodies cannot simply be read in a biological way, since their meaning is culturally constructed. Black curly hair and black bodies are thus symbolic expressions of black culture in Brazil, functioning as symbols of sociocultural resistance, but also of oppression (2006). By the end of my fieldwork, almost a year later, Lilian was content with the result of her naturally grown hair and had stopped covering it.

Although her father was a black activist, for the most of her life Lilian had been blind to racial discrimination: 'I was living our racial democracy, thinking that I am white as my mother is white.' It was only quite recently when Lilian entered public university to obtain her master's degree in education, that she first had a very strong feeling of not belonging due to the majority of students looking a lot whiter and more European than she did. At university Lilian got in touch with black activists, who offered her a perspective on race-related questions that was new to her. Luiz, her supervisor, described her as shy and scared when taking her university admission exam, ready to be refused. During her time at university (2014–16), Lilian dedicated herself to studying and debating and started to think of herself as *negra*, while at the same time developing the feeling that she needed to do something in order to change black people's lives. In her practice as an educator, Lilian uses knowledge gained at university and within the research group that allows her to think more critically about the curriculum she is conveying to her pupils. She advocates racial quotas at public universities and visits various schools to talk to pupils who are applying to university about the opportunities, controversies and issues surrounding racial quotas, always weaving her personal experience into the narrative.

Another primary school history teacher present at the meeting, Jackie, described herself as being in a very similar situation to that of Lilian. In my view, she is a brown-skinned woman who, the first time I saw her, asked Lilian about her hair transformation while still straightening her own hair. Her words to Lilian were encouraging and admiring, but she smiled timidly and told us she would not be brave enough to start the process of growing back her own naturally wavy hair. At the meeting Jackie told us that she identifies as *negra*, but that her mother, whose skin is slightly darker, disagrees and keeps telling her that she is *morena* [brown, mixed]. When Jackie is outside the context of people who identify as black or see value in being black, she says that she continues to think of herself as *morena*. Sheriff (2001) argues that the favela dwellers she worked with readily recognise a basic social distinction between white and non-white, despite the complex range of colour terms used in Brazil. Furthermore, referring to the national census, Telles states that inequalities between *pardos* [browns] and whites are almost identical to those between *pretos* [blacks] and whites (cited in Selka, 2007, p. 14).

However, during her life, Jackie claimed, she had never suffered any prejudice as she always 'passed for *morena*' and was not treated in the derogatory way that she imagines *negros* are. This demonstrates that Jackie politically identifies as *negra*, standing up against racial discrimination and fighting for the implementation of law 10.639/03. However, she does not feel comfortable in fully claiming her *negra* identity in contexts in which being black might be regarded as disadvantageous. Jackie may also not feel entitled to call herself *negra*, given her impression that she had never been treated negatively due to the colour of her skin and her appearance. Her skin complexion and straightened hair equip her with the flexibility to shift between her *negra* and *morena* identity, without fully committing to either.

In her profession as a primary school teacher, Jackie found a way to express and develop her *negra* identity. For her political project she started to work with *abayomis*, little dolls made out of cotton fabric that represent the dolls made by enslaved African mothers out of their own garments. Through the production of such dolls she introduces pupils to the Brazilian history of slavery from an angle that stresses the caring and creative qualities of African mothers and thus diverges from traditionally pejorative narratives about slavery, which often portray enslaved Africans as primitive, cultureless and mere victims. When Jackie presented her *abayomis* at the research group's first meeting of the year, she was highly emotional and started crying (which happened again six months later at another meeting). She seemed to be moved not only by the idea of enslaved mothers giving joy to enslaved children by creatively using the little they had, but also by the idea of reaching her pupils in a playful way. For her, this opened up the possibility of reaching hundreds of other pupils though her efforts and making them receptive to the abundance of African and Afrobrazilian culture and history.

Júlio, another teacher who attended the research group's meeting, opened up about his past as a police officer, a personal fact he had not told anyone in this group before. Given his known history of being a highly active member of the trade union Central Única dos Trabalhadores (CUT)[Unified Workers' Central], which has very close ties to the Movimento dos Trabalhadores Rurais Sem Terra (MST) [Worker's Party and the Landless Workers' Movement], imagining Júlio in a police uniform elicited puzzled faces and astonished looks. Despite what I would describe as his curly black hair and brown skin, Júlio, who is now in his late forties, grew up believing in his whiteness and that it was impossible for him to date a woman who was not white. He remembered his mother always telling him and his brothers that they were white. Like Lilian, he only came to think of himself as black when he was an adult and entered university:

> It wasn't easy, I also started this process of becoming *enegrecer* [black] very late in my life. You have to find it very weird how in a country full of black people these people have to become black. It is a tense process. I discovered myself as black when I was an adult. My mother had several children and called none of us black, and we didn't either. She would always say 'limpar o útero' ['clean/whiten the uterus']. We were three boys and we always heard her say this.

The accounts above demonstrate a certain flexibility of racial and ethnic identities. Cicalo (2012) discusses the terminological flexibility of racial terms that Brazilians use for everyday identification. Jackie's concurrent identification as *negra* and *morena*, depending on the context, demonstrates that the usage of racial terms is strongly influenced by the specific contextual framework in which people interact (p. 94). Lilian, Jackie and Júlio all assumed a *negra* identity when they entered university, an environment in which they learned about racial discrimination and law 10.639/03 and got in touch with black activists. Júlio calls this process of claiming a *negro* identity 'becoming black'. In the following part we will see that this terminology is also shared by white Brazilians.

Becoming black

Clara, Úrsula and Ana Paula, the only women at the meeting whom I would describe as white, stated that they did not learn about racial discrimination before they were adults either. Their perception of themselves as being white has not changed however. Similarly to Júlio, Clara, who is a history teacher at a public high school, used the term *enegrecer* ['becoming black']. She had grown up believing she lived in a racial democracy, despite her father having prohibited her to go out with a black person. Until she entered high school as a teacher in 2009, she had associated the term *negro* with slave. When one of the coordinators of her school at that time assigned her to a project that was meant to further the implementation of law 10.639/03 and discuss the deconstruction of the myth of racial democracy, she started to question the beliefs she had grown up with. Consequently, in her teaching practice she became more aware of the reproduction of racist narratives and centred her continuing university studies on the implementation of the law.

Clara used the term *enegrecer* when she referred to the process of learning about racial inequality in Brazil. As Clara identifies as white, when she uses the term it does not carry the same meaning as when Júlio says it. Clara refers to her *acordar* [awakening] from the belief of living in a 'racial democracy', whereas the way Júlio uses it goes beyond the re-conception of society and history in terms of injustice and racial discrimination and refers to him becoming conscious about his own racial identity. Ana Paula, another white teacher at the meeting, put it in the following way: 'There are people who *descobrir como negro* [discover themselves as black]. I became *enegrecer*. White people become black.' She describes the (re-)construction of her identity process as having begun in 2006, the year she started to work at a municipal education secretariat in one of the municipalities close to the city of Rio de Janeiro where she oversaw the implementation of the project 'A Cor da Cultura' [The Colour of Culture][11] in 35 municipal schools. Although Ana Paula describes her history studies at the prestigious UFRJ as having taught her to examine society in a critical way and to reflect on inequality, they failed to make her look beyond social class and made her blind to racial inequality. She stresses the importance of getting to know and being around social activists who fight against racism. Through them she learned to question the meaning and privilege of being white in Brazil and discovered herself as a social activist against racism in the domain of education; on the one hand, using her work as a teacher to reach her pupils, and on the other, educating herself further. She told me one day that to her it is essential that the white population recognises its advantages and privilege compared to other ethnicities. She thinks the only way to get there is love, affection and admiration of anything considered to be *negro*. When I asked her explicitly about becoming *enegrecer* she answered:

> When you ask me about the moment that I became black, I can tell you that it is through each learning experience, social activism, altruism, solidarity and the wish for social justice for *negros* and for any other subaltern segment. Every time another person's pain hits me, it makes me sad and this sadness transforms into strength to work and denounce the injuries to the subaltern parts of the population caused by those in power. I think that every white person should have the possibility to live and feel the importance of this displacement. In order to create a different world it is necessary to *enegrecer* your soul.

According to Ana-Paula's words, becoming black goes beyond the perception and understanding of the existence of racial injustice and discrimination, and entails an element of empathy and embodied knowledge in the shape of the ability to put oneself into the position of the subaltern. Úrsula, who grew up and lived in an impoverished area until she got married and moved to a white upper-middle-class neighbourhood, put it the following way:

---

11 The project 'A Cor da Cultura' [The Colour of Culture] was funded in 2004 by the education ministry's Secretaria Especial de Políticas de Promoção da Igualdade Racial (SEPPIR) [Special Secretariat for Policies that Promote Racial Equality], Petrobras, Canal Futura, TV Globo and the Centro de Informação e Documentação do Artista Negro (CIDAN) [Centre for Information and the Documentation of the Black Artist]. It has been producing videos, children's books and teaching materials since 2004, and has started to collaborate with universities, NGOs and other institutions to provide teacher education with regard to the requirements of the law in 2010.

> I never regarded myself as *negra*, but I am Afrodescendant, I am a white woman. [...] A woman of the [education] secretariat stopped her chemical hair treatment, let her hair grow naturally. This is a process, for other people and the individual. [...] It is not just to fall asleep white and wake up black. It is a painful process that I have not lived but I see it through other people that I know. A five-year-old girl, suffering and discovering her body, her identity.

Even though Úrsula describes herself as Afrodescendant, she does not identify as *negra* as she does not consider her physical appearance to be that of a *negra* person: she has very light skin, straight hair and no physical traits that would mark her as non-white. Her African descent stems from having a grandmother she considers to be *negra*, which, in her eyes does not say anything about her own colour/race, which she bases on her physical aspects/markers.

Thus, in Brazil it is possible to become black without being black, at least in some contexts. Becoming black can signify becoming conscious of one's black racial identity or cultural ancestry, but it can also mean claiming a political identity/social activism based on awareness of the prejudice against black people in Brazilian society or a strong feeling of empathy. When Clara uses the term of *enegrecer* it describes the process she went through from being a white woman denying racism to a white woman identifying with the struggle of *negros* and the black movement. Júlio, who today identifies as *negro* and looks a lot less European than Clara, uses the term in a slightly different context. His mother raised him to be blind to racial discrimination, while telling him that he was white. *Enegrecer* describes the moment that he came to see his own misconceptions about racism and assumed his place in society as *negro* and not a white man. He decided to fight racial discrimination, accompanied by a process of claiming a political, symbolic and personal *negro* identity. Being *negro* is usually seen as an ontological category of being; here it is an experiential category of becoming, which focuses on the centrality of knowledge. Like Jackie, Júlio's light skin provides him with the option of switching between a *negro* and *moreno* identity, just as it gave his mother the power to raise him in the belief that he was a white boy. In this sense, choosing his *negro* identity is a political statement, in a way that Clara's 'blackened' identity cannot be.

Whereas learning about racial inequality can evoke empathy among white and black people, for black people this process is often closely tied to a transformation of their racial consciousness. White people develop racial consciousness and continue to be white, even if they politically identify as black. However, black people who previously identified as white or *pardo*, develop racial consciousness and go through a process of becoming black – politically and often aesthetically. What de facto differentiates them is the position from which they experience racial discrimination, which can have implications when it comes to building anti-racist coalitions and alliances. Even though white people associating themselves closely with political blackness did not evoke resentment or astonishment in the research group or the teacher education class at UFRRJ, it was not met with comprehension everywhere.

The incommensurability of discrimination and *negro* leadership

Apart from claiming one's *negro* identity, becoming black can carry the notion of becoming an ally to black people, by understanding how racial discrimination works in society. However, as we will see it can also evoke the idea of having experienced any type of discrimination or prejudice. Talking about the pain that black people feel due to systemic racial discrimination encouraged other participants in Luiz's class at UFRRJ, who identify as white, to open up about their personal experiences with discrimination. Clara, who is originally from Pernambuco, an impoverished state in the north east of Brazil, which had vast plantations and received a large number of enslaved Africans until the first half of the 19th century, said she suffers from discrimination because of her origin. There have been repeated waves of migrants from the north east to the metropolises of São Paulo and Rio de Janeiro in search of employment and a better life. Often, the population in the north east is said to be lazy and fond of partying, and hence subject to similar stereotypes as black people in general. After various black students talked about their process of becoming black and the pain involved in this process, Clara responded: 'Being Nordestina, I feel like being part of an excluded group, because I am Nordestina. Black people are being excluded and discriminated against, but there is a similar prejudice against people of the Diáspora Nordestina.' Interestingly enough, no one seemed irritated by Clara's comparison between discrimination against black people and being discriminated against as a phenotypically white Nordestina. Úrsula shared a similar experience. Today she lives a few blocks away from Clara in the wealthy neighbourhood Grajaú, but she grew up in the Baixada Fluminense, an impoverished, crime-ridden suburb of Rio de Janeiro, and found it therefore difficult to navigate social relations in the city of Rio de Janeiro as her origin makes people look at her differently. During Luiz's class she said:

> We suffer as women [and] as we are from the Baixada Fluminense. We suffer prejudice but not as severely. I was never denied a job but I am not rich and fancy. I have three jobs so my family can travel. My black grandmother married a white man to *limpar a família* [lighten the family], after that no one was allowed to marry a *negro*. When I look at this painting [another girl had shown a picture of the painting *A Redenção de Cam*[12] to demonstrate whitening politics in Brazil] I think about my

---

12 This painting, *The Redemption of Ham* (Modesto Brocos, 1895), which shows a dark-skinned elderly woman, her lighter-skinned daughter with a white man and a white baby, can be understood as the synthesis of *branqueamento* politics in Brazil. The title is a reference to a passage in the Bible in which Noah curses his son Ham through a curse laid upon Ham's son Canaan. According to the book of Genesis, all humankind descends from Ham and his

grandmother who isn't even alive anymore.

While Úrsula shared her personal experience of being treated differently because of the area she was raised in, she acknowledges that there is a difference between the discrimination that a white and a black person experience in terms of securing work. That her grandmother wanted to have a lighter-skinned family infuriates and hurts her as it represents the unequal treatment black people continue to experience, and the deprecation of African and Afrobrazilian culture and history, while at the same time it representing a mother's wish to better her children's lives, which she only imagines to be possible through the whitening of their skin.

Another girl who identifies as white, Viviane, had had an accident years ago in which a high percentage of her skin had been burnt. She is a white woman with straight blond hair. In class, she elaborated in detail on her life after her accident and how people looked at her and treated her differently. For years she was not able to return to her previous routine, as she felt bad about her appearance and people's reactions to it. She became highly emotional and cried while sharing her story. Ana Paula joined in, and the two women cried together while the latter told Viviane how proud she was of her transformation and of how she had regained confidence. As a response to the women speaking up about the discrimination they experience, Rodrigo, a very dark-skinned elderly man, told the class how even after so many decades of teaching, pupils would still stare at him on the first day of school. They did not expect a dark-skinned man to be their teacher. He did not have tears in his eyes but he seemed highly emotional when speaking. All of their stories were met with great sympathy and encouraging words.

Jackie, who identifies as *negra*, addressed the class as a response to Clara talking about her work at her high school and being a white woman talking about the law. She said that there are *espaços negros* [black spaces] in which white people cannot enter or participate, like in a research and activist group at the State University of Rio de Janeiro. This is something she does not agree with. 'If you are white you cannot enter, but how can anyone choose who gets to talk about this? If it wasn't for Clara at [her school] Colégio Pedro II, then who would? If it wasn't Úrsula in the Baixada, then who would? Politically they identify as *negra*, they became *enegreceram* [black], they talk for or about it and spread this [discussion] in their networks.' Her comment started a brief discussion about white people being able to speak with *negros*, but never for them.

After the end of the term, I asked Luiz, the teacher of the course, about this particular moment and how he interpreted the students' reactions to the people who shared their personal experiences of discrimination and prejudice:

---

brothers. Haynes (2002) discusses the controversial question of the extent to which Europeans used Noah's Curse to justify the enslavement of Africans, as Ham and Canaan are often imagined to be of dark skin.

I remember, yeah I remember. That was a difficult class. I think this class was very productive, because sometimes you don't need to express intellectually or rationally a condition, and in that moment, I'm not sure whether you will agree, it wasn't even the individual but the collective subject that was manifesting itself. When I speak of collective subject I mean that diverse oppressions of Brazilian society were expressing themselves and people were showing how it operates. I think Viviane left an impression, Viviane who is very white, who shows the conditions, a *padrão identidário* [norm] that Brazilian society cultivates. It's a hetero, masculine, white, adult norm, and then the beauty norms that are built around this. For Viviane, for example, she does not conform to Brazilian society's understanding of standard beauty. So there is a big system of norms behind all of this, the condition of the woman, of the homosexual, of the *negro*, and Úrsula's perception goes hand-in-hand with the regional condition, like in Clara's case (being Nordestina) that she works in the Baixada Fluminense, even being Christian. Other oppressions that people are living were mobilised through this condition that we have to face, the discussion of it. [...] I'm saying this to say I know how this stirs up people's emotions, and this is why Viviane made this statement, this expression was only possible in this space, it would've never happened in 2013. [It was] an environment that increasingly gave her a little bit more security. It stirs up people's identity, and I think the way Viviane expressed it that day really helped to illustrate what the racial situation is for people.

No critical voices came forward in Luiz's class, or in any of the research group's meetings, rejecting white people's claim to understanding racial discrimination based on empathy and their personal experiences with other types of discrimination. However, divergent opinions about the role of non-black people in the black movement surfaced when Clara gave me a lift into the city centre after one of Luiz's classes. I asked her about the Núcleo de Estudos Afro-Brasileiros (NEAB), which is a research entity usually found at public universities, and which is dedicated to issues concerning Afrobrazilians. Clara's high school is unique since it is the only one that has its own NEAB. She told me that she had been crucial in the research entity's founding phase but made it clear that she felt the group's coordinator, a woman called Alessandra, could not be trusted. She said she had decided to leave the NEAB as it was not a democratically led group, but built around Alessandra's narcissism and thirst for power and attention. She believed Alessandra's speeches to be too radical and sarcastic, scaring people off. According to Clara, the NEAB did not hold elections, meaning Alessandra could stay in control as long as she wanted to.

When Alessandra and Artur, a history teacher and founding member of the NEAB, told me separately about how it came to life, and about the initial struggle to even get it started, Clara's name was not mentioned. When I next met Alessandra at an event on gender equality, I expected her to be cold and reserved. Instead I found a remarkably lively, approachable and helpful woman, who seemed to be highly popular among students and some teachers. During one of our last encounters, Alessandra told me about a teacher who had left the NEAB because of her, without mentioning Clara's name:

> It was a personal matter. She put that into her letter of resignation, because she thought that the NEAB had to be more democratic. She believed in a collective. I signalled to her that this collective she believed had to exist, is a white collective. And the NEAB is a *negro* group, by the way the only one in the school. It is difficult for these people to accept that the NEAB has to have a black leader. So, this did a lot to their sense of honour. It became a matter that was dragged into the personal, as in 'Alessandra wants to be seen, Alessandra has this event that is unnecessarily big, because she wants to be seen'. The difficulty of understanding that there has to be black leadership operating throughout the school was very significant. This resulted in confusion, fuss, many discussions and arguments.

Alessandra said that three teachers had wanted to be part of the NEAB but could not accept its black leadership, two of them white and one of them black. The black teacher did not like the NEAB identifying the privileges white people have and thought that the group was being racist against white people. However, Alessandra explained that she did not want white people to be the leaders of the NEAB, as they could take that role anywhere else. When she stood firm it was a problem for those three teachers. Repeatedly, Alessandra told me about white and black people who think of themselves as anti-racist, but cannot deal with *negros* being in a leadership position. Furthermore, that she was a woman and that she was a pedagogical coordinator and not a teacher (although she used to teach for many years in state schools in a suburb of Rio de Janeiro) troubled a lot of people. Thus, Alessandra, as a black female pedagogical coordinator, made some people uncomfortable, and they responded to the NEAB by ignoring it. When I told Alessandra about students in Luiz's class comparing their personal experiences to different types of prejudice she responded:

> Whiteness thinks it knows what racism is. They minimise it, compare it. This makes the struggle more difficult. It turns into a debate about who suffers more. It isn't very common for *negros* to speak out loudly enough to question the suffering of whiteness. They suffer together. White bodies cause a bigger commotion. Even for black people, unfortunately. Who would say something against this, do you think? It would have to be someone very secure, very engaged.

I heard Alessandra speak to students and teachers at the sociology teachers' event on gender equality. Indeed, her speech was extremely direct, full of sarcasm and unapologetic. However, the students seemed highly enthusiastic about it and were engaged in the discussion afterwards. The sociology teachers I worked with, four white teachers, referred to the NEAB and to Alessandra as a point of authority and a source of knowledge. Unlike those attending Luiz's class, Alessandra was greatly outspoken about the incommensurability of a white and a black person suffering different types of prejudice and discrimination.

She interpreted what Luiz called the 'collective subject manifesting different oppressions of Brazilian society' as white peoples' need to take centre stage in the narrative of racial discrimination, and as the absence of a black person who feels secure enough to tell other students off in this particular context. Whereas the teachers who identify as *negro* in the research group let white allies decide rather freely what position to take in the anti-racist struggle, the same cannot be said about the NEAB. In one context Clara is regarded as an anti-racist activist, while in the other she is perceived as perpetuating racial hierarchies.

Conclusion

Luiz frequently calls himself and his colleagues who work on the implementation of the law *agentes da lei* [law enforcement]. During the military dictatorship this term had a negative connotation as it was used for politicians, the police and anyone who worked for the state and could arrest regime opponents. Today, the situation is reversed and Luiz and his colleagues as *agentes da lei* go to schools and summon the leadership teams there to follow law 11.645/08. This chapter demonstrates that supporters of the law can leverage its legal authority to advance their agenda and get education officials and school leaders to make concessions. As there are several different levels of the public education system operating in Brazil (municipal, state and federal), as well as private schools, supporters of the law have to be creative and come up with innovative ways to make their concerns heard. Without doubt, the emergence of laws 10.639/03 and 11.645/08 has resulted in the creation of various spaces and preconditions, which facilitate collaboration, conflict and negotiation between teachers, education professionals, students, social activists and academics who want to challenge the status quo of institutionalised education in one way or another.

Exploring the experiences that turned a group of teachers into advocates of the law and anti-racist activists can provide a vantage point from which to think about the effectiveness of the law and ways of urging more education officials to advance its goals. It took most of the educators I talked to until they reached their adult life to understand their place within a differentiated racial framework that structurally puts white people at an advantage compared to black people. Issues arising around the formation of ethnic-racial identity demonstrate that identity formation is a crucial aspect contributing to the meaningfulness of law 11.645/08. It is striking that white and black people became conscious of their racial identification once they came into contact with black activists, often working on the implementation of law 11.645/08. In this sense, the implementation of law 11.645/08 has been transformative and has proven to be a way of fostering self-esteem in underprivileged groups (Taylor, 1994). These findings emphasise the need for educational spaces in which students and educational staff can share their experiences of ethnic-racial identity formation and racism.

To some of the teachers, the embodied knowledge of the pain and suffering resulting from any type of discrimination has been crucial in their understanding of racism. If the commitment to anti-racism is thus closely tied to such personal experiences and beliefs, creating space for similar experiences and beliefs to develop inside schools may be a useful approach to implementing the law and fostering anti-racist attitudes among students and staff. This also poses the question of who implements the law (whether they are black, white, female, male, and so on) and what difference this might make. It is not always clear what role white allies and anti-racism teachers should take or what anti-racist activism should look like in order to most effectively support its intended beneficiaries. On the one hand, white history teacher Clara was criticised for trying to adopt too central a role in the black struggle. On the other, her work was praised and deemed necessary, because in many white spaces, such as Colégio Pedro II, not many black representatives could do this work. There are limits to how far a white ally can truly empathise with victims of racism, in ways which might shape the way educational policy can be implemented, something that needs further investigation.

Bibliography

Akkari, A. (2012) 'Intercultural education in Brazil: between conservatism and radical transformations', *Prospects*, 42: 161–75.

Burdick, J. (1998) *Blessed Anastácia: Women, Race, and Popular Christianity in Brazil* (New York: Routledge).

Cicalo, A. (2012) *Urban Encounters: Affirmative Action and Black Identities in Brazil* (New York: Palgrave Macmillan).

Da Costa, Emboaba, A. (2014) *Reimagining Black Difference and Politics in Brazil: From Racial Democracy to Multiculturalism* (New York: Palgrave Macmillan).

Damatta, R. (1987) *Relativizando. Uma introdução à antropologia brasileira* (Rio de Janeiro: Rocco).

Dávila, J. (2003) *Diploma of Whiteness: Race and Social Policy in Brazil, 1917–1945* (Durham, NC: Duke University Press).

Flyvbjerg, B. (1998) 'Rationality and power', in S. Campbell and S.S. Fainstein (eds.), *Readings in Planning Theory* (Oxford: Blackwell).

Gillborn, D. (1994) 'The micro-politics of macro reform', *British Journal of Sociology of Education*, 15 (2): 147–64.

Gomes, N.L. (2001) 'Educação Cidadã, etnia e raça: o trato pedagógico da diversidade', in Cavalleiro, E. (ed.), *Racismo e antirracismo na educação: repensando nossa escola* (São Paulo: Selo Negro Edições).

— (2006) *Sem perder a raiz: corpo e cabelo como símbolos da identidade negra* (Belo Horizonte, MG: Autêntica).

Gomes, N.L. and R.E. d. Jesus (2013) 'As práticas pedagógicas de trabalho com relações étnico-raciais na escola na perspectiva de Lei 10.639/2003: desafios para a política educacional e indagações para a pesquisa', *Educar em Revista*, 47: 19–33.

Haynes, S.R. (2002) *Noah's Curse: The Biblical Justification of American Slavery* (New York: Oxford University Press).

Hofbauer, A. (1995) *Afro-Brasilien* (Vienna: Promedia).

Ferreira, A. de J. (2008) *PEAB – Projeto De Estudos Afro-Bracsileiros: Contexto, Resultados de Pesquisas e Relatos de Experiências* (Paraná: Cascavel).

Júnior, A.X.B. and J.G. da Silva (2013) 'Brief overview on compliance of the Law 10.639 in Maceió/AL', *Identitdade!*, 18 (1): 112–21.

Oliveira, A.G. de (2005) 'O silenciamento do livro didático sobre a questão étnico-cultural na primeira etapa do ensino fundamental', *Jornal Bolando Aula*, 66: 5–7.

Oliveira, L.F. de (2012) *História da África e dos africanos na escola. Desafios políticos, epistemológicos e identitários para a formação dos professores de história* (Rio de Janeiro: Imperial Novo Milênio).

Palácio do Planalto. Presidência da República (2008) LEI Nº 11.645, DE 10 MARÇO DE 2008, available at: http://www.planalto.gov.br/ccivil_03/_ato2007-2010/2008/lei/l11645.htm (accessed 31 March 2019).

Paschel, T.S. (2016) *Becoming Black Political Subjects: Movements and Ethno-Racial Rights in Colombia and Brazil* (Princeton, NJ: Princeton University Press).

Pereira, A.A. (2011) 'A Lei 10.639/03 e o movimento negro: aspectos da luta pela reavaliação do papel do negro na história do Brasil', *Cadernos de História*, 12 (17): 25–45.

Pereira, A.M. (2003) 'Guerrilha na educação: a ação pedagógica do Movimento Negro na escola pública', *Educação em Debate*, 2: 26–35.

Pinho, P. de S. (2009) 'White but not quite: tones and overtones of whiteness in Brazil', *Small Axe*, 29: 40–56.

Prefeitura de São Paulo (2004) *Diretrizes curriculares nacionais para a educação das relações etnico-raciais e para o ensino de história e cultura afrobrasileira e africana* (Brasília).

Selka, S. (2007) *Religion and the Politics of Ethnic Identity in Bahia, Brazil* (Gainesville, FL: University Press of Florida).

Sheriff, R.E. (2001) *Dreaming Equality: Color, Race, and Racism in Urban Brazil* (New Brunswick, NJ: Rutgers University Press).

Soeterik, I.M. (2013) 'Policy discourses and multi-scalar interactions in curriculum development: institutionalizing and translating ethnicity/race issues in Brazilian education' (Amsterdam: Amsterdam Institute for Social Science Research PhD thesis) available at: http://dare.uva.nl/record/1/400258 (accessed 30 March 2019).

Taylor, C. (1994) *Multiculturalism and "The Politics of Recognition"* (Princeton, NJ: Princeton University Press).

Telles, E.E. (2004) *Race in Another America: The Significance of Skin Color in Brazil* (Princeton, NJ: Princeton University Press).

Wade, P. (2010) 'The presence and absence of race', *Patterns of Prejudice*, 44 (1): 43–60.

Warren, J.W. and C.A. Sue (2011) 'Comparative racisms: what anti-racists can learn from Latin America', *Ethnicities*, 11 (1): 32–58.

7. The last in a country of forgotten people: ancestry, music and identity among Bolivia's Afro population

Lena Schubmann

We are the last in a country of forgotten people. We have an indigenous government, but we are not considered indigenous, and we are not part of the white minority, of course. So we are just forgotten. But we are not slaves any more: we are free people, free farmers. We're poor but free, and we would like the country to know – the world to know – that we exist.[1]

Julio Bonifaz Pinedo

In 2007, Julio Bonifaz Pinedo was crowned by the Bolivian government in La Paz as king and official representative of the Afrobolivians, an event followed by a large festival of Afrobolivian Saya music. Previously, members of the Afrobolivian community had traced back Pinedo's ancestry to the royal family of a West African tribe, enslaved and brought to Bolivia in the 1820s (Maconde, 2006). The Bonifaz monarchy as well as the unique sound of Saya music have given increased visibility to the Afrobolivian community at a national level. The formation of a national Afrobolivian council, the Consejo Nacional del Pueblo Afroboliviano (CONAFRO) in 2011, the establishment of the cultural institute Casa Real Afroboliviana (CRA) in 2012 and the proclamation of 23 September as national day of Afrobolivian culture in 2011 are evidence of this recent development. The increased presence and legal recognition of Afrobolivians is often conceptualised as a direct outcome of more inclusive policies promoted by Evo Morales, Bolivia's first self-proclaimed indigenous president, and his party Movimiento al Socialismo (MAS) (Comunidad Andina, 2011; Käss, 2010; UNESCO, 2013; Toledo, 2013). Since Morales' election in 2006, his government has made it a priority to fight institutional racism and include historically excluded ethnic groups in policy-making.

This chapter contributes to literature on Afrobolivian cultural production by focusing on recent political developments in Bolivia since the election of Evo Morales. Rather than conceptualising the greater visibility of Afrobolivian culture as the direct outcome of anti-racist state policies, however, this chapter

---

1   Cited in Schipani (2009).

L. Schubmann, 'The last in a country of forgotten people: ancestry, music and identity among Bolivia's Afro population', in P. Wade, J. Scorer and I. Aguiló (eds.), *Cultures of Anti-Racism in Latin America and the Caribbean* (London: Institute of Latin American Studies, 2019), pp. 147–66. License: CC-BY-NC-ND 4.0.

critically analyses the dynamic and reciprocal interaction between the Bolivian state and the Afrobolivian community. First, the chapter gives an overview of the historic marginalisation of Afrobolivians from Bolivian statehood. It then reveals that the government discourse about ethnicity and ethnic rights is centred on ancestral links to physical and social space, creating a contrast between Bolivia's indigenous and white populations. This discourse leaves no clear space for Afrobolivians and provokes the perception that they are displaced.

By analysing the sociopolitical significance of Afrobolivian Saya music as well as the Bonifaz monarchy, this chapter shows that Afrobolivians mobilise their cultural uniqueness to claim the same rights to land titles and heritage protection as indigenous peoples and therefore justify their legitimate access to ethnic rights. Building on David Goldberg's (2002) conceptualisation of the racial state, this chapter shows how Afrobolivian efforts to comply with the state's discourse on ethnicity reproduces structures of racialisation. It reveals that the Afrobolivian claim for 'ethnic authenticity' discourages mixture, reinforcing a discourse of ethnic conflict by encouraging groups to compete for scarce rights distributed by the state. It concludes that rather than a reaction to a less oppressive and more inclusive government, increased cultural production among Afrobolivians is a response to the narrow definition of ethnicity and ethnic rights promoted by the MAS government.

Introducing Afrobolivians

The election of Evo Morales in 2005 was followed by a set of constitutional changes facilitating the inclusion of indigenous and aboriginal groups in the Bolivian state. With the aim of taking a bottom-up approach to the drafting of the new constitution, the new government created a constituent assembly, including representatives from Bolivia's various social movements at the time and from various geographical departments. After 14 months of drafting, the new constitution was put to a national referendum and came into force in January 2009. In the preamble to the constitution, Morales identifies the main problem of contemporary Bolivian society as the concentration of wealth in the hands of the 'new' inhabitants, referring to those who settled in Bolivia after the Spanish conquest, and the exclusion of Bolivia's 'originary' peoples from economic and political power (Morales, 2009, pp. 1–2). According to Morales (p. 2), the new constitution aims to 'end racism, discrimination and exclusion' by building a 'plurinational, democratic and intercultural state', which will secure the equal status of all Bolivians (pp. 2–3).

One of the reforms aiming to guarantee legal protection of indigenous peoples is the recognition of communal land ownership and the self-governance of indigenous groups (Constitution: Art. 2). The recognition of 'ancestral' lands for Bolivia's indigenous groups means that a certain territory is guaranteed to a specific ethnic group without the need for any financial acquisition. The land reforms of the MAS government clearly define who qualifies for the distribution of land titles and who does not. Accordingly, the constitution defines 36 ethnic groups whose ancestral lands and traditions are recognised and protected by the Plurinational State (Constitution: Art. 30). Afrobolivians are one of these recognised ethnic groups. However, how exactly they fit into the government's notion of the poor indigenous majority oppressed by a small white or mestizo elite is not clear in the constitution. It is apparent that Afrobolivians belong to neither of the groups whose dichotomous opposition is fundamental to the political reforms promoted by the Morales government. They certainly do not belong to Bolivia's white or mestizo elites who have historically monopolised Bolivia's economic and political power. At the same time, however, they are not an indigenous group with ancestral rights based on pre-Columbian presence.

Despite their constitutional recognition, Afrobolivians do not fit into the ethnic discourse the constitution is based on, and therefore do not qualify for the same rights as indigenous peoples. While Afrobolivians are constitutionally guaranteed the same legal status as indigenous groups (Constitution: Art. 32), they were not initially included in the constituent assembly which allegedly included representatives of all of Bolivia's different ethnic groups (Medina, 2013). During pre-assembly dialogues, Afrobolivians were accused of being too few to be a priority in the constituent assembly. In response, more than 500 Afrobolivians played Saya music in front of the building where negotiations took place, until they were included in political dialogues on an equal footing with other groups (Medina, 2013). As in King Julio Pinedo's words, cited in the epigraph, Afrobolivians are indeed virtually forgotten in political dialogues in Bolivia. Through protests and Saya music, however, Afrobolivians make themselves visible on the national level.

The history of Afrobolivians goes back to the 16th century, when West African inhabitants were enslaved and brought to the Spanish empire in order to work in the tin and silver mines in the Bolivian department of Potosí (Maconde, 2006). The slave trade in what then was part of the Viceroyalty of Peru is not well documented or studied and the total number of Africans brought to Potosí is uncertain. As letters reveal, in 1608 the governor of Potosí asked the Spanish Crown to send 1,500 to 2,000 slaves annually to work in the mines. Most slaves were brought from what is now Senegal (2006). However, slaves brought to Bolivia did not predominantly come from one specific region or ethnic group, but from a large variety of different cultural, linguistic and religious groups. Afrobolivian historian Juan Angola Maconde identifies traces of Kikongo, Mani Kongo, Luba, Ndongo, Lingala and other languages in documented speech in the 17th century. Because of this linguistic diversity among slaves, Spanish soon became the unifying language among them and original African languages almost entirely disappeared. Aside from language, Maconde states that there were no identifiable cultural or religious characteristics shared by all or most Africans brought to Bolivia as slaves. Their forced transport across continents and the denial of their humanity linked to their status as slaves by colonialists was consequently the main unifying element in early Afrobolivian history.

Slavery was officially abolished in 1831 by Bolivian president Manuel Isidoro Belzú (Klein, 2011). After their emancipation, a large number of Afrobolivians migrated from the highlands to a region called the Yungas, located between the Andean highlands and the Amazon region at an altitude between 1,000m and 1,500m. According to Bolivian historians Arturo Cuenca and Max Ortiz, this migration was the result of the cold and hostile environment in the Potosí region which lies at an altitude of 4,000m to 5,000m (Ortíz, 1978; Cuenca, 1977). Before the agrarian reforms following Bolivia's national revolution of 1952, most Afrobolivian and indigenous people served mestizo landowners under *pongueaje*, the Bolivian serfdom system. With the abolition of *pongueaje* in 1952, many Afrobolivians gained access to land titles and became coffee and coca-leaf farmers in the Yungas (Morales, 2010, p. 12).

Nowadays, most Afrobolivians' livelihoods depend on agricultural production, making the state's distribution of land titles economically relevant and attractive. The Yungas are part of the department of La Paz, administratively divided into Nor and Sud Yungas. With an average annual income of US$1,500 per household, the Yungas is one of Bolivia's poorest regions overall (Jiménez Zamora, 2007, p. 67). According to a recent survey (INE, 2012), 22,777 Bolivian citizens self-identify as Afrobolivian. Approximately 60 per cent of these self-identified Afrobolivians reside in the Yungas region, while most of the other 40 per cent live in Cochabamba, Santa Cruz and La Paz, Bolivia's three largest cities (2012). The Yungas have a total population of approximately 100,000 inhabitants. Of the region's inhabitants, 68 per cent of Yunguean inhabitants live by agriculture, and 81 per cent of this sector's total revenue comes from growing coca leaves (UMSA, 2012, p. 42). Previous demands to recognise land in the Yungas as Afrobolivian territory were rejected by the government in 1994 and 2006 (Choque, 2014). This was a central issue of CONAFRO's foundational meetings in 2011. CONAFRO's introduction to its strategic plan (2011, p. 20) states that the recognition of ancestral rights is its key target. It further specifies that these ancestral rights refer to the recognition of ancestral Afrobolivian territory in the Yungas. While the report praises the recognition of Afrobolivian existence by the MAS government, it criticises the lack of land distribution to Afrobolivians in the Yungas. Achieving the legal recognition of 'ancestral Afrobolivian' territory is highlighted as CONAFRO's main agenda up to 2020 (p. 32).

The politics of ethnicity and authenticity in the plurinational state of Bolivia

In the Bolivian Yungas, problems and risks associated with the distribution of land titles based on ethnic criteria are particularly obvious. According to Alison Spedding (1994), anthropologist and ethnographer of the Yungas, social and territorial boundaries between different ethnic groups residing in the Yungas are fluid and under constant renegotiation. She claims that the Yungas is one of Bolivia's most diverse regions, influenced by people of Aymara, Afrobolivian and mestizo heritage. There are no clearly defined regions where either Afrobolivian, Aymara or mestizo populations predominate. Chicaloma and Coroico, the towns with the highest numbers of Afrobolivian inhabitants, both have an even higher amount of self-identified Aymaras. The same is true for the rural Yungas. Members of different ethnic groups live side by side and without clear boundaries. Furthermore, the extent to which one can clearly distinguish between members of different 'ethnic groups' in the Yungas is not always clear. Many self-identified Afrobolivians speak Aymara, wear traditional Aymara dress and practise Aymara rituals, such as the sacrifice of coca leaves. Rather than a fixed category, Afrobolivian identity is fluid and socially constructed within the local context of the Yungas.

Intentionally anti-racist cultural production, particularly the efforts to make Saya music and the Bonifaz monarchy visible on a national level, shows how Afrobolivians position themselves in relation to the state's discourse about ethnicity and ethnic rights. Robert Templeman (1998, p. 437) claims that the Bolivian state recognises Afrobolivians as part of the Bolivian nation thanks to their expression of cultural heritage in the form of Saya music. Chuck Sturtevant (2017) conceptualises Afrobolivian cultural production within a framework of local community-making in the Yunguean town of Chicaloma. By representing this cultural production as African heritage, Afrobolivians construct Chicaloma as a black social space that is 'ethnoracially marked as ancestrally African' (ibid., p. 7). According to Sturtevant (p. 20), the performance of Afrobolivian ethnicity through Saya music 'fits awkwardly' with national expectations of ethnic identity as it emphasises African ancestry and at the same time evokes stereotypes of African drumming and rhythmic dancing. Linguist John Lipski (2008) documents and analyses Afrobolivian dialect, identifying several semantic and phonetic characteristics which most likely derive from Kikongo, a Bantu language spoken in south-western Africa. Together with Maconde, Lipski is creating an archive of digital recordings to conserve the endangered dialect. He furthermore supports the promotion of poetry written in the traditional dialect by Maconde, hoping that 'appreciation for linguistic expression becomes part of the Afrodescendents' struggle for recognition' (ibid., p. 195). While these authors do not draw a direct link between state policy and Afrobolivian cultural production, they emphasise the potential of the latter for increasing recognition and visibility in Bolivia. Afrobolivian visibility through cultural production is seen as a contributing factor and a first step towards combating marginalisation and racism against Afrobolivians.

Theoretical contributions analysing the link between ethnic groups, and state policies directed at ethnic minorities, conceptualise their relationship more critically. While many authors analyse obviously racist states, such as apartheid South Africa, Goldberg analyses racist and racial characteristics of modern 'multicultural' or 'colour-blind' states. According to Goldberg (2002, p. 10), any attempt by the state to include ethnic minorities inherently comes with the possibility of their exclusion. The tolerance and promotion of heterogeneity at state level necessarily requires homogeneity at local level. Any state calling itself multicultural assumes a variety of distinct ethnic groups living within state borders. Identifying distinct ethnic groups is itself a racialising act and often a top-down imposition. The distribution of ethnic rights, such as access to certain resources or cultural heritage recognition, requires the assignment of individual citizens to different ethnic groups. As available categories are decided by the state, this is true even when censuses are based on self-identification. However, minority ethnic groups can potentially design these categories according to their own purposes. The racial structures underlying ethnically heterogeneous states are the same as those underlying nation states built on assumed ethnic homogeneity. The discourse and practice of local ethnic homogeneity constitutes racial structures of the state as well as the concept of race itself (ibid., p. 5).

Rather than an exclusively structural phenomenon operating independently from individual actors, Goldberg (p. 249) conceptualises the state as reproducer and reinforcer of certain institutional and social values. He compares the role of the state to the role of the conductor of an orchestra (p. 249). Despite not producing any music themselves, conductors define the rules and guidelines for the players. To become legitimate members in the orchestra musicians play according to the conductor's instructions. Equally, to become visible citizens with access to social welfare programmes, individuals act according to the state's definition of ethnicity and ethnic rights. Goldberg here refers to race and racialisation as the connection between conductor and musicians. Successful communication between citizens and the state is possible if the state deals with individuals in racialised ethnic categories to which citizens assign themselves.

In the Bolivian case, Goldberg's reference to the conductor and the orchestra is more than just an analogy. As Michelle Bigenho (2002, p. 17) argues, music performances are an essential part of indigenous nation-building in Bolivia and of their struggle 'to be recognised officially by the state as an indigenous collectivity'. The following analysis conceptualises the Bolivian state as an institutional body with the power to distribute land rights to Afrobolivians, an ethnic minority claiming access to these rights. It dialogues with Goldberg's critical approach to interactions between ethnic groups and state institutions by conceptualising ethnicisation as a dynamic interaction between racialising state policies and Afrobolivian claim-making. Rather than being passive victims of the state's policies, Afrobolivians publicly address the Bolivian state, claiming rights and the recognition of their cultural heritage. The following analysis shows not only how this racialised space is constructed through cultural production, but also how this process creates social and physical boundaries and sources for ethnic conflict and competition.

Furthermore, this chapter contributes to literature on Afrobolivian cultural production by focusing on recent political developments in Bolivia since the election of Evo Morales. It analyses the increased performance of Saya music as well as the crowning of Julio Pinedo I in 2007 in relation to the supposedly anti-racist politics of ethnicity by the plurinational Bolivian state. This will reveal the paradox fundamental to Afrobolivian identity: to be recognised as a legitimate ethnic group by the plurinational state, and hence claim belonging to Bolivia, Afrobolivians emphasise how their African roots inspired their unique cultural heritage. At the same time, however, this perpetuates the perception that Afrobolivians are out of place in Bolivia. Consequently, activists claiming Afrobolivian ancestral land rights in the Yungas find themselves in a constant contradiction between ethnic authenticity and national belonging, which this chapter explores in more detail.

The mobilisation of Saya music for the recognition of Afrobolivian territoriality

The following section analyses a selection of the Saya songs that have been most frequently performed publicly and in the presence of state authorities since the inauguration of Bolivia's new constitution in 2009. Rather than analysing Saya music itself, this chapter focuses on the content represented by the lyrics of Saya, specifically how traditional Saya music emphasises Afrobolivian territoriality in the Yungas. This claim for territoriality is then analysed in the context of Afrobolivian land claims, revealing how Afrobolivian organisations politicise territorial belonging expressed in Saya music to claim land ownership from the state. Considering the state's discourse on ethnicity and ethnic rights elaborated above, this reveals the fundamental contradiction of Afrobolivian identity politics: to be recognised as an ethnic group by the plurinational state, Afrobolivians culturally perform and constitute a racialised and biologised notion of the African diaspora localised in the Yungas.

According to Afrobolivian activist Mónica Rey, Saya derives from the word 'Nsaya', meaning 'common work or labour' in Kikongo (Choque Gutiérrez, 2017). The songs consist of several stanzas of four to six verses of text which each contain eight syllables. One stanza is defined as the chorus which is repeated after each stanza of the verses. Traditionally, the chorus is sung by women while the other verses are sung by men. There is one male and one female leader during performances, who wear bells around their ankles. Men generally play two or three differently voiced drums as well as differently sized *guaches* [shakers], guided by the male leader. The female leader guides the dancing (Arias, 2009). Probably the most frequently performed Saya song, 'Se presenta el afroboliviano' by the group Saya Unión Afro (SAU), opens with the verse:

> *Todos somos coroiceños*
> *Traemos lindas tonadas*
> *Reciban fuertes abrazos*
> *Del Grupo Afroboliviano*[2]

Coroico is the capital city of the Northern Yungas province and the largest city in the entire Yungas region. The verse emphasises the importance of Coroico as the physical and social centre of Afrobolivianness. Coroico is portrayed as Afrobolivian territory, underlining associations of the city with Afrobolivian people and their cultural heritage. Afrobolivianness is spatialised, expressing Afrobolivians' territorial belonging to the Yungas. Through the public performance of these songs, Afrobolivianness is literally 'mapped onto Bolivian territory' (Busdiecker, 2009b, p. 127).

Another traditional Saya song, composed by Vicente Gemio, repeats the verse (see Templeman, 2001, p. 449):

> *Todo es de fruta*
> *Café y coca*
> *El lugar donde vivimos*
> *Se llama Coroico*[3]

The reference to coffee and coca, Afrobolivians' main source of income, and crops which in Bolivia can only be grown in the Yungas, emphasises the socioeconomic importance of Yunguean territory. The geographical region of the Yungas is portrayed as essential to Afrobolivian economic, social and cultural life. Afrobolivian intellectual and activist Maconde (2006) states that Afrobolivian culture 'flourishes in the Yungas' because its geographical landscape serves as an inspiration for Saya music. Claims for support for communal projects, particularly in the agricultural sector, stress the responsibility of the state to support the development of the Yungas for environmental as well as cultural reasons, indicating the importance of the Yungas for Afrobolivian heritage (CONAFRO, 2011, p. 2). Consequently, the recognition of Afrobolivian land is portrayed as a precondition for the protection of Afrobolivian cultural heritage.

---

2   We are all Coroiceños / We bring beautiful tunes / Receive strong hugs / From the Afrobolivian Group.
3   Everything is fruit / Coffee and coca / The place where we live / Is called Coroico.

The Saya song 'Si yo fuera presidente', by Afrobolivian composer Manuel Barra, opens with the verses:

Yo vengo de Coroico
El pueblo más querido
Con toda su gente linda
Caramba, ¡viva Bolivia!

Si yo fuera presidente
Formaría un puente
Formaría un puente, ¡caray!
De Coroico hasta La Paz[4]

In addition to the emphasis on Coroico and the Yungas, this song shows how Afrobolivians claim belonging to Bolivia. The patriotic expression 'viva Bolivia', as well as the metaphorical notion of forming a bridge between the Yungas and La Paz, Bolivia's capital city, highlight that Afrobolivians present themselves as part of the Bolivian nation. Jorge Medina Barra, the first Afrobolivian member of parliament, calls public Saya performances an instrument to show that Afrobolivians have 'their own culture' (Medina, 2014). The lyrics clearly emphasise that this uniquely Afrobolivian cultural identity, expressed through Saya, does not contradict a Bolivian national identity. Despite criticising Afrobolivian marginalisation within dominant Bolivian national identity templates, Saya lyrics express Afrobolivian willingness to enrich rather than alter Bolivian nationality. By combining the cultural and socioeconomic importance of the Yungas, Saya performances clearly demonstrate Afrobolivian territoriality and social attachment to the region. Simultaneously highlighting their belonging to Bolivia reveals how Afrobolivians portray their cultural heritage as eligible to be protected by the Bolivian state in the form of guaranteed land titles.

Afrobolivians' claim for state recognition as an ethnic group has been partly successful. Following Afrobolivian demands, the MAS government integrated the Law against Racism and All Forms of Discrimination into the constitution (Constitution: Art. 45). In the most recent ethnic survey (INE, 2012), 'Afrobolivian' was for the first time listed as a separate ethnicity. Moreover, in 2014 the government included Afrobolivian history and culture in the Yunguean school curriculum (CONAFRO, 2014a). However, CONAFRO's most important aim, the recognition of land in the Yungas as ancestral Afrobolivian territory, has not yet received attention from the MAS government.

Simultaneously, the Afrobolivians' claim on the state for the recognition of them as an ethnic group caused an increase in ethnic differentiation and conflict within the Yungas. The high level of cultural diversity and mixture

4   I come from Coroico / The most beloved town / With all its beautiful people / Caramba, long live Bolivia! // If I were president / I would build a bridge / I would build a bridge, Good Heavens! / From Coroico to La Paz.

in the Yungas makes it hard to distinguish between ancestral Aymara and Afrobolivian territory. The distribution of land titles by the state, however, requires a clear territorial demarcation between Aymara and Afrobolivian land. As the legal recognition of land titles is based on the sociocultural meaning attached to territory by one ethnic group, the clear separation between Aymara and Afrobolivian land and culture is a precondition for any territorial demarcation. Due to the limited amount of land available for distribution to ethnic groups, Aymaras and Afrobolivians find themselves in a competition over whose ethnic identity is more 'original' and 'authentic', and hence requires state protection in the form of guaranteed land.

Afrobolivians define clear boundaries between Afrobolivian and Aymara heritage in Saya music. When Los Kjarkas, a popular Bolivian folklore band, mixed traditional Saya songs with *caporal* rhythms and pan flute sounds associated with Aymara music, the Afrobolivian composer Santos Reynal wrote the following Saya verse:

> *Los Kjarkas están confundiendo*
> *La saya y el caporal*
> *Lo qué ahora están escuchando*
> *Es saya original*[5]

This reveals that Saya music is not seen as original when it is appropriated by non-Afrobolivians and mixed with sounds and rhythms associated with Aymara music (Céspedes, 1993, p. 55). Afrobolivian dancers emphasise that non-Afrobolivians may learn how to dance and perform Saya, but they 'never feel the same connection to the music as Afrobolivians', making performances 'less authentic' (Busdiecker, 2009b, p. 129; Rossbach, 2007, p. 187). This self-ascription of Saya to Afrobolivian identity portrays music as inherent and essential to Afrobolivianness. As Afrobolivianness itself is defined in racial terms, the ability to produce and perform Saya is treated as directly linked to an African bloodline.

The differentiation of Aymara culture by Afrobolivians is not only expressed in music, but also in legal terms. In 2014, Afrobolivian activists demanded a nationwide prohibition of *tundiqui*, a carnival dance usually performed by Quechua or Aymara dancers who dress as African slaves and imitate African dances (Buechler, 1980, p. 42). Current director of CONAFRO, Juan Carlos Ballivián, justifies the demand for a prohibition of *tundiqui* with the argument that this imitation represents 'distortions of Saya and Afrobolivian culture' (Cuevas, 2014). The imitation and appropriation of Afrobolivian history and music by non-Afrobolivians blurs the boundary between indigenous and Afro ethnicity, impeding the recognition of Afrobolivians as a distinct ethnic group associated with a unique ancestral and cultural heritage. Claiming ethnic

5   The Kjarkas are confusing / The Saya and the *caporal* / What you are listening to now / Is original Saya.

authenticity by differentiating themselves from indigenous culture is therefore a precondition for the recognition of Afrobolivian territory by the state.

Furthermore, the purposefully constructed link between 'authentic Afrobolivianness' and the Yungas leads to increased invisibility and marginalisation of Afrobolivians living in other parts of the country. The state's emphasis on ancestry and territoriality to qualify as an ethnic group – as well as Afrobolivian activism demonstrating these characteristics systematically – excludes the 40 per cent of self-identified Afrobolivians who live in urban areas outside the Yungas. The importance given to ancestral land recognition by the Bolivian state monopolises the political negotiation between Afrobolivians and state authorities. Other issues which primarily concern Afrobolivians outside the Yungas, such as discrimination in urban labour markets, are neglected. The focus on land ownership manifests and perpetuates Afrobolivians' role in Bolivian society as coffee and coca farmers. Consequently, demands made by Afrobolivians that do not relate to land ownership in the framework of ethnic rights are marginalised.

The Bonifaz monarchy and its relevance for Afrobolivian identity

In addition to Saya, Afrobolivian heritage has gained national and international visibility through the crowning of an Afrobolivian king and the formal establishment of an Afrobolivian monarchy. This section shows how the monarchy reinforces the notion of Afrobolivian uniqueness and simultaneously creates a bridge between the Yungas and La Paz by claiming formal recognition of the monarchy in the plurinational constitution. At the same time, however, the monarchy is built on African origins fundamentally different from indigenous or mestizo Bolivia, provoking perceptions of geographical and social displacement.

The common African ancestry of Afrobolivians was first celebrated in 1932 when Bonifacio Pinedo was crowned as Afrobolivian king by the Afrobolivian population of the Yungas. Bonifacio Pinedo, also known as Bonifacio the First, was a direct descendant of the Kikongo Prince Uchicho, who was enslaved and brought to Bolivia just before slavery was abolished in the early 19th century (CONAFRO, 2014b). Prince Uchicho was identified as a member of the royal family by other Afrobolivians while he was washing himself in a river. They recognised distinctive marks on Bonifacio's body, received in his early childhood before enslavement, which were associated with West African royal families (Revilla, 2014). The current Afrobolivian king Julio Bonifaz Pinedo is Bonifacio the First's grandson.

Following Afrobolivian demands, the mayor of the department of La Paz Alejandro Zapata invited Julio Pinedo and the entire Afrobolivian population to participate in an official coronation organised by the MAS government in

2007 (Schipani, 2007). In addition to the nationwide awareness of Afrobolivian ancestry raised by this coronation, Julio Pinedo's status as Afrobolivian king was legally recognised by the department of La Paz, which institutionalised and legitimised his position (CRA, 2011). A resolution of November 2007 states that Julio Pinedo is to be 'treated with respect and recognition of his status as Afrobolivian king by the Bolivian authorities' (Consejo Departamental, 2007). In 2012, the CRA was founded to provide official information about the Afrobolivian monarchy and manage issues regarding inheritance of the crown. According to the CRA (2017), the public promotion of the Bonifaz monarchy serves to 'show support for cultural initiatives in favour of the identity and tradition of Afrobolivians'.

The idea of a common African ancestry, embodied by the Bonifaz monarchy, supports CONAFRO's claims for ancestral land rights in the Yungas. CONAFRO localises King Bonifaz Pinedo's symbolic authority in the Yungas and therefore emphasises the significance of the region for Afrobolivian cultural and political identity. The Bonifaz monarchy links Afrobolivianness with time and space. Generations of ancestors and their connections to the Yungas, represented by King Bonifaz Pinedo, are portrayed as the foundation of Afrobolivian identity. The claim for territoriality and ancestry reinforce a notion of Afrobolivian belonging to Bolivia. Consequently, Afrobolivianness is inscribed into Bolivian territory as well as history. This reinforces Afrobolivian ancestral attachment to the Yungas. Rather than passively accepting that this definition of ethnicity does not include Afrobolivians, due to their ancestral and territorial roots in Africa and not Bolivia, they take agency and claim belonging to the Bolivian nation. Their territorial attachment to the Yungas supports their recognition as an ethnic group by the state and hence their eligibility for land ownership rights. This makes Afrobolivian land claims in the Yungas feasible for the Bolivian state. It is hereby not implied that the Afrobolivian monarchy is merely a strategic instrument to gain land rights. Instead, the monarchy reinforces the notion of a shared Afrobolivian historical past and rootedness within Bolivian territory. This aligns with the government's distribution of land rights based on ethnic criteria designed as a legal basis for territorial claims by indigenous groups.

Their claim for ethnic uniqueness by giving importance to African origins, however, counters the perception of their rootedness in Bolivia, perpetuating the notion of Afrobolivians as displaced in Bolivia. Reflecting Sara Busdiecker's (2009a) critical approach to the negotiation of Afrobolivian identity in relation to space and place, the localisation of Afrobolivianness into a certain region creates clear assumptions about where Afrodescendants can be found outside Africa. Consequently, they can be 'out of place' in other regions (p. 113). In order to differentiate themselves from Bolivia's indigenous majority, Afrobolivians claim a unique African heritage which constructs the perception that they are socially, historically, physically and culturally out of place in Bolivia (p. 106).

At the same time, however, the emphasis on 'ancestral Afro-Yunguean land' and 'ancestral traditions and territory' (CONAFRO, 2011, pp. 2, 5) ignores the African origins of Afrobolivian identity. Instead, it starts the clock when black people first settled in the Yungas in the late 18th century. This reveals the conflicting dynamics at the core of Afrobolivian identity performance. The emphasis on African origins of the Bonifaz monarchy, as well as Saya music, seems to contradict their claim to belonging and rootedness in the Yungas. At the same time, African origins allow Afrobolivians to distinguish themselves from mestizo or indigenous ethnicities in the Yungas. This separation is necessary to make Afrobolivians identifiable on the state level and eligible for ethnic land claims. Paradoxically, the way for Afrobolivians to be recognised as an ethnic group and be part of Bolivia's plurinational state is to emphasise their geographical and social displacement, reinforcing a racialised and biologised notion of the African diaspora.

Through legal recognition and symbolic representation of the Bonifaz monarchy, Afrobolivian ancestry is institutionalised into the official structures of the Bolivian state. Consequently, Afrobolivians are recognised as a distinct ethnic group by both the Bolivian state and the majority of the Bolivian public. The emphasis on a common ancestry reveals the racial foundation of Afrobolivian identity. According to the CRA (2011), a common African bloodline qualifies certain Bolivian citizens to be represented by the Afro monarchy. The symbolic representation by a monarchy is portrayed as essential to Bolivians sharing this African bloodline. Due to the lack of official documents about the former slave trade, African ancestry in most cases can only be identified by the physical appearance of blackness. The narrative of a common Afrobolivian culture resulting from a common history is fundamentally based on common physical appearance. Afrobolivians' claim-making to the state therefore constitutes structures of racialisation among Bolivia's society. Consequently, membership in the Afrobolivian community and representation by King Julio Bonifaz Pinedo I is defined in racial terms.

Afrobolivians' connections to Africa create a common history and origins in the local diaspora population, which is not unusual among Afro-Latin Americans. The figure of the king, however, adds something specific and ambiguous to this. The crown, sceptre and red-and-white cape King Bonifacio wears at public events resemble the traditional clothing of European monarchs. Oral history claims that these royal items were sent to Prince Uchicho before the death of his father in Africa in the early 19th century (CRA, 2017). The items were stolen shortly after and replicated for the crowning of Bonifacio Pinedo in 1932 (ibid.; Templeman, 1998, p. 427). While it is unclear where exactly the items originate, they appear to be a simulation of traditional European royal dress. This, in combination with the recognition of Julio Pinedo I's authority as Afrobolivian king by the La Paz prefecture, seems ambivalent in the context of Evo Morales' alleged anti-colonial and socialist government. The hierarchical and authoritarian societal structures associated with traditional monarchies seem to contradict the discourse of equality and minority empowerment by the MAS government and Afrobolivian activists.

These seeming contradictions reveal that the Bonifaz monarchy does not aim to establish political or societal structures of a kingdom. Instead, the monarchy facilitates Afrobolivian visibility on the national level by ascribing distinctive and conspicuous characteristics to Afrobolivianness. This reveals the importance of ethnic uniqueness for official and legal state recognition. Despite not being mentioned explicitly in government discourse, the importance given to the Afrobolivian monarchy suggests that ethnic uniqueness is a fundamental factor for the recognition of ethnic rights.

The risks and costs of the Plurinational State's definition of 36 distinct ethnic groups in Bolivia is particularly obvious in the case of performed Afrobolivian identity within Bolivia. In order to qualify as a distinct ethnic group, Afrobolivians differentiate themselves from other ethnic groups in Bolivia by emphasising their unique roots and links to Africa. To be recognised as legitimate citizens of the Bolivian plurinational state, Afrobolivians demonstrate their collective ancestry and unique heritage. Claims to being legitimate ethnic citizens rest on claims to rootedness within Bolivia. At the same time, they emphasise their roots in Africa to demonstrate their common history and unity as a group and consequently their unique Afrobolivian ethnicity. By highlighting their African origins, however, they undermine their claim to rootedness in Bolivia. This contradiction is particularly visible in Afrobolivian cultural production. While Afrobolivians emphasise the African origins of Saya instruments, rhythms and dance, its lyrics clearly demonstrate Afrobolivian rootedness in the Yungas. Likewise, the Bonifaz monarchy gains legitimacy because of African origin. However, it clearly gains meaning for Afrobolivians due to its recognition by the Bolivian state and the way it helps to justify ancestral Afrobolivian land claims in the Yungas. This contradiction seems to be constitutive of Afrobolivian ethnicity itself.

How state visibility on the national level through the Afrobolivian monarchy relates to anti-racism is equally ambiguous. In order to empower the Afrobolivian minority within Bolivia by granting them visibility and the possibility of claiming ethnic rights, it seems necessary to reinforce common stereotypes about black people. Drumming and dancing are often directly associated with blackness. This bears the risk that Afrobolivians are exclusively regarded as entertainers but neglected in strategic and political decision-making processes in state institutions. The government publicity around the Bonifaz monarchy potentially evokes the perception of fundamental political incompatibility with national politics. Rather than the cultural expressions of Afrobolivians themselves, however, it is the publicity and importance the Bolivian state gives to these aspects in relation to legal recognition which perpetuates racialisation.

What seems like a more tolerant approach towards cultural and ethnic heterogeneity by the Bolivian government at the same time reinforces discourses of ethnic purism at the local level. By reinforcing the importance of African heritage for Afrobolivian identity, the Bonifaz monarchy draws racial boundaries between the ethnically diverse populations of the Bolivian Yungas. Any mixture and kinship relations between Afrobolivians and Bolivia's indigenous or mestizo population blurs this visible Afrobolivian identity. Mixture therefore hinders the identification of Afrobolivians as a clearly visible and distinct ethnic group. Resembling Goldberg's conceptualisation of the racial state, the promotion of ethnic heterogeneity by the state requires homogeneity within the separate ethnic groups. Racialisation and exclusion are required and reproduced by ethnically heterogeneous just as much as homogenous states.

Conclusion: the conflicting dynamics constituting Afrobolivian identity

This chapter has argued that Afrobolivian cultural and political activism aims to portray Afrobolivianness as a 'distinct' and hence 'authentic' ethnic identity. By ascribing ancestry defined by a common African bloodline and a unique cultural heritage localised in the Yungas to Afrobolivian ethnicity, Afrobolivians socially and geographically differentiate themselves from other ethnic groups. Mixture and syncretism between Afrobolivian and Aymara languages, ethnicity and culture is regarded as a threat to the possibility of the legal recognition of Afrobolivian land and the economic benefits associated with it. The link between blackness, Saya music and the Yungas is portrayed as inherent and natural.

This performance of ethnicity by demonstrating territoriality and ancestry reveals the interaction of racialising and anti-racist dynamics which constitute Afrobolivian identity and ethnicity. On the one hand, Afrobolivians claim ancestral rootedness in a region in Bolivia, which aligns them to dominant and state ideas about ethnicity in Bolivia. They make claims about ancestry and territoriality and use Saya music and dance to make these claims visible on a national level. On the other hand, they claim ancestral roots in Africa, which undermines their claim to Bolivian rootedness and contradicts the state's definitions of ethnicity. Claims to being legitimate ethnic citizens in plurinational Bolivia rest on claims to rootedness within Bolivia. Claims to ethnic uniqueness and authenticity, however, rest on their African roots. By showing common history and thus unity as a group through emphasising Africa, they undermine their claims to rootedness in Bolivia. This irreducible tension and contradiction is constitutive of the Afrobolivian condition.

The relevance of increased performances of Saya, as well as the publicity surrounding King Julio Pinedo I, are constructed in relation to policies implemented by the MAS government. Resembling Goldberg's concept of the 'racial state', the Bolivian plurinational state defines distinct ethnic groups based on racial categories. In the Bolivian case, the definition of a distinct ancestry and territoriality initially neglected Afrobolivians. The politicisation of this cultural production by Afrobolivian activists, however, reveals how Afrobolivian ancestral territoriality in the Yungas is highlighted and instrumentalised with the aim of qualifying for land ownership rights granted by the state. The racialisation of Afrobolivians is therefore not a by-product, but a necessary step to achieve the recognition of Afrobolivian ancestral territory. To counter the invisibility of Afrobolivians highlighted by King Julio Pinedo, Afrobolivian activists follow and therefore reproduce the structures of ethnic separation and racial identification defined by the state. By adhering to the state's definition of ethnicity, Afrobolivians reproduce the same racial structures which led to their exclusion from Bolivian society.

The consequences of these conflicting dynamics of Afrobolivian identity are reflected by the politics of Afrobolivian land claims to the Bolivian state. No significant land has been granted as ancestral Afrobolivian land. Despite CONAFRO's insistence on the declaration of part of the Yungas as such, these claims have until now had little success compared with indigenous land claims. While some forms of structural recognition of Afrobolivian communities by the plurinational state have been achieved, the question of ancestral territory and Afrobolivian land rights has yet to be resolved.

The analysis of Saya music and the Bonifaz monarchy has revealed two main causes for the continuing inequality and political disadvantage of Afrobolivians. First, the emphasis on Afrobolivians' ancestral and cultural roots in Africa perpetuates the perception of them as displaced within Bolivian society. The demonstration of Afrobolivian territoriality in the Yungas through the lyrics of Saya music and CONAFRO's political activism has not yet countered this perception. The emphasis on their African ancestry means they are not regarded as an 'authentic' ethnic group, nor as a group which originally owned land but were dispossessed of it by conquest. Afrobolivians are not seen as sufficiently ancestrally rooted within Bolivia by the plurinational state. Second, the public demonstration of a common and unique Afrobolivian ancestry and territoriality portrays them as an internally homogenous ethnic group. Consequently, land claims are made by the Afrobolivian community as a whole, politically represented by CONAFRO. Members of the Afrobolivian community, however, are spread across Bolivia and live in the Yungas as well as the cities of La Paz and Santa Cruz. A collective Afrobolivian claim for ancestral territory in the Yungas is weakened by the fact that the Yungas are not exclusively inhabited by Afrobolivians and they do not exclusively reside there. Indigenous land claims, however, are made by certain villages which associate themselves with an indigenous ethnicity. Land claims are not made by the ethnic group, but by villages with clear territorial borders. From the state's perspective, indigenous land claims are more feasible than Afrobolivian land claims.

This chapter has attempted to move beyond the discourse of states' victimisation of ethnic minorities by showing Afrobolivians' agency in claiming belonging and citizenship in plurinational Bolivia. Analysing cultural and political claims, however, it has found that the state's vision of Afrobolivians as an ethnic group and Afrobolivians' own claim-making both constitute their racialisation and separation from other Bolivians. At the local level, allegedly heterogeneous states engage just as much in nation-building as ethnically homogenous states. It should be emphasised that this chapter does not criticise Afrobolivians for demonstrating their cultural expressions and uniqueness. Instead, it criticises the relevance given to these aspects by the plurinational state in relation to the legal recognition of ethnicity and ethnic rights.

It is therefore necessary to fundamentally reform the political and analytical definitions of ethnicity and ethnic groups. The change from a Bolivian nation state into a plurinational state has promoted tolerance towards distinct ethnicities. However, it has not altered the discourse of internal homogeneity that underlies the identification of different ethnic groups. Rather than fundamentally challenging it, Afrobolivian claim-making reveals that the plurinational state has reduced nation-building from the state to the local level. Instead of further reducing the size of internally homogenous categories identifiable by states, however, it is necessary to find a way to counter the negative associations of ethnic mixture and hybridity regarding legal and political recognition.

Bibliography

Aliaga, F. and E. Aliaga (1991) *Rhythmes noirs de Pérou: historique et présentation de musiques et chants enregistrés á Lima-Pérou* (Paris: Lierre & Coudier).

Ardito, L. (2007) 'Pensar lo musical como correlato de lo social: el caso de la música popular afrolatinoamericana' (Santiago de Chile, University of Chile undergraduate thesis).

Arias, S. (2009) *Una cultura de la resistencia. La Voz de los Sin Voz Programa*, vol. 4: *Afrodescendientes*. Buenos Aires: Ministerio de Relaciones Exteriores, Comercio Internacional y Culto.

Barra, M. (1998) 'Si yo fuera presidente', performed by Movimiento Cultural Saya Afroboliviana 2006 in La Paz, available at: https://www.youtube.com/watch?v=Oo54TVsrHmM (accessed 12 Feb. 2017).

Bigenho, M. (2002) *Sounding Indigenous: Authenticity in Bolivian Music Performance* (New York: Palgrave).

Buechler, H.C. (1980) *The Masked Media: Aymara Fiestas and Social Interaction in the Bolivian Highlands* (The Hague: Mouton).

Busdiecker, S. (2009a) 'Where blackness resides: Afrobolivians and the spatializing and racializing of the African diaspora', *Radical History Review*, 103: 105–16.

— (2009b) 'The emergence and evolving character of contemporary Afrobolivian mobilization', in L. Mullings (ed.), *New Social Movements in the African Diaspora* (New York: Palgrave Macmillan), pp. 121–37.

Casa Real Afroboliviana (CRA) (2012–2017), official website, http://www.casarealafroboliviana.org (accessed 12 Feb. 2017).

Céspedes, G.W. (1993) 'Huayño, saya, and chuntunqui: Bolivian identity in the music of Los Kjarkas', *Latin American Music Review/Revista de Música Latinoamericana* 14 (1): 52–101.

Choque, F. (2014) 'Afrobolivianos quieres revalorizar y fortalecer su cultura e historia', *La Razón*, 21 Sept., La Paz.

Choque Gutiérrez, H. (2017) 'Saya afroboliviana', in *Gran Poder 2017* available at: http://www.minculturas.gob.bo/index.php/prensa/gran-poder-2017/2980-saya-afroboliviana (accessed 14 Oct. 2017).

Comunidad Andina (2011) 'Políticas de desarrollo social en la Comunidad Andina', *Revista de la Integración*, 8 (Nov.) (Lima).

CONAFRO, Consejo Nacional del Pueblo Afroboliviano (2011) *Plan Estratégico 2014–2020* (La Paz: CONAFRO).

— (2014a) *Currículo regionalizado del pueblo afroboliviano* (La Paz: CONAFRO) available at: http://www.minedu.gob.bo/files/publicaciones/upiip/cr-afroboliviano.pdf (accessed 12 Feb. 2017).

— (2014b) *Historia, cultura y economía del pueblo afroboliviano* (Cochabamba: FUNPROEIB Publicaciones).

Consejo Departamental (2007) 'Resolution No. 2033, Resolución oficial de proclamación del rey afroboliviano', Consejo Departamental, Prefectura del Departamento de La Paz, 15 Nov. 2007.

Constitution (2009) Political Constitution of the Plurinational State of Bolivia, approved 7 Feb. 2009, La Paz.

Cuenca, A.P. (1977) *La cultura negra en Bolivia* (La Paz: Ediciones Isla).

Cuevas, A. (2014) 'Exigen eliminar los elementos racistas en baile del tundiqui', *Página Siete*, 31 July 2014 available at: https://www.paginasiete.bo/sociedad/2014/8/1/exigen-eliminar-elementos-racistas-baile-tundiqui-28241.html (accessed 17 May 2019).

Goldberg, D.T. (2002) *The Racial State* (Malden, MA:. Blackwell).

INE, Instituto Nacional de Estadística de Bolivia (2012) *Censo nacional* available at: http://www.ine.gob.bo:8081/censo2012/PDF/resultadosCPV2012.pdf (accessed 16 March 2017).

Jiménez Zamora, E. (2007) 'La diversificación de los ingresos rurales en Bolivia', Íconos: Revista de Ciencias Sociales, 29: 63–76

Käss, S. (ed.) (2010) *Bolivia en la senda de la implementación de la ley marco de autonomías y descentralización (LMAD), Evaluación, análisis crítico y perspectivas futuras* (La Paz: Fundación Konrad Adenauer).

Klein, H.S. (2011) *A Concise History of Bolivia* (Cambridge: Cambridge University Press).

Lipski, J.M. (2008) *Afrobolivian Spanish* (Madrid, Frankfurt: Iberoamericana, Editorial Vervuert).

Maconde, J. (2000) *Raíces de un pueblo: cultura afroboliviana* (La Paz: Producciones CIMA).

— (2006) 'Dónde está mi pueblo?', *Afrociudadanizando*, 6 Sept. 2006, La Paz.

Medina, J. (2013) 'En Bolivia hay discriminación muy solapada', *La Razón*, 22 Sept. 2013, La Paz.

MOCUSABOL (Movimiento Cultural Saya Afroboliviano) (2006) *Propuesta de los temas a discutirse en la Asamblea Constituyente* available at http://www.foroconstituyente.info/files/propuestas/propuestaafrobolivianos.pdf (accessed 12 Feb. 2017).

Morales, E. (2009) Preamble to the Constitution, Political Constitution of the Plurinational State of Bolivia, approved 7th Feb. 2009, La Paz, available at: https://www.constituteproject.org/constitution/Bolivia_2009.pdf (accessed 17 May 2019).

Morales, W.Q. (2010) *A Brief History of Bolivia* (New York: Infobase Publishing).

Ortiz, M.P. (1978) *La esclavitud negra en las épocas colonial y nacional de Bolivia* (La Paz: Instituto Boliviano de Cultura).

Rossbach, L. (2007) 'Expresiones controvertidas: Afrobolivianos y su cultura entre presentaciones y representaciones', *Indiana* 35 (2): 173–90.

Schipani, A. (2007) 'Bolivia's African king', *The Guardian*, 10 Dec. 2007.

— (2009) 'Hidden kingdom of the Afrobolivians', BBC News, 17 April 2009, available at: http://news.bbc.co.uk/1/hi/world/americas/7958783.stm (accessed 12 Feb. 2017).

Spedding, A. (1994) *Wachu wachu: cultivo de coca e identidad en los Yunkas de La Paz* (La Paz: CIPCA).

Sturtevant, C. (2017) 'Claiming belonging, constructing social spaces: citizenship practices in an Afrobolivian town', *Critique of Anthropology*, 37 (1): 3–26.

Templeman, R.W. (1998) 'We are the people of the *Yungas*, we are the *Saya* race', in N.E. Whitten and A. Torres (eds.) *Blackness in Latin America and the Caribbean: Social Dynamics and Cultural Transformations*, vol. 1, *Central America and Northern and Western South America* (Bloomington, IL: Indiana University Press), pp. 400–26.

— (2001) 'Women in the world of music: Latin America, Native America and the African Diaspora', in K.A. Pendle (ed.), *Women and Music: A History* (Bloomington, IL: Indiana University Press), pp. 438–59.

Toledo, C. (2013), *ELLA Guide: Promoting Indigenous and Ethnic Minority Rights in Latin America* (Lima: ELLA, Practical Action Consulting).

Revilla, P. (2014) 'De coronaciones y otras memorias: afrobolivianos y el estado plurinacional', *Tinkazos*, 17 (36): 121–31.

UMSA (2012) *Encuesta socio-demográfica – Yungas estadística por municipio* (La Paz: Universidad Mayor de San Andrés).

UNESCO (2013) 'Pueblo afroboliviano inaugura su Instituto de Lengua y Cultura en Tocana', Servicio de Prensa en Quitó, available at: http://www.unesco.org/new/es/media-services/single-view/news/pueblo_afroboliviano_inaugura_su_instituto_de_lengua_y_cultu/ (accessed 12 Feb. 2017).

SAU Saya Unión Afro (2016) 'Se presenta el afroboliviano', available at: https://www.youtube.com/watch?v=WJB8G7EW8rc (accessed 12 Feb. 2017).

8. White *cholos*? Discourses around race, whiteness and Lima's fusion music

Fiorella Montero-Diaz

Historically the traditional upper classes in Lima have been described by scholars and the general public as manipulative, distant and hegemonic, and as a group that has maintained social, racial and cultural hierarchies to perpetuate its powers (for example, Durand, 2007; Galindo, 1994; Kogan, 2009; Bruce, 2007; Ardito, 2010). This image has not changed much over the years and is reinforced by segregation between wealthy and working-class areas and lack of contact between different strata. But who are the traditional upper classes? Peruvian scholars use different terms in reference to the white *limeño* [people from Lima] upper classes. Liuba Kogan uses words such as *viejas elites* [old elites] and *oligarquía tradicional* [traditional oligarchy]; Rolando Arellano uses *grupos tradicionales A, B* [traditional A, B groups] and *Lima tradicional* [traditional Lima]; while Gonzalo Portocarrero uses *clases altas criollas* [creole upper classes]. The word 'traditional' is common in academic as well as popular discourse when referring to the Lima upper classes that predate the 20th-century peaks in Andean migration to the capital.[1] This means that the 'traditional' upper classes are of predominantly European descent, which is synonymous with white in the Peruvian imaginary, and associated with urban coastal culture and lifestyle.

History and the dominant discourses have also cemented associations between money and whiteness. Of course, not all whom most Peruvians would perceive as part of the white upper class in Lima self-define as white upper class, often due to negative social connotations, such as white arrogance, social and economic privilege, lack of Peruvianness (that is, being hyper-white or carrying Peruvian un-whiteness, cf. Turner, 2014) and the snobbish attitude associated

---

[1] The migration peaks were due mainly to labour shortages in the capital (1880), disruptions caused by agricultural reforms (1940–60) and displacement by internal violence (1980–2000). With the increased presence of Andean migrants in Lima's historic centre, the upper classes left their traditional areas for new homes in Magdalena, Miraflores, San Isidro and later La Molina. But they were rapidly encircled because accelerated population growth meant that Lima was surrounded by peripheral emergent districts predominantly inhabited by internally displaced people (North Lima, East Lima and South Lima).

F. Montero-Diaz, 'White *cholos*? Discourses around race, whiteness and Lima's fusion music', in P. Wade, J. Scorer and I. Aguiló (eds.), *Cultures of Anti-Racism in Latin America and the Caribbean* (London: Institute of Latin American Studies, 2019), pp. 167–90. License: CC-BY-NC-ND 4.0.

with discrimination against *gente no como uno* [people unlike oneself]. However, others do define themselves as white upper class and terms like GCU, short for *gente como uno*, or *gente bien* [people of good standing] are used by certain sections of the elite and upper classes when referring informally to themselves. This difference in self-perception gives rise to the division between 'alternatives' and 'non-alternatives' discussed later in this chapter.

In 1994 a survey was conducted among students at the private Lima university Pontificia Universidad Católica del Perú (PUCP). It featured the question 'Which Peruvian groups hinder the country's development?' The group cited most often was the traditional upper classes (for example, 'the upper classes', 'the big capitalists', 'the ones who transfer their profit out of the country', 'the ones who exploit the rest'); the next most cited were the 'terrorists' (for example, the Shining Path) involved in Peru's 20-year internal war (1980–2000) in which, according to the Peruvian truth and reconciliation commission, an estimated 70,000 people were killed or disappeared;[2] and the third group was politicians and bureaucrats (Venturo, 2001, p. 56). Though this was a small sample it was a telling ranking, which triggered academic interest in studying youth political culture. How do upper-class young adults (20–25 years old) tackle being portrayed, even in their own imaginary, as 'worse than terrorists' for Peru's development? Very few scholarly resources are available to answer this question, but an examination of the fusion genres in music that emerged in post-war Lima gives us a partial answer.

This chapter focuses on fusion styles that combine what most Peruvians generally perceive as traditional music, and music originating elsewhere (for example, Afro-jazz, *huayno*-rock, Peruvian electro-*cumbia*). It also looks at the social roles this music plays for white upper-class audiences and musicians.[3] The discussion maps the contemporary intercultural popular fusion scene in Lima, from the work of the pioneers in the 1960s to the current scene, following the work of upper-class fusion musicians (not all of whom are from the white upper classes), as well as their white upper-class audience.[4] I examine how fusion constitutes a resource for personal reflection, social agency and the

2   This war paralysed the country's economy and cultural scene; it restricted individual freedom of movement and further divided an already conflict-ridden Peru.

3   For more details on fusion music see Montero-Diaz (2016, p. 192).

4   In order to limit its scope to the 'traditional white upper classes', this chapter takes into consideration common variables found in what *limeños* described (or imagined) as the 'traditional white upper classes': people with a light skin tone or European phenotype, who either have well-known upper-class last names and are historically associated with the intellectual or economic upper classes, or they have been part of the upper classes for generations, have attended wealthy private schools and universities, live in affluent districts, such as Barranco, Miraflores, La Molina, Surco, San Borja or San Isidro, and attend upper-class exclusive venues for leisure and entertainment (clubs, parties, venues and beach houses). It does not take self-identification into consideration, because, as noted, that proved problematic for the upper classes. Nor are household income classifications used, as it would have been impossible to obtain income figures from interviewees and survey respondents. Moreover, few

elaboration of new forms of citizenship among upper-class whites. It is worth noting that in Lima fusion and similar trends existed before the period and case studies in focus here (for example, the band El Polen in the 1970s). However, previous fusion projects attempted to rediscover the essence of the imagined indigenous nation by looking at the internal 'other' instead of continuing to engage with foreign music aesthetics, taking a quasi-*indigenista* approach.[5] In contrast, some of the contemporary fusion music initiatives serve as a platform for upper-class personal reflection, a journey towards social responsibility through engagement in intercultural creative dialogues via human coexistence, and rapprochement with previously marginalised music genres to ultimately belong to and actively participate in an imagined nation.

It seems that for some, the period of internal conflict sparked intense personal soul-searching as well as a collective pursuit of a more 'cohesive' identity. This is reflected in the increase in interethnic and cross-class collaborations after 2005 (see Montero-Diaz, 2016), and the proliferation and success of fusion albums.[6] For Lalo Ponce, CEO of Phantom Peru, the fusion music boom in 2005 helped Peruvian music to top the charts, as before 2005 'it was rare to find local albums leading the charts, [but] now [in 2010] over 50 per cent of the bestselling ones are always local'.[7]

Drawing on ethnographic examples gathered between 2010 and 2011 in Lima, Peru, this chapter offers a problematisation of racial tensions as experienced by white upper-class performers themselves, especially because research on ordinary white upper-class daily lives and reflections on their own racialised identities through cultural participation are scarce. It analyses how race and phenotype constitute barriers to the creativity and mobility of musicians, and problematise the discourse used by white upper-class musicians to validate their new fused identities as they negotiate empathy, social solidarity, authenticity and racial colour blindness while advocating social change. This chapter aims to contribute to the growing literature about the link between whiteness and racism in Latin America (for example, Moreno, 2010; Telles and Flores, 2013; Wade, 2010) by providing the perspective of young, white upper-class allies (cf. Frankenberg, 1993; Bishop, 2002).

    musicians actually earn enough to be part of the higher *limeño* strata, based on income alone, but their education, network and family history do match the profile.

5 President Velasco's unofficial ban on 'foreign capitalist genres' in 1968 led several rock musicians, who suddenly found themselves barred from pursuing their passion for rock, to explore more local sounds. The ban was not official, as it did not explicitly forbid foreign music. However, some foreign bands' concerts were cancelled while Peruvian traditional music was prioritised. There are testimonies from the period of the Morales Bermúdez presidency of the army categorising people dressed in rock fashion as drug dealers (Riveros, 2012, p. 149).

6 'Almost all the 25 bestselling albums of 2007 and 2008 were fusion' (José Luis Cárdenas, CEO of Play Music & Video record label, interview, Nov. 2010).

7 Interview with Lalo Ponce, Nov. 2010.

A monolithic upper class in Lima?

When it comes to contemporary sociological study of the middle and upper class in Peru post-1960, the list of scholars contributing extensively can arguably be whittled down to four.[8] Gonzalo Portocarrero (1998) focused on the Peruvian middle classes, while Norma Fuller (1993, 1997) and Maruja Barrig (1979, 1981) dealt with gender in the middle and upper classes. Only Liuba Kogan (2009) has produced recent sociological research on the *sectores altos* [upper classes], in which she paid special attention to the old elites, or the traditional oligarchy, approaching her research from a gender identity perspective.[9] This paucity of academic scrutiny reflects a generalised avoidance of contemporary academic debate about the 'traditional white upper classes'. In his prologue to Kogan's *Regias y conservadores* (2009), the Peruvian journalist and writer Rafo León observes that Peru's traditional upper classes have:

> never [been] studied or analysed as anything but agents of evil, beings without personality, soul or feelings; mere machines engaged in racist money making; epigones of a feudal system, which Velasco[10] did away with, though only with its trappings, because the rich are like cockroaches, withstanding even the worst catastrophes, outliving the human species. (my translation)

Kogan's research is important as a pioneering contemporary sociological study of the traditional upper classes. However, her research also depicts the traditional upper-class elites as white *pitucos* [posh], superficial, naïve, conservative, arrogant and deeply religious. This is crystallised even in Kogan's book title *Regias y conservadores: mujeres y hombres de clase alta en la Lima de los noventa* [Fabulous and conservative: upper-class women and men in 1990s Lima]. Elsewhere in Latin America, research on local white elite cultural consumption is also rare, but two studies are of special note: Edwin Chuquimia, Ronal Jemio and Alex López's work (2006) on the cultural identity of the *jailones* – the elites of the city of La Paz, Bolivia, and Eugenia Iturriaga Acevedo's analysis (2011) of white elite racism and ethnic discrimination in Mérida (Yucatán, Mexico).

---

8   In Peru there are studies and portrayals of the upper classes that take different approaches including focusing on their role in history and the economy (Durand, 1982, 1994, 2003, 2004a, 2004b), journalistic approaches (Malpica, 1990), market-oriented research (Arellano and Burgos 2004; Arellano 2010), humorous fictional social commentaries (León, 2000, 2004, 2006) and political caricature (Acevedo, 2009). However, the upper classes have not been extensively studied from a sociological/anthropological perspective.

9   I would also like to acknowledge Rolando Arellano's contributions to the understanding of class from the perspective of market research and business management (Arellano and Burgos 2004; Arellano 2010).

10   Former President of Peru (1968–75). Juan Velasco Alvarado, a left-wing army general, was responsible for a number of nationalist reforms such as the nationalisation of various industries, implementation of bilingual education, prohibition of the term 'Indian' and the promotion of traditional music in the media.

Most Peruvians' perceptions of the 'traditional white upper-classes' in Lima are negative ones. This is rooted in history: colonial, racial and economic tensions, hegemonic power, symbolic violence, racism and discrimination towards Andeans, and systematic appropriations of Andean culture. Lima as a city has also been historically described by influential thinkers as a white cluster (Eakin, 2007, p. 187), *hija de la Conquista sin raíces en el pasado autóctono* [daughter of the Conquest without roots in the native past] (Mariátegui, 1970, p. 254), *centro de irradiación de la ideología racista* [a centre from which racist ideology spreads] (Galindo, 1994, p. 235), and a city with a 'desire for adaptation to the European culture … because Cuzco already existed when the Conquistador arrived, and Lima was created by him' (Valcárcel, 1972 [1927], quoted in and translated by García, 2005, p. 18).

There is still little nuance in how the Peruvian upper classes are described and perceived in literature and public discourse. They are considered and discussed as a homogenous block, but this is, of course, not accurate. While conducting fieldwork in Lima in 2010/11, I noticed that upper-class youths were a diverse group and seemed to express their class and racial identity in several ways. However, in our conversations one major division was highlighted repeatedly: some like belonging to the upper class, flaunt status and wealth, and describe themselves in interviews as high-class white people. Others (whom I term 'the alternatives') mainly identify with moderate left-wing politics, are more liberal, reject notions of exclusivity and superiority, and are generally more involved in their respective local communities. While this divide is not fixed, it is a noticeable internal classification.

One of my online surveys disseminated among white upper-class individuals between 20 and 35 years of age (2010), made it clear that each upper-class sub-group attended a different music venue in Lima. For example, of the respondents who preferred Gótica and Aura (very exclusive night clubs in the affluent Miraflores district of Lima) as many as 70 per cent described themselves as white, while those who preferred Sargento Pimienta (in Barranco) described themselves as mestizos or did not specify their ethnicity.[11] The differences between these two groups are also expressed in youth discourse through word

---

11 Barranco is a district well known for its bohemian, artistic and leftist intellectual inhabitants. Among the white upper classes themselves, Gótica and Aura are considered the most exclusive discos in Lima, while Sargento Pimienta, Dragón and La Noche (all in Barranco) were presented as more mixed; they are where upper-class 'alternatives' gather to listen to their favourite bands. The music programme in Sargento Pimienta is also diverse: classic rock, reggae, salsa and fusion are often on the bill. An advantage of Sargento Pimienta is its size and lack of tables; this enables people to move around freely, dance, drink, jump and express themselves without restrictions of space. Also, groups like La Mente have used the space to incorporate new elements into their shows, such as bringing *sikuri* [pan pipe] troupes to play and dance among the audience. People do not dress as smartly as they would for other venues; they are distinctly underdressed, even compared with La Noche's relaxed audience. During concerts it is not uncommon to overhear jokes and negative comments directed at overdressed attendants, even from their own friends: 'Where do you think you are, in Aura? [laughter].

play with the names of these two venues and the locations in Lima. There is a music scene and circuit for each lifestyle. 'Alternative' wealthy youth predominantly favour Barranco district's music scene (for example, Sargento Pimienta), and are hence known as *barrancoides* or *barranqueros*, whereas the youth who frequent the exclusive clubs are called *gotiqueros*.

There are other names too, mostly pejorative and associated with political preference and ideology, such as *progre* or *caviar* [champagne socialist]: someone from the upper class who has a wealthy lifestyle, but claims to understand 'the people' and sympathise with leftist ideology. When asking wealthy *limeños* whether there really is such a stark divide, the replies came without hesitation:

> They're totally different, I consider myself *barrancoide*, but I went to Gótica two weeks ago and to tell you the truth I'm ashamed to go to Gótica, because I don't have anything in common with the people who go there, the music is all 107.7 [reference to Radio Planeta – music in English and mostly from major US labels]. *Barrancoide* people are like '*así no más*' [they maintain their distance] with *gótica* people and they don't mix because a *gotiquero* works at a bank and has a different life, different aspirations, they want to marry quickly. We share the same social class, but the *barrancoides*, for example ... are people who don't go to Starbucks, they don't do the '*cafecito*' [let's go for a coffee] thing, they're totally underground ... they drink *chela* [beer]. (Jorge 26, focus group, December 2010)

For the 'alternatives', fusion music is a clear marker of their 'alternative' identity and an opportunity to explore other cultures and interact with them, a phenomenon Hopenhayn (1999, p. 25) labels 'transcultural self-recreation', 'a way to self-recreate oneself through the interaction with the "other"'. For example, Joaquín Mariátegui, former lead guitarist of well-known group Bareto, clearly felt the clash between his musical taste and his reality:[12]

> I would love to know and speak Quechua and, damn, play *yaravíes* the way Manuelcha Prado [well-known Andean guitarist from Ayacucho] does. Again, I'm not Manuelcha Prado, I mean, I'm a *colorao* ['red', a more affectionate euphemism for 'white' than *blanco*] [...] I'm not a liar. I'm not Manuelcha Prado, but, damn, I'm not Eric Clapton either, I'm not Bob Marley either ... shit ... where am I, WHO AM I? I think that for me music has become a way of finding myself on the map, basically, music for me is like a compass and it tells me who I am. (interview, September 2010)

Poor sod, you look lost, there's nowhere to put your Johnny Walker here. Get with it, here you come in pyjamas and *ojotas* [car tyre sandals]' (female, 24, Sargento Pimienta).

12 In 2009–10 Bareto was hailed in the media as the 'most democratic' band in Lima, because its music was heard by many Peruvians, regardless of ethnicity and social class. Bareto's social impact was evidenced with descriptions such as 'the band that united Peru through music' or 'the band that broke down social barriers in Peru'. See these interviews as examples: Sonidos del Mundo, conducted by Mabela Martinez (15 Feb. 2009), http://www.youtube.com/watch?v=-GFQbBHkB-g&feature=related [accessed 6 June 2016]; Cuarto poder (25 Jan. 2009), http://www.youtube.com/watch?v=IzFWQ28zktg [accessed 6 June 2016].

Figure 8.1. Joaquín Mariátegui – Bareto's former lead guitarist. (Photographer: Alonso Molina. Used with permission of Joaquín Mariátegui and Alonso Molina.)

Through music, Joaquín 'finds himself on the map'. Fusion music then becomes the tool he needs in order to discover himself and later reconstruct himself as an alternative wealthy *chichero* musician.[13] Joaquín embraces this categorisation, one that in the past would have been perceived as an insult to a white upper-class musician, as *chicha* music was associated with marginality, *serranos* [highlanders] and bad taste (Romero, 2007, p. 31; Bailón, 2004, p. 58–9; Ramos-García, 2003, p. 201).

The aftermath of the Peruvian internal conflict (1980–2000) played a significant role in fostering the feeling of 'togetherness' that motivated my collaborators[14] to approach previously rejected musical styles and individuals through cultural consumption and interracial/interclass onstage collaborations (Montero-Diaz, 2016). The rise of this music among white upper-class youth in 2005–6 indicated a new taste for previously marginalised genres. This crossing of racialised boundaries allowed for empathetic musical interactions,

---

13 Person who plays *chicha* music. The word is not always used pejoratively, yet in upper- and middle-class Lima it is mainly used as a derogatory term to refer to musicians from the provinces, regardless of whether they play *chicha*. *Chicha* is the musical product of waves of migration from the hinterland to the capital, as Andeans in Lima mixed one expression of their *huayno* [traditional music] with foreign rhythms such as *cumbia, mambo, guarachas*. A new genre of popular music emerged featuring electric guitars and synthesisers as iconic instruments.

14 I have chosen to use the term 'collaborators' instead of 'informants', as I find that the former more accurately describes the role of the individuals I spoke to in the course of the fieldwork. Informant seems to indicate a more distant and unequal relationship with the researcher.

reconfigurations of white upper-class identity, and new hybrid self-representations, for instance, as 'white *cholos*'.[15] Phrases such as: 'I'm white, but I'm black inside' (Miki González); 'I love *huaynos*, I must have Andean blood somewhere' (Pepita García-Miró); or 'I'm a proud *cholo* and white *chichero*' (Joaquín Mariátegui, Bareto) are often used when white fusionists describe their engagement with more traditional Peruvian music as a way to embody racialised musical identities (cf. Wade, 2005, p. 248–9). However, there is a tension between the whiteness and class of fusion musicians and audiences on the one hand, and their commitment to social equality through music on the other.

'Alternatives' do not feel like 'regular' upper-class youths, but most do not feel part of a broader Lima either. Many say that other *limeños* reject their perspectives because they have not experienced marginality or 'real' hardship. One collaborator said:

> I just want to be me, I don't want to be like my parents or like other snobs, but I can't escape my class totally. I am a lefty, I study anthropology, have diverse friends ... but still some people think I am fake, too idealistic, empty, [a] naïve spoiled *pituco*, and this is because I am still white and I still live in Miraflores. For me fusion music is the soundtrack of Peru, not just of the elites, or the working classes, it represents an ideal Peru, where everyone is treated the same and can make music together [...] Do I have to paint my face, leave my home and university to prove I am genuine, that I am not a liar? [his voice breaks]. (Male aged 25, interview, 10 March 2011).

Even fusion fandom is seen by many in their own class and lower classes as a consumerist, appropriative fad, a 'hipster' act. However, some 'alternatives' I interviewed made a distinction between upper-class fusion 'fans' and 'followers' by knowledge and social identity, much like the categories defined by Tulloch and Jenkins (1995). 'Followers' engage with fusion erratically and inconsistently, while fusion 'fans', many of whom are 'alternatives', engage not only with the aesthetics, but also, and principally, with the message and ideals of fusion (interculturality, celebration of diversity, social and personal transformation) (Montero-Diaz, 2016); this distinction is an attempt to

---

15 *Cholo* is originally a pejorative term used to refer to Andean-mestizo urban residents and people born in cities who have Andean ethnicity, background, phenotype or cultural traits. However, from the mid 2000s, hand in hand with the growing popularity of fusion music and the tendency to embrace previously marginalised genres among the middle and upper classes, a new sense of 'Choloness' (*choledad*) emerged in Lima. Redefined as a form of celebratory non-assimilative *mestizaje*, this describes a proud fusion of cultural traits between the Andes and the coast, giving rise to a distinctive *cholo* identity. *Cholo/a blanco* [white *cholo*] is a term used by white musicians when giving reasons for their engagement with music not traditionally associated with white upper-class taste.

validate their hybrid identities by differentiating the fad (hipsterism) from sincere musical engagement.[16]

Through intercultural contact and friendship, 'alternative' fusion musicians explore their city outside the fixed trappings of race and social class. Many play at both exclusive venues and at mass popular events, challenging the 'allowed spaces' of their class in search of something more 'real'. I coined the term *espacios permitidos* [allowed spaces] as an analytical tool to examine what the white upper classes perceive as safe poverty-free places for them to live and travel around 'comfortably'. For most *limeños* the experience of their city is limited to spaces where one is comfortable among people who share one's habits, purchasing power, prejudices and fears. These spaces are perpetuated as 'allowed spaces' passed down from parents to children.[17] The way fusionists challenge 'allowed spaces' hints at what Arellano (2010, p. 172) calls an 'inverse aspiration process', in which the white upper classes reject social distance and aspire to feel socially included in the city.

> I think we have grown up looking abroad a lot, don't you? We go out for a *Coca-Cola* [she puts on an American accent], we go for *hamburgers* … finally Peruvians, and I wouldn't say that it is just the upper classes, look at themselves and say 'ok, my *chicha* is bloody brilliant' … yeah sure Michael Jackson is cool, but listen, Grupo 5 [*cumbia norteña* band] is brilliant, I love it. So I also think it's a kind of better self-esteem, but I see it like that, I don't see it as a longing, but like taking a look inside, when you suddenly look at yourself and say 'I like myself'. (Pamela Rodríguez, interview, Miraflores, Lima, 4 March 2011)

This interaction through mixing genres brings issues of participation and agency to the fore. Who has the right to mix and play this music? Who has agency to represent themselves? Are these sincere attempts at dialogue or just another way to ignore differences and pretend that everything is fine? White upper-class performers have to grapple not only with the *limeño* audiences' imaginaries and ideas of what they 'should' be doing or performing, but also with their relationships with fellow musicians, the scene and academics. Multiple pressures have forced some of them to change genres, bands or even rethink their music careers, an indication that discrimination, exclusion and racism in Lima are complex and merit examination across the whole ethnic spectrum.

---

16 Arguably fandom is always performative, sometimes defined as 'an identity which is disclaimed and which performs cultural work' (Hills, 2002, p. xi).

17 For examples, see the undergraduate thesis on Lima's imaginary city limits by Eduardo González Cueva (1994).

Whiteness in Lima: a tangled tale

According to several Peruvian studies (Bruce, 2007, pp. 70–3; Drzewieniecki, 2004, pp. 13–17; Portocarrero, 1993, p. 218) and other studies in Latin America (for example, Hale, 2006; Stepan, 1991; Telles, 2014; Van Dijk, 2005; Wade, 1997, 2008), a white person is situated at the top of the socioeconomic pyramid and is often associated with favourable traits: intelligence, cleanliness, education, good looks and so on. Even today in Lima, there are those parents who will try to get their children to marry a white person so as to *mejorar la raza* [improve the race]. These positive connotations are reinforced when a white person is, or is imagined to be, wealthy – money and whiteness often go together in *limeño* imaginaries. Yet, this positive discourse coexists with the derogatory stereotype of the white *pitucos* [posh] – the white wealthy elites, who are commonly perceived as shallow, naïve and conservative. Only very few scholars have briefly discussed what they refer to as racial discrimination against whites (Bruce, 2007, p. 43; Degregori, 2000, pp. 31, 33) and white stereotypes in Peru (Turino, 1993, pp. 192, 237).

According to Alastair Bonnett (2000, pp. 21–6), whiteness has been the central signifier of European superiority, a 'talisman of the natural whose power appeared to enable them [Europeans] to impose their will on the world'. In Peru this perception was established in colonial times and remains the norm today. He continues that whiteness has always been approached as a naturalised normative, and is therefore seen as a static, inflexible category, an essentialism that needs to be identified and challenged. In Peru, anti-racist scholars, several of whom happen to be white and from the upper classes, have adopted this same essentialist approach, often ignoring the sociological dissection of whiteness and class and critiquing the elite's role without problematising its current context, individual lifestyles, ordinary lives, youth movements and subversions from within. This reinforces the notion that their white upper-class identity is immutable, impervious to social or political transformation. This may be one reason why academics and public commentators lambast the white upper classes for their alleged indifference and distance from national social issues, while simultaneously branding those who do get involved through culture or protest (white allies) as *caviares*, fake, naïve or superficial hipsters. This reinforces the idea of whiteness as a fixed condition with negative moral values, linked to congenital ignorance of Peru's social problems. According to Modood (1990) and Bonnet (2000), such imaginaries of whiteness position whites as nothing but racist, silencing, discriminating oppressors, in turn reducing non-white people to victims who suffer white attitudes and actions, and whose identities are created merely in opposition to white lives. This reifies whiteness as almighty and powerful and reinforces one of the major social 'myths of whiteness' (Bonnett, 2000, p. 121).

Moreover, academics in Lima and public commentary strengthened the idea that racism is a 'white problem', thereby making invisible the responsibilities of non-white people in the anti-racist agenda. There is growing awareness in Lima that racist portrayals of Andean people and themes in movies, TV and daily life are not acceptable. However, few if any appear to notice let alone speak out against stereotyped portrayals of whites as empty, emotionally damaged, addicts, naïve, spoiled, selfish and culturally ignorant. Josué Méndez, the director of *Dioses* (2008), a movie portraying the emotional and intellectual emptiness of the Lima white upper classes, said he wanted to portray:

> a high class that is not well known in Lima because it is very hermetic, they live in closed zones and very few people interact with them. People create an image of them that has nothing to do with real life, you become disappointed because you think they are intellectuals when they only talk rubbish ... they only talk about flowers and don't worry about problems.[18]

Not an eyebrow was raised at this movie, in sharp contrast with reactions to the film *Madeinusa* (2006), directed by Claudia Llosa, a white upper-class filmmaker, released only two years before *Dioses*.[19] This fictional narrative, set in the Andes with the protagonist played by Magaly Solier, was lambasted by Peruvian academics and public commentary as racist, a stereotyped inaccurate depiction of the Andes and Andeans. Regarding the widely different reactions towards two movies with problematic racial/ethnic portrayals, Josué Méndez commented:

> What happens in the Andean world causes more controversy. The high class is not that important, and the elite don't care about seeing themselves portrayed. Maybe they will only think: why am I going to worry about this little movie? However, there will always be the Andes protectors who think they know what is right for the poor.[20]

Méndez portrays the upper classes as distant, cold, indifferent to their own social image, an 'empty' group unconcerned with the visibility of their whiteness or how their experience and identities are racialised (cf. Byrne, 2006; Garner,

18 'Josué Méndez cuestiona a la clase alta del Perú', *El Comercio*, 23 Sept. 2008, http://elcomercio.pe/ediciononline/html/2008-09-23/josue-mendez-cuestiona-clase-alta-peru.html (accessed 12 Aug. 2015).

19 *Madeinusa*'s plot, as described on Claudia Llosa's website, is as follows: '*Madeinusa* is set in the fictional indigenous village of Manayaycuna ("the town no-one can enter" in Quechua) in the Peruvian Andes. The story covers three days in the lives of the villagers and a stranger from Lima. The stranger, Salvador, is unwelcome because he has arrived at the beginning of the "Holy Time," a syncretic religious festival spanning Good Friday and Easter Sunday. The villagers of Manayaycuna believe that during "Holy Time" God, symbolized by an effigy of Christ, is dead and, therefore, nothing is a sin. The drama centres on the encounter of the eponymous Madeinusa, a teenaged girl selected as the festival's Mater Dolorosa and daughter of the village mayor' (https://hollywoodandhistory.wordpress.com/tag/quechua/).

20 'El cine peruano no existe', interview with Josué Méndez by Mario Castro Cobos and Fernando Vilchez, 20 Feb. 2007, http://lacinefilianoespatriota.blogspot.com/2007/02/dioses-la-segunda-pelcula-de-josu-mndez.html (accessed 26 March 2019).

2007), a group that 'only talk[s] rubbish' (Méndez, 2008). This resonates with Drzewieniecki's (2004) discussion of 'resistance to the idea that discrimination against or mistreatment of *blancos* was worth considering'. This notion is also evident on the music scene.

These observations should not be read as an attempt to downplay the social harm of systematic white upper-class racism and discrimination against others or to mask the fact that such regular social practices mobilise a system of power inequalities. But the complexities of class and race relations in Lima merit closer scrutiny. Social interactions through music can offer clues to a fuller understanding from different sides of the spectrum.

Being white in Lima: a music ethnography

Pamela Rodríguez is a 34-year-old white singer and composer from Lima. She hails from a family of musicians and cites her main influences as Chabuca Granda and Susana Baca, two Peruvian *criollo* musicians from different socioeconomic and racial backgrounds. Chabuca Granda was a white upper-class Peruvian composer (1920–83) who collaborated with Afroperuvian and *criollo* musicians to innovate in traditional *limeño criollo* genres, such as the *vals peruano*, by including Afroperuvian harmonic and rhythmic elements. Susana Baca, a black Afroperuvian singer, was her protégée. After Chabuca's death, Susana continued to develop these harmonic innovations in *criolla* and Afroperuvian music. Between the early 1980s and mid 1990s, Susana focused on more traditional Afroperuvian song. After 1995, and already under the aegis of David Byrne (Scottish-born American musician, founder of Talking Heads and later world music producer), Susana would develop her characteristic minimalistic sound, which she would consolidate throughout the 2000s under the musical direction of David Pinto. Susana would prove a great influence on young white upper-class fusion artists, especially on the Afro-jazz scene.

Rodríguez chose this scene for her performances, adopting Chabuca and Susana as her main influences. *Criollo* music was for Rodríguez a way to explore her Peruvianness in traditional music, drawing out her interactions with popular culture:[21]

> I explored Peruvianness in *lo afro* [the Afro] and the *lo andino* [Andean] cultures. I began to learn the *landó, zamacueca, marinera* rhythms, harmonies, melodies. I mean, I really broke it all down on a theoretical level, because, of course, I hadn't grown up in *peñas*[22] and that was my frustration at one point, right? Why didn't I grow up in those cultural centres and why didn't my family take me to that? Why have I been living listening to a type of music [foreign music], which is awesome, yes, but why haven't I experienced Peruvianness the way other people have? [in an

---

21 It is worth noting that even though Chabuca Granda was a white upper-class singer/composer of *criollo* music, no studies exist which address her whiteness in the *criollo* scene.

22 Clubs where people can sing and dance to Afroperuvian and *criollo* music.

indignant tone]. (interview, Miraflores, Lima, 4 March 2011)

Rodríguez abandoned her formal music studies in Texas and returned to Peru to continue exploring more Peruvian genres and later mix them with jazz music structures. In Afroperuvian music she says she found her 'Peruvian gene' and several Afro-jazz pieces emerged. She released two albums of contemporary Afroperuvian music: *Peru blue* (2005) and *En la orilla* (2007).

> I returned [to Peru] and I went to the *peñas* every day … EVERY day and I danced in the streets, because I was born a party girl (*jaranera*) … I felt repressed at home to a certain point … I grew up in a family of girls from [the exclusive private school] San Silvestre, with parents who are all that … when I could step out of the box, I did and from then on I lived by my own rules … I have always been irritated by the inflexibility of the Lima white upper class, I'm really sick of it. (interview, Miraflores, Lima, 4 March 2011)

Rodríguez describes her class background as repressive and makes it clear that she would prefer to distance herself from the 'standard' Lima upper-class lifestyle. Given that the Afroperuvian scene is predominantly black, Rodríguez usually performed with well-known black musicians. She states that being blonde and white on the Afroperuvian scene made things complicated and that she encountered difficulties with some performers, composers and even academics:

> You are the silly blonde daddy's girl who doesn't fight for anything [pause]. But you know what? It stopped hurting, 'cause I got street smart [laughter]. (interview, Miraflores, Lima, 4 March 2011)

As a composer of *criollo* music, which is perceived as a nationalist genre (Turino, 2003, p. 198), Pamela somehow did not fit in; people did not associate her with what they perceived as 'authentically Peruvian'.

> I feel that my physical stereotype doesn't help me [when making music], because there is a stereotype based on my physical traits … of girls from European-Peruvian families, who go to such-and-such a school, have money and are racist … no, the word racism is not one I know, I mean, it isn't in my dictionary. (interview, Miraflores-Lima, 4 March 2011)

Rodríguez, while acknowledging the commonly perceived monolithic identity of the white, rich racist, distances herself from racism; she acknowledges her own racialised identity and problematises its consequences, while addressing her whiteness and class through empathetic inter-racial music collaborations. In her discourse, the artist directly emphasises racial authenticity, repeatedly validating her own engagement with the Afroperuvian tradition by mentioning that she plays with 'authentic performers'. She does not make much explicit reference to ideas or concepts that Kimberly Davis (2014, p. 78) would term racial sincerity – an act of 'sincere commitment to undermine white supremacy, to learn from the creative work of people of colour, to work empathetically in solidarity with marginalised people, and to remain self-aware of how [her] own whiteness ... complicates [her] role in the struggle against racism'.

Following a passionate discussion with friends in Lima about Peru's diversity, multiculturalism and integration, Rodríguez composed a *criollo* fusion, 'Perú a voces', an optimistic anthem for social change in Lima:[23]

El Perú que me canta,	*The Peru that sings to me,*
con sus voces me encanta,	*with its voices charms me,*
es el coro de color multicolor.	*is the choir of multicoloured colour.*
Viva la voz de la igualdad,	*Long live the voice of equality,*
canta la libertad.	*freedom sings.*
Un país de confluencias,	*A country made of confluences,*
de sangre bellas y diversas,	*of beautiful and diverse bloodlines,*
gente que con tolerancia,	*people who with tolerance,*
olvidó sus diferencias.	*forgot their differences.*
El Perú que me canta,	*The Peru that sings to me,*
con sus voces me encanta,	*with its voices charms me,*
es el coro de color multicolor,	*is the choir of multicoloured colour,*
voces dispuestas a sonar,	*voices ready to sound,*
heridas que van a sanar.	*wounds that will heal.*

This composition was criticised by other composers and academics arguing that it was naïve and ignored poverty and suffering in Peru – something Rodríguez could not understand, not having experienced living on the margins. Coincidentally, other upper-class fusion performers have also been described as 'naïve', a term *limeños* commonly associate with sheltered and privileged backgrounds. The not-so-subtle implication is that they cannot possibly speak of racial or class issues with any credibility, as they have been cosseted, do not know what it is like to face true adversity and are distanced from *la gente* [the people]. However, most contemporary white upper-class fusion performers contest this stereotype by playing genres associated with being 'street smart' and with understanding 'the people', even though they may not belong to 'the people', and in this way make their musical creations more authentic.

> I love Peru in general. If I didn't like Peru so much I wouldn't have wrecked my brain trying to figure out how to make my music taste like *combi* [popular public transport], like the knife sharpener, the little newsstand instead of something else, so ... that passion is really in fashion, but in jazz, right? What made me fall out of love a little [with jazz] was that there was no popular connection, right? I'm not talking about fame, or concerts with thousands of people, I'm talking about 'mmm *qué rico* mama, that is bloody brilliant' [putting on a more working-class intonation]. It didn't have that, I didn't want to take that ingredient out of what I do ... I love that ... I believe that this need to include ourselves is

23 Source and permission: Pamela Rodríguez.

something all generations have in common. I see my poshest friends who know the people who work with them, and through them I think they have gotten to know a lot. (Joaquín Mariátegui, lead guitarist of Bareto, interview, September 2010)

However, as Cepeda (2010, p. 129) discusses in his examination of Carlos Vives, a white upper-class Colombian performer of *vallenato*,

> upon defending his place in the genre [as a white performer], Vives swiftly falls into the type of *vallenato* posturing that is based on one's knowledge of certain people and places ... thereby to some extent engaging in the same superficial tests of authenticity as his detractors.

Rodríguez's views of a 'multi-coloured' country, 'made of confluences, of diverse bloodlines, with tolerant people who forget their differences', can be interpreted as a colour-blind stance, an avoidance of seeing the realities of racism and racial inequality (colour and power evasiveness, in the terms of Frankenberg, 1993, p. 14). But perhaps Rodríguez's colour-blindness is part of an initial emotional response to inserting herself in racialised inequality. Whites in Lima are not often exposed to social situations that force them to decide whether to empathise, sympathise or 'betray'[24] their own whiteness. However, through inter-racial music and socialising across this scene, some are exposed to emotional responses to the reality of racialised identities, compelling them to reflect on their social position and make an informed decision about their interaction with other racialised people, be they black, indigenous, or other white individuals (Montero-Diaz, 2016, p. 199).

Leslie Patten, a well-known young fusion percussionist who often collaborates with different fusion groups, also felt *encajonada* [pigeonholed] in an upper-class stereotype, even branded by a well-known composer as '*la blanquita de la percusión*' [the little white girl on percussion].

> It happened to me a whole lot, with my own album too, I mean, what is this little white girl doing playing black stuff or what is a woman doing playing the *cajón*? ... or what is this kid doing recording an album? (interview, November 2010)

Patten expresses feeling limited by racialised stereotyping on several occasions, an experience she shares with other white upper-class musicians I have interviewed. In fact, it even led Patten to stop playing in certain bands. Interestingly, she not only experienced discrimination from people considered 'inside' the tradition and therefore perceived as 'authentic' performers, but also from other white upper-class fusion musicians, who maligned her in an effort to acquire credibility, or a 'from the *barrio*' image and sound. For them, Patten lacked *calle* ['street cred']; ordinary people could not relate to her music, which they saw as lacking

---

24 This is a reference to Richard Delgado's discussion (1996, pp. 31–6) of the idea of transforming white empathy into racial treason in order to resist and renounce white privilege and racist structures. The term 'racial traitor' was coined by Noel Ignatiev and John Garvey (1993) as a path towards the abolition of whiteness.

a 'physical presence', which should have been there in her movements, audience interaction and choice of rhythmic patterns. Patten was told she was *muy exacta* [too accurate], *muy pituca* [too posh] and *muy tiesa* [too stiff] to play popular Peruvian genres such as *huayno*, *chicha* or Peruvian *cumbia*. As these are seen as 'popular' working-class genres, rhythmic precision and melodic clarity were seen as unnecessary – too academic, too sophisticated. Objections extended to the way she swayed to the rhythm on stage, which for some was 'too white'. It appears that in Lima the notion remains embedded that some people are 'natural biological bearers of culture', and therefore predisposed to playing certain genres better (as 'primitives') (Haynes, 2013, pp. 51–2). It is worth mentioning that all the performers noted as 'authentic' in most interviews with white upper-class fusionists fitted the racialised stereotype of the genre they played. So black performers were perceived as 'authentic', while whites were not. For Haynes (2013, pp. 51–2), this reinforces essentialist notions of cultural identity as something 'pure and authentic'. But, if indigeneity and blackness are the 'authentic' culture, are there any 'authentic' contemporary white Peruvian traditions?

White fusion performers acknowledge the change in Lima's music scene, where upper-class musicians and audiences are starting to enjoy and embrace Andean and Peruvian traditional music, re-evaluating certain genres previously perceived as being in bad taste, due to their popularity among indigenous audiences and the working classes, and attempting to free them of stigma.[25] However, since our conversations, Pamela Rodríguez has moved into pop music, leaving Afroperuvian genres behind. In describing her album *ReconoceR* (2011), she wrote: 'there is nothing more valuable and beautiful than being yourself, loving yourself on your own terms and accepting yourself the way you are', which is perhaps tacitly revealing.[26] Is she choosing to embrace her limiting whiteness, returning to the pigeonhole her phenotype and perceived social position would confine her to? By 2011–12, Leslie Patten was mainly focusing on her personal music projects and her music school for children, Kalimbá. This suggests that racialisation and stereotyping may have led both performers to move into different areas and re-think how they engage with musical genres, musicians, venues and audiences.

It seems that some white upper-class fusion musicians' attempts to recreate themselves start with collaboration and a desire to blend different musical aesthetics. The musical pose, attitude and style they adopt is their way of claiming – sonically – that they belong to the city, possess *calle dura* ['street cred'], are part of a *rico barrio* [marginal neighbourhood], and can perform with *rico veneno* [a flavour of the streets]. However, such attempts are often viewed with mistrust by non-white and other white musicians alike. Certain

---

25 For more on the racialisation of musical genres and Andean imaginaries of Lima's upper classes see Montero-Diaz (2017, pp. 74–94).

26 La Mula, 26 Jan. 2012, http://lamula.pe/2012/01/24/pamela-rodriguez-en-crudo-y-en-directo/lamula (accessed 26 March 2019).

members of the 'alternative' white upper classes I interviewed during fieldwork acknowledged that although they had not shared the marginal experiences of most residents in Lima, they nevertheless sought to share in the city they have in common, trying to find a place for and to validate their experiences and identities in order not to remain on the privileged fringes, but to really share in the city, its politics, its protests, its daily life. In many cases, music becomes a tool to enact racial betrayal and escape the markers of whiteness – to transcend musical aesthetics in search of a real music experience and to expand the narrow social and geographical sphere white upper-class musicians usually navigate – their 'allowed spaces'. In this way, 'music becomes a source of collective consciousness which promotes group cohesion and social activities that in turn wield political consequences' (Frith, 2000, p. 317).

> Prejudice is something instilled in or imposed on you, right? And you grow up with that, but the rest, what's out there, you absorb that, whether you want to or not, whether it is good or bad, the violence of the *combi* driver, the corruption of the police officer, these are things that you absorb when you are little and you wind up becoming a person who has consumed all these nutrients. (Nicolás Duarte, leader of La Mente, interview, 24 November 2010) [27]

But some musicians go further than crossing the racialised borders of music (Davis, 2014, pp. 27–36). What comes after inter-racial sincerity, acknowledging racialised whiteness, and problematising one's own social role in society? What can white upper-class musicians do to change the status quo, transform themselves and engage in anti-racist action?

Sabor y Control, a *salsa dura* orchestra founded by white upper-class saxophonist Bruno Macher, a musician with experience of the fusion scene (for example, as saxophonist of La Mente) but now distanced from it, is an interesting example. Macher has led various social projects as the frontman of a band that seeks to 'define the *barrio*, the street, the corner, putting all those experiences into its interpretations, closely linked to our customs and daily life; that is why this orchestra's genre can be catalogued as "Peruvian Salsa"'.[28]

Sabor y Control has released seven albums, and song titles include: *El Bravo* [Badass], *La Calle está sabrosa* [the street has got flavour], *Alta peligrosidad* [highly dangerous], *Barrio bendito* [blessed *barrio*], and *Cruda realidad* [harsh reality]. These titles showcase the group's 'street cred' and interest in marginal and dangerous experiences in the city. However, Macher lives in one of the wealthiest areas of Lima, physically and culturally far away from the places

---

27 La Mente, a much-favoured band among the 'alternatives', released its first CD in 2007: *Sonidos del sistema La Mente – electropical*. The singers in the group, Nicolás Duarte and Ricardo Wiesse, found in La Mente a 'more liberating space for their lyrics and communication' (Nicolás Duarte, leader of La Mente, interview, Barranco, Lima, 24 Nov. 2010). They started playing ska, rock, reggae and *cumbia*, including live electronic.

28 Sabor y Control's website: http://www.saborycontrol.com/# (accessed 26 March 2019).

described in his music. So, as a way to approach the *barrio* and act on the orchestra's ideals of cohesion, Macher and Sabor y Control created a social project called 'Salsa a la Calle' [Salsa to the Streets]. People from working-class neighbourhoods could contact the orchestra to co-arrange with the musicians free live outdoor afternoon concerts coupled with workshops for local youth.[29] In this way, Macher and other members of Sabor y Control transcend their own leafy neighbourhoods in search of the community and gritty street experience they lacked growing up, while also showing respect for it, advocating peace among neighbourhoods, encouraging youth involvement in music, and promoting *barrio* values of cohesion and community building. These values of cohesion, inclusion and brother- and sisterhood start with the relationship between the members of the orchestra itself, as they also come from different neighbourhoods, ethnicities and social strata (Sabor y Control documentary, 2015). This evidences the anti-racist motivation of their projects. Moreover, as Sabor y Control attracts a broad white upper-class audience, as well as a following from marginal and impoverished neighbourhoods in Lima, the dissemination of their inclusive, anti-racist message transcends race, social strata and geographical origin.

Some of these marginal audiences appreciate having the band visit their neighbourhood, not as an exotic setting, but as real community engagement through social action:

> Brunito is a *gringo*, but he is really a *cholo gringo*. We are his '*señitos*' [neighbourhood matriarchs] and we love it when he comes to Rimac and you see he is sincere when he jokes around, hugs us, plays barrio songs and swears heartily. He might be a *colorado*, but he has got more street and *sabor* than many who live here. This always is and will be his *barrio bendito*! [blessed *barrio*]. (Dulce, resident of El Rimac neighbourhood, email communication, March 2016).

Joaquín Mariátegui, music director of Bareto, also highlights this appreciation and links it to the process of cross-over:

> I am a *limeño* and like a good *limeño* you have prejudices and things … I think that I have far fewer, now that I know Peru more, I think that the prejudice comes from ignorance, to a large extent, and when you know, your fear disappears. After that, working-class people receive me as a brother, so for me that is the most beautiful thing that can happen to me in my life, that they don't treat me like a posh whitey. (interview, Miraflores, Lima, 11 September 2010)

Fieldwork with focus groups, and extensive interviews with upper-class youths after events such as protests and marches, show that the impact of the music of Bareto, La Mente and Sabor y Control has led to the formation of new

29 'Salsa a la Calle' was planned as an annual concert in marginal neighbourhoods, usually three concerts a day for one or two days. They took place from 2010 to 2013. Concurrently and afterwards other projects were started, such as 'Salsa a la Cárcel' [salsa to the prison] and 'Conciertos de Pacificación' [peace concerts].

youth citizenships and political consciousness, amounting to the establishment of a white anti-racist agenda. This agenda goes beyond 'racial treason' (Ignatiev and Garvey, 1996) to transform whiteness through the transgression of 'allowed spaces', and the formation of real quotidian interaction and friendship.

> This isn't a white protest, we aren't kicking up a fuss in our privileged spheres. We're joining many other Peruvians, who aren't satisfied with the reality in which we live, with human rights violations, with poverty, discrimination. We're the privileged children of those who lead big private businesses and pernicious companies; we have a duty to rise up, for ourselves, for others. We don't agree with the shit our grandparents did, our parents … we won't prolong it. (Xavier, 26 years old, Lima, March 2012)

There seems to be no need to abolish whiteness, but there is an urge to recreate it in order to transform its monolithic meaning into a diverse non-passive fluid identity. The awareness of white privilege not only comes from empathy with non-white others, or from adopting a white ally attitude, but also from empathy with themselves, as they see themselves disfigured by privilege; they are aware of how harmful this is, so they take responsibility for change and respond through musical/political actions.

Conclusion

Andean musicians have long been stigmatised, together with the music they play. This is slowly changing and in previous research (Montero-Diaz, 2017, 2016) I argued that one of the many factors underpinning this change is the fact that intercultural, interracial and inter-social music projects are becoming more visible, which itself fosters the social transformation of white upper-class musicians/audiences, triggering an anti-racist discourse, and in some cases action. Still, many of these white musicians, especially young women, experience prejudice and are 'pigeonholed' in certain genres, mainly foreign – a fact that is often played down, even by the performers grappling with these issues. This brings to mind the words of film director Josué Méndez (2008, p. 214): 'the high class has a titanium shell, nothing affects them, they don't take it personally. It's very difficult to reach the soul, because they don't feel affected at all'.

While white performers should not and cannot be viewed as victims of any systematic institutionalised discrimination, acknowledging two-way tensions of racial segregation is essential. Most white upper-class Peruvians do not talk publicly about their journey through Peruvianness and experiences of segregation, but this does not mean that they are not affected, as Méndez claims. The racial segregation that white upper-class musicians experience is not systematic; it cannot and need not be categorised as racism. Nonetheless, such cultural segregation upholds inequality and reinforces resentment and *revanchista* [vindictive] discourse, leading to further unnecessary racial tension.

Sincere interracial music collaborations, dialogue and the coexistence of musicians of different ethnicities, classes and phenotypes[30] – the ones that conceptually go beyond validating the musical engagement created by simply playing with 'authentic' performers – can be a first step for white performers and audiences to experience the limitations of a racialised identity. In some cases these musicians' attempts to challenge segregation can seem naïve and are verbalised in colour-blind statements and racial stereotyping. Others characterise themselves as 'down and marginal' whites in order to validate their efforts to transgress racialised spaces. For most, this constitutes their first personal experience of racialisation, and can catalyse empathy with others who are systematically discriminated against in Lima. They can also catalyse empathy with themselves as they become aware of the legacy and damage still done by their own white privilege.

It is essential to address racism, segregation, exclusion and stereotyping from all angles without discriminating against any particular testimony. As long as it remains normal to say that 'white girls can't play,' the notion that people can be judged by the colour of their skin remains alive.

Bibliography

Acevedo Fernandez de Paredes, J. (2009 [1983]) *Ciudad de los Reyes* (2nd edn, Lima: Contracultura).

Ardito, W. (2010) 'La experiencia de la mesa contra el racismo', Universidad del Pacífico, Peru (draft shared by the author).

Arellano, R. (2010) *Al medio hay sitio. El crecimiento social según los estilos de vida* (Lima: Planeta).

Arellano, R. and D. Burgos (2004) *La Ciudad de los Reyes, de los Chávez, de los Quispe...* (Lima: Arellano IM).

Bailón, J. (2004) 'La chicha no muere ni se destruye, solo se transforma. Vida, historia y milagros de la cumbia peruana', *Iconos*, 18: 53–62.

Barrig, M. (1979) *Cinturón de castidad. La mujer de clase media en el Perú* (Lima: Mosca Azul).

— (1981) 'Pitucas y maracas en la nueva narrativa peruana', *Hueso Humero*, 9: 73–89.

Bishop, A. (2002 [1994]) *Becoming an Ally: Breaking the Cycle of Oppression* (Halifax, NS: Fernwood Publishing).

Bonnet, A. (2000) *White Identities: Historical and International Perspectives* (Cambridge: Pearson Education).

---

30 For more information on interracial fusion collaborations see Montero-Diaz (2017).

Bruce, J. (2007) *Nos habíamos choleado tanto. Psicoanálisis y racismo* (Lima: Universidad de San Martin de Porres).

Byrne, B. (2006) *White Lives: The Interplay of 'Race', Class and Gender in Everyday Life* (London: Routledge).

Cepeda, M.E. (2010) *Musical ImagiNation: US Colombian Identity and the Latin Music Boom* (New York: New York University Press).

Chuquimia, E., R. Jemio and A. López (2006) *Jailones: En torno a la identidad cultural de los jóvenes de la elite paceña* (La Paz: Fundación PIEB).

Davis, K.C. (2014) *Beyond the White Negro: Empathy and Anti-Racist Reading* (Urbana, IL: University of Illinois Press).

Degregori, C.I. (2000) *No hay país más diverso: Compendio de antropología peruana* (Lima: Red Para el Desarrollo de las Ciencias Sociales en el Perú).

Delgado, R. (1996) *The Coming Race War? And Other Apocalyptic Tales of America after Affirmative Action and Welfare* (New York: New York University Press).

Drzewieniecki, J. (2004) 'Peruvian youth and racism. The category of "race" remains strong'. Paper presented at the Meeting of the Latin American Studies Association. Las Vegas, Nevada, 7–9 Oct. 2004.

Durand, F. (1982) *Los industriales y el poder* (Lima: DESCO).

— (1994) *Business and Politics in Peru* (Boulder, CO: Westview Press).

— (2003) *Riqueza económica y pobreza política: Reflexiones sobre las elites del poder en un país instable* (Lima: Fondo Editorial de la PUCP).

— (2004a) *El poder incierto: Trayectoria económica y política del empresariado peruano* (Lima: Fondo Editorial del Congreso del Perú).

— (2004b) 'Los nuevos dueños del Perú', *Quehacer*, Oct./Nov., available at: http://www.rebelion.org/docs/9442.pdf (accessed 31 March 2019).

— (2007) 'La cultura criolla ha muerto', *Diario La Primera*, 29 Jan. 2007.

Eakin, M.C. (2007) *The History of Latin America: Collision of Cultures* (New York: Palgrave Macmillan).

Frankenberg, R. (1993) *White Women, Race Matters: The Social Construction of Whiteness* (Minneapolis, MN: University of Minnesota Press).

Frith, S. (2000) 'The discourse of world music', in G. Born and D. Hesmondhalgh (eds.), *Western Music and its Others: Difference, Representation and Appropriation in Music* (Berkeley, CA: University of California Press), pp. 305–22.

Fuller, N. (1993) *Dilemas de la femineidad: Mujeres de clase media en el Perú* (Lima: Pontificia Universidad Católica del Perú).

— (1997) *Identidades masculinas: varones de clase media en el Perú* (Lima: Pontificia Universidad Católica del Perú).

Galindo Flores, A. (1994 [1986]) *Buscando un inca. Identidad y utopía en los Andes* (Lima: Horizonte).

García, M.E. (2005) *Making Indigenous Citizens* (Stanford, CA: Stanford University Press).

Garner, S. (2007) *Whiteness: An Introduction* (London: Routledge).

González Cueva, E. (1994) 'Ciudades paralelas: una investigación sobre el imaginario urbano' (Lima: Pontificia Universidad Católica del Perú BA dissertation).

Hale, C. (2006) *Más que un indio: Racial Ambivalence and Neoliberal Multiculturalism in Guatemala* (Santa Fe, NM: School of American Research Press).

Haynes, J. (2013) *Music, Difference and the Residue of Race* (London: Routledge).

Hills, M. (2002) *Fan Cultures* (London: Routledge).

Hopenhayn, M. (1999) 'La aldea global entre la utopía transcultural y el ratio mercantil: paradojas de la globalización cultural', in C.I. Degregori and G. Portocarrero (eds.), *Cultura y globalización* (Lima: Red para el Desarrollo de las Ciencias Sociales en el Perú), pp. 17–35.

Ignatiev, N. and J. Garvey, (eds.) (1996) *Race Traitor* (New York: Routledge).

Iturriaga Acevedo, E. (2011) 'Las elites de la Ciudad Blanca: racismo, prácticas y discriminación étnica en Mérida, Yucatán' (Mexico: Universidad Nacional Autónoma de México PhD thesis).

Kogan, L. (2009) *Regias y conservadores: mujeres y hombres de clase alta en la Lima de los noventa* (Lima: Fondo Editorial del Congreso del Peru).

León, R. (2000) *La China Tudela: antologia de sus crónicas* (Lima: Apoyo).

— (2004) *La China Tudela y la panaca real* (Lima: Grupo Editorial Norma).

— (2006) *La expulsión del paraíso (según la China Tudela)* (Lima: Planeta).

Malpica, C. (1990) *El poder económico en el Perú* (Lima: Mosca Azul Editores).

Mariátegui, J.C. (1970) *Siete ensayos de interpretación de la realidad peruana* (Lima: Amauta).

Méndez, J. (2008) *Dioses* (Lima: Santillana S.A).

Modood, T. (1990) 'Catching up with Jesse Jackson: being oppressed and being somebody', *New Community*, 17 (1): 397–404.

Montero-Diaz, F. (2016) 'Singing the war: reconfiguring white upper-class identity through fusion music in post-war Lima', *Ethnomusicology Forum*, 25 (2): 191–209.

— (2017) 'YouTubing the "other": Lima's upper classes and Andean imaginaries', in T. Hilder, S.E Tan and H. Stobart (eds.), *Music, Indigeneity, Digital Media* (Rochester, NY: University of Rochester Press), pp. 74–94.

Moreno Figueroa, M. (2010) 'Distributed intensities: whiteness, mestizaje and the logics of Mexican racism', *Ethnicities* 10 (3): 387–401.

Portocarrero, G. (1993) *Racismo y mestizaje* (Lima: Ediciones Sur).

— (ed.) (1998) *Las clases medias: entre la pretensión y la incertidumbre* (Lima: Ediciones Sur).

Ramos-García, L. (2003) 'Rock 'n' roll in Peru's popular quarters: cultural identity, hybridity and transculturation', in F.R. Aparicio and C.F. Jaquez (eds.), *Musical Migrations: Transnationalism and Cultural Hybridity in Latin America*, vol. I (New York: Palgrave Macmillan), pp. 199–206.

Riveros Vásquez, C. (2012*)* 'Formas de organización de las escenas musicales alternas en Lima. El caso de las bandas ska del bar Bernabé', (Lima: Pontificia Universidad Católica del Perú BA dissertation).

Romero, R.R. (2007) *Andinos y tropicales: La cumbia peruana en la ciudad global* (Lima: Instituto de Etnomusicología Andina, Pontificia Universidad Católica del Perú).

Stepan, N.L. (1991) *'The Hour of Eugenics': Race, Gender and Nation in Latin America* (Ithaca, NY: Cornell University Press).

Telles, E. and Project on Ethnicity and Race in Latin America (2014), *Pigmentocracies: Ethnicity, Race and Color in Latin America* (Chapel Hill, NC: University of North Carolina Press).

Telles, E. and R. Flores (2013) 'Not just color: whiteness, nation, and status in Latin America', *Hispanic American Historical Review*, 93 (3): 411– 49.

Tulloch, J. and H. Jenkins (1995) *Science Fiction Audiences: Watching 'Doctor Who' and 'Star Trek'* (London: Routledge).

Turino, T. (1993) *Moving Away from Silence: Music of the Peruvian Altiplano and the Experiment of Urban Migration* (Chicago, IL: University of Chicago Press).

— (2003) 'Nationalism and Latin American music: selected case studies and theoretical considerations', *Latin American Music Review,* 24 (2): 169–209.

Turner, J. (2014) 'Uma cultura atrasada: the Luso-Baroque *manezinha*, hyperwhiteness, and the modern middle classes in Florianópolis, Brazil', *Journal of Latin American and Caribbean Anthropology*, 19 (1): 84–102.

Van Dijk, T.A. (2005) *Racism and Discourse in Spain and Latin America* (Amsterdam: John Benjamins Publishing Company).

Venturo Schultz, S. (2001) *Contrajuventud: Ensayos sobre juventud y participación política en Lima* (Lima: IEP).

Wade, P. (1997) *Race and Ethnicity in Latin America* (Chicago, IL: Pluto Press).

— (2005) 'Rethinking mestizaje: ideology and lived experience', *Journal of Latin American Studies*, 37: 239–57.

— (2008) 'Race in Latin America', in D. Poole (ed.), *A Companion to Latin American Anthropology* (Oxford: Blackwell Publishing), pp. 177–92.

— (2010) 'The presence and absence of race', *Patterns of Prejudice*, 44 (1): 43–60.

Discography

Rodriguez, P. (2005) Peru Blue. IEMPSA. IEM-75000573 (Peru).

— (2007) En la Orilla. IEMPSA. IEM-0647-2 (Peru).

— (2011) ReconoceR. Mamacha Productions Sac (Peru).

Sabor y Control (2006) El Guapo Soy Yo. Independent Label (Lima, Peru).

— (2008) Cuchillo en los Ojos (Lima, Peru).

— (2009) Alta Peligrosidad (Lima, Peru).

— (2010) Barrio Bendito (Lima, Peru).

— (2011) El Más Buscado (Lima, Peru).

— (2012) Cruda Realidad (Lima, Peru).

— (2014) Humildad (Lima, Peru).

Filmography

Dioses (2008) Josué Méndez. Prod. Enid Campos. Chullachaki Cine (Peru), Lagarto Cine (Argentina), TS Productions (France), Mil Colores Media & Cachoeira Films (Germany).

Madeinusa (2006) Claudia Llosa. Prod. José María Morales, Antonio Chavarrías and Claudia Llosa. Vela Films (Lima, Peru), Wanda Visión (Madrid, Spain) and Oberón Cinematográfica (Barcelona, Spain).

Sabor y Control. Revolución por la Paz. 'Un documental dedicado a los barrios' (2015) Sabor y Control. Play Music & Video (Lima, Peru).

9. Bolivia's anti-racism law: transforming a culture?*

Henry Stobart

The catalyst for Bolivia's 2010 law 'against racism and all forms of discrimination' (law 045) is conventionally and officially identified with a large-scale incident that took place in the city of Sucre (Bolivia's constitutional capital) on 24 May 2008 – a date later declared as the national day against racism and discrimination (law 139 of 2011). In this ugly episode, some 40 *originario* ['native'] people from the provinces who had travelled to the city to welcome president Evo Morales, and take possession of ambulances gifted from Spain, were rounded up by a huge mob of townspeople, forced to strip to the waist and led to the central square. Here, they were made to kneel in humiliation beside the entrance of the Casa de la Libertad [House of Liberty]. Their *wiphala* flags – symbolising native identity – were burnt, they were subjected to verbal and physical abuse and they were forced to kiss the flag of Sucre in an act of submission.[1] The scale, violence and unprecedented nature of this attack, which provoked widespread national and international condemnation, was shocking and remains hard to reconcile with Sucre's usual reputation as a sleepy backwater, beloved by tourists, where 'nothing happens'.

Sucre's 'racist' incident can be interpreted in the context of the rise to power of Evo Morales in 2006, as Bolivia's first 'indigenous president', and the tensions that surrounded the Sucre-based writing of the country's new constitution.[2] In its final stages, in November 2007, this process erupted into violence, tragedy and a wave of destruction which undoubtedly prefigured

---

* My thanks to the late Gregorio Mamani, his family and the many other friends in Bolivia who so generously contributed to this research. Gratitude is also due to Cassandra Torrico, who first suggested focusing my research on Gregorio. The patience, astute comments and editing of Peter Wade and James Scorer are especially appreciated, as is the understanding and support of my wife Diura. I gratefully acknowledge the support towards the research featured in this chapter that was received from the British Academy and the UK Arts and Humanities Research Council.

1 See also Calla et al. (2011, p. 311) and Gotkowitz (2011, pp. 35–6).

2 See, e.g., Gotkowitz (2011), Calla and Muruchi (2011), Calla et al. (2011) and Ströbele-Gregor (2011). Morales was brought up in a native community and is widely identified as 'indigenous'. However, this subject position has sometimes been questioned, and even denied by Morales himself, who often prefers to stress his labour union background. See 'Evo "nunca" se consideró un presidente indígena', *Página siete*, 25 Sept. 2011.

H. Stobart, 'Bolivia's anti-racism law: transforming a culture?', in P. Wade, J. Scorer and I. Aguiló (eds.), *Cultures of Anti-Racism in Latin America and the Caribbean* (London: Institute of Latin American Studies, 2019), pp. 191–212. License: CC-BY-NC-ND 4.0.

Figure 9.1. Burning tyres on the streets of Sucre on 25 November 2007 on the morning after the deaths of three capitalía *protesters. (Photo by Henry Stobart.)*

and, in part, motivated the actions of 24 May 2008 (see fig 9.1). At the heart of this conflict was Sucre's demand that Bolivia's seat of government be returned to the city from La Paz, where it was relocated following the Liberal War of 1899. An extended official enquiry was undertaken into the incident of 24 May, lasting many years, and in 2016 12 ex-authorities who had been involved in the incident were sentenced to jail terms, mainly of six years.[3] All 12 defendants then appealed, rejecting the ruling as unfair and political, and have avoided serving prison terms for the incident.[4] Since 2008 several of these defendants have held high-profile civic and political positions in Sucre, clearly with strong local support, which raises questions about how much attitudes and the underlying political climate have changed.

The incident of 24 May has also been understood in the context of a long history of 'silent racism of a structural and quotidian nature' (Calla and Muruchi, 2011, p. 300). Such an approach suggests that racism has a deep and persistent aspect that is embedded in multiple cultural dimensions. Indeed, scholars have long viewed culture as a key basis for racist thought and practices, although attitudes to how this intersects with biology have shifted over time. In the 21st century, according to Laura Gotkowitz (2011, p. 9), 'culture is racism's dominant figure; it lies at the center of racist rhetoric and practice'. If culture and racism are so intimately entwined, it is perhaps not surprising that of the many laws created by Evo Morales during his second term as president, none 'produced as much dissent and strife' as law 045 (Calla et al., 2011, p. 314). According to Pamela Calla and the Observatorio del Racismo research group (2011), critics expressed concerns about the law's potential effectiveness, its punitive nature, and the way it reserved the most severe penalties for public officials, rather than taking a more holistic approach. The most heated objections came from journalists, who viewed certain articles as infringing freedom of expression. For example, Article 16 states that 'Communications media that authorise and publicise racist or discriminatory ideas will be subject to economic sanctions and suspension of operating licenses.' A nationwide hunger strike by journalists was, however, unsuccessful and the law was passed with the original wording (Calla et al., 2011, p. 315).

Newspaper reports from 2014 characterised the law as 'not worth the paper it was written on', arguing that there had been no prosecutions, despite the hundreds of complaints received by the vice-ministry of decolonisation, which is responsible for enacting the law. The Afrobolivian congressman, Jorge Medina, who had promoted the law, countered these criticisms by stressing the need for conciliation, where an apology from an aggressor was favoured over punishment, and arguing that the spirit of the law was 'not to

---

3   'Los sentenciados rechazaron el fallo por considerarlo injusto y político. Anunciaron la apelación del fallo', *Página siete*, 2 March 2016.

4   See 'Caso de 24 Mayo: los 12 sentenciados siguen libres', *Cambio*, 6 April 2017.

fill the prisons with those who discriminate.'⁵ In October 2016 the law was reinforced by the launch of the smartphone app *No Racismo*, created jointly by Bolivia's ministry of communications and vice-ministry of decolonisation. This provides a phone or chat line to report acts of racism or discrimination, alongside news items, reports, statistics, photos, videos and details of the law. New technology of this kind suggests a strategic focus on students and young people among whom smartphone ownership has grown exponentially in recent years. This stress on younger people and students, who were identified as the primary perpetrators of the violence in Sucre, has also been manifested in the initiative of Student Brigades against Racism and Discrimination. The second national meeting of this organisation, held in Santa Cruz in May 2017, was attended by more than 2,000 school students from around the country and officially opened by Evo Morales. In his speech, Morales claimed that Bolivia had 'managed to recover its identity through recognising its 36 native-peasant nations in the constitution as well as through respect for their culture, clothing, music, dance and language'. He went on to observe that 'the only way to decolonise ourselves is through recovering our dress, our lifeways, and our music. The music's content that is sung is for unity, for the Mother Earth.'⁶ Thus, in the context of a major national event dedicated to combatting racism and discrimination, it was cultural expressions that Morales highlighted, pointing in particular to the unifying nature of native music and its connection with the environment. Wilma Alanoca, Bolivia's minister for culture and tourism, also spoke at this meeting's inauguration, emphasising the progress made in the 'process of change' over the 11 years of Morales' presidency. In her view, nothing now blocked the advance of the cultural revolution. Both these key government representatives related combatting racism and discrimination to transforming culture. What, then, might such cultural transformation involve?

When Morales spoke of achieving decolonisation through recovering native-peasant dress, lifeways and music, characterising these as 'our' expressions, questions emerge about *who* this includes and what 'recovery' might mean. Is this an inclusive 'all Bolivians'? Is he suggesting that a form of unity results when cultural expressions, such as music, dance and dress, are 'recovered' from native-peasant peoples, so that all Bolivians can sing, dance and dress up in them together? Images of massive and colourful urban folklore parades spring to mind, alongside a sense of national(istic) unity (Bigenho and Stobart, 2016). Let's not forget, Morales formerly played the trumpet in Oruro-based brass bands that accompanied these large folklore parades. If this is what he was alluding to in his speech, it sounds strikingly reminiscent of Bolivia's 1952 national revolutionary project, which aimed to create a mestizo

5   Franz Chávez, 'Bolivia's anti-racism law – not worth the paper it's written on?', *Inter Press Service,* 13 Feb. 2014.
6   Ministry of culture and tourism (minculturas.gob.bo) news report: 'En 11 años de gobierno Bolivia rompe barreras contra el racismo y la discriminación', 23 May 2017.

nation, represented by a national folklore derived from native-peasant sources, adapted according to European-orientated aesthetics and values to make it 'safe for the nation' (Bigenho, 2005). As elsewhere in Latin America, this 1952 vision of turning all Bolivians into mestizo citizens certainly spoke to an anti-racist agenda or post-racial imaginary. Combatting discrimination was also manifested in the policy of replacing the racist term *indio* ['Indian'] with *campesino* [peasant], thereby erasing ethnic and racial differences in favour of workers' rights and unionism. In this former revolutionary context, native culture became a rich and colourful resource to be mined in order to construct a national folklore culture.

However, from the perspective of contemporary indigenous politics, the 'recovery' of cultural expressions (or their mining for national folklore) looks like 'appropriation' or 'plagiarism'. When Morales speaks of having managed to recover Bolivia's identity through 'recognising its 36 native-peasant nations in the Constitution', he is invoking the official recognition of the country's multiple indigenous peoples in the 2009 constitution – and the re-founding of the country as the 'Plurinational State of Bolivia'.[7] (As a reminder, it was conflicts surrounding the creation of this document in Sucre, between August 2006 and November 2007, which prefigured the violence of 24 May). The 2009 constitution not only recognises the existence of the country's 'indigenous native peasant nations and peoples' but also officially protects their cultural expressions and safeguards their intangible rights over such expressions.[8] When we return to the question of what *recovery* of native-peasant traditions might mean, and who the *we* Morales invokes might – or might not – include, it quickly becomes apparent that expressions of native music, dance and dress are deeply interwoven with the politics of identity and alterity. So, should 'recovery' simply be understood as native culture-bearers making their traditions more visible and maintaining control over them? Might such visibility involve or resist commercialisation? Is adaptation to be welcomed or opposed? As we pose these questions, we quickly discover that we are in deeply contested territory, with long histories of discriminatory practices. For example, as in many other countries, Bolivia's 1992 copyright law cast native music as national property, thereby giving (non-native) citizens liberty to adapt, register and commercialise it as their own (Sanchez, 2001; Bigenho, 2002, p. 221; Brown, 2003). To what extent, then, might 'maintaining control' involve native people employing legal measures to exclude or require payment from non-natives? Can we talk of a

7   The Bolivian political constitution was ratified by national referendum in Jan. 2009.

8   According to article 100 of the 2009 constitution: (i) The world views, myths, oral history, dances, cultural practices, knowledge and traditional technologies are the heritage of the indigenous native peasant nations and peoples. This patrimony forms part of the expression and identity of the state. (ii) The state will protect this wisdom and knowledge through the registration of intellectual property which safeguards the intangible rights of indigenous native peasant nations and peoples, and of intercultural and Afrobolivian communities. In article 102, it is stated that both individual and collective property rights will be protected.

kind of 'payback' time? – one that employs some of the very same weapons of exclusion. Viewed from such a perspective, we might ask: do the practices and discourses surrounding native-peasant cultural expressions – such as music, dance and dress – contribute to perpetuating and even hardening the structures of racism and other forms of discrimination? Alternatively, as Morales' speech suggested, should we look to native-peasant cultural expressions for solutions to Bolivia's deep-seated structures of racism and discrimination? These questions form the central focus for the reflections in this chapter.

My perspective on these questions draws on my encounters with a number of Sucre-based musicians, most especially Gregorio Mamani Villacorta (1960–2011), who formed the central focus of my research over 11 months in Sucre in 2007–8. How did this *originario* ('native') artist and indigenous activist, from a humble rural background, negotiate the socially uneven terrains he inhabited? What were the implications of Evo Morales' rise to power for native people like Gregorio[9], and how did race, class and other forms of social difference shape his opportunities and challenges? I then turn to the impact of Morales' presidency on urban mestizo musicians, whose perspectives we hear before a final concluding section dedicated to a tourist-focused culture show in Sucre. But first let us explore the background to the incident of 24 May.

Evo Morales and the Sucre *capitalía* protests

It is perhaps unsurprising that the rise to power of Evo Morales in 2006, as Bolivia's first 'indigenous president', would provoke a strong backlash from certain quarters of the population. The most extreme opposition came from the gas- and soya-rich Eastern lowland departments of the so-called *media luna* [half-moon-shaped area], especially Santa Cruz, which had already been proposing autonomy from highland Bolivia (Ballvé, 2005; Dunkerley, 2007). Under Morales, indigenous people became paradigmatic citizens who occupied a 'privileged position vis-à-vis the state' (Canessa, 2012, p. 204), thus overturning long-established structures of political power, and challenging naturalised understandings of social hierarchy, privilege and identity. From the perspective of Sucre's privileged classes 'giving power to the "*indios*" or allowing them to participate politically mean[t] to relinquish the country to the less civilized, the uneducated, the inept, the inferior' (Ströbele-Gregor, 2011, p. 83). Despite such views, in 2005 Chuquisaca department, of which Sucre is capital, had strongly supported Morales' election with 54 per cent of the vote. It was also one of only three departments to elect a government-supported Movimiento al Socialismo (MAS) prefect, David Sánchez. However, only three years later, in 2008, following the violent so-called *capitalía* protests, demanding

---

9   I use Gregorio's first name to reflect the close friendship we developed and my status as *compadre* [co-parent] to the family, as a sponsor (with my wife) of his eldest daughter's wedding cake.

that the seat of government be returned to the city, Sucre had transformed into an important centre of government opposition. Indeed, in the 2008 recall election Morales was rejected by 67 per cent of Sucre's population (Centellas, 2010, p. 162). These conflicts also led Chuquisaca to become highly polarised between city and countryside, with opposition to Morales centred on the urban population.

In Sucre, local people often refer to their city as the 'capital'. Indeed, it is Bolivia's official constitutional and judicial capital, and hence was host to the constitutional assembly convened to write a new constitution. Losing its historical status as 'full capital', following the civil war in 1899, has long been a source of resentment in Sucre and is used to explain the city's lack of economic dynamism and other woes; complaints that I have heard on and off since first visiting the city in the 1980s. The theme of returning Sucre to 'full capital' status arose a few months after the inauguration of the constitutional assembly (6 August 2006) and was reiterated on several occasions during 2007.[10] In March 2007, a so-called 'citizen interest group' began to mobilise in the form of the 'interinstitutional committee' represented by civic leaders and business interests, led by the rector of the university, Jaime Barrón (Defensor, 2008, p. 79).[11] The strong support for the *capitalía* proposal, voiced by opposition assembly members from eastern lowland departments, was undoubtedly less aimed at benefiting Sucre than harming La Paz; its primary object was to derail the work of the constitutional assembly.

Government attempts to veto discussion of the full capital proposal by the assembly were clumsily handled, further exacerbating tensions.[12] By late September 2007, when I arrived in Sucre with my family to commence research, *capitalía* demonstrations and marches through the city were a daily occurrence, and bands of university students regularly gathered outside the Gran Mariscal theatre to obstruct the work of constituent assembly members. A particular target for harassment and racist insults were Aymara assembly members who wore the *pollera* (Carrasco and Albó, 2008, p. 121). Many of the students involved came from other parts of the country, a particularly thuggish element being the Union Juvenil Cruceñista, a youth wing of the Comité Civico of Santa Cruz (Ströbele-Gregor, 2011, p. 78). This ongoing intimidation and obstruction of access to the Gran Mariscal theatre provoked organisations

10 Fabio Porcél of the opposition party Podemos, raised the topic of returning Sucre to 'full capital' status during an assembly meeting on 2 Nov. 2006 (Carrasco and Albó, 2008, p. 103; Plaza et al., 2014, p. 266). A formal proposal from Sucre's inter-institutional committee was then made in March 2007, and proposed again by a group of nine opposition assembly members, mainly from the lowland regions of Santa Cruz, Beni, Pando and Tarija in June 2007 (Carrasco and Albó, 2008).

11 Key civic authorities represented on this committee included the city's mayor (Aidé Nava), its civic committee president (John Cava) and its municipal council president (Fidel Herrera).

12 Large-scale mobilisations vehemently rejecting Sucre's proposal were organised in La Paz and El Alto, where huge crowds chanted the slogan *la sede no se mueve* [the seat will not move].

allied to the MAS government to bring groups of indigenous people to Sucre to hold peaceful vigils intended to enable the constituent assembly to continue its work. These vigils were often violently dislodged by the pro-*capitalía* students and – in an attempt to quickly finalise the draft constitution – on 23 November the constituent assembly was relocated to the military training school (Liceo Militar) on the outskirts of the city. On the afternoon of 24 November, and through the night, crowds of *capitalía* protesters attempted to reach the Liceo Militar, which was surrounded by a largely indigenous pro-government vigil. A police cordon, separating the groups, used tear gas and rubber bullets to hold the protesters back, but the violent skirmishes with the police resulted in three deaths among the protesters, who have become known in Sucre as the 'martyrs of Calancha'. Gradually, through the night, the assembly members were evacuated – a draft text having been agreed for the new constitution – and the vigil dispersed. The next day the police retreated from the city, which then descended into lawlessness and mayhem (see fig. 9.1). In retribution for the deaths, *capitalía* protesters focused their anger on police property, ransacking, looting and burning the city's police stations, and destroying police vehicles.

This eruption of violence, tragedy and destruction in November 2007, that surrounded the drafting of Bolivia's new constitution, is a primary context for understanding the incident of 24 May 2008. The intimidation and attacks on rural people from the Chuquisaca provinces, visiting the city to receive ambulances from Evo Morales, may also be understood in terms of punishment for their support of the government's constitutional process and failure to back Sucre's *capitalía* cause. Looking closely at the video footage of these attacks, it is notable that the perpetrators are often difficult to distinguish phenotypically from their victims, although economic and cultural differences are evident from their dress. Those inflicting the punishment on the rural people appear to have been a racially diverse mix, including children or grandchildren of rural Chuquisaqueños. However, although this discriminatory violence may be related to culturalist distinctions (including class, politics, rural/urban residence, occupation and education), these aspects are historically intimately interwoven with ideas about racial differences and are played out discursively in racial language, despite a paradoxical tendency to deny racism (De la Cadena, 2001). Some perpetrators undoubtedly came from families whose homes employ housemaids, nannies and gardeners from the rural provinces; a deeply ingrained sense of racialised superiority is commonplace among such families (Ströbele-Gregor, 2011, p. 83). Bullying and abuse of domestic employees is well documented (Peñaranda et al., 2006), and the events of 24 May partially resemble a large-scale public version of this kind of domestic discrimination and maltreatment.

The challenges and opportunities of turning the tables

My research project in Sucre focused on the work of the regionally celebrated *originario* musician, music entrepreneur and activist Gregorio Mamani Villacorta (see fig. 9.2). Gregorio is a good example of how Morales' rise to power put race centre stage, creating new opportunities and new challenges. Gregorio had grown up and lived, until around the age of 30, in the rural community of Tomaykuri, near Macha in northern Potosí. His long trajectory as a recording artist dated back to the late 1980s, and my project involved working with him in his low-budget home studio on the production of several music videos (Stobart, 2011). He was an outspoken campaigner for *originario* musicians and against media piracy, and often presented himself as a revolutionary, styling himself on the 19th-century indigenous insurgent hero Tomás Katari, also from the Macha region.

Gregorio was a household name among rural people and indigenous urban migrants of the region, and stalls in Sucre's Mercado Campesino [peasant market] offered many of his recordings. However, when I enquired, none of the music stall holders of Sucre's Central Market – who mainly sell national and international genres – had heard of him. This highlights the social-racial structuring of Sucre's urban space, where people perceiving themselves as belonging to 'civilised urban society' occupy the centre, with its beautiful white colonial architecture, and see the indigenous population as relegated to the periphery (Ströbele-Gregor, 2011, p. 71; Defensor, 2008, p. 28). Nonetheless, as evidenced by Sucre's diverse musical landscape, the city's socio-racial and class structures are considerably more complex than this duality might suggest.

Gregorio played an active part in Morales' election campaign and in the MAS party, releasing a music video of influential campaign songs.[13] In particular, the song 'Evo Evo Presidente' became ubiquitous at MAS campaign meetings around the country.[14] This campaign anthem was on everyone's lips, but few people knew the identity of the composer. Nonetheless, the regional branch of the MAS recognised Gregorio's contribution and in 2006 appointed him as director of the Servicio de Fortalecimiento Municipal y Comunitario [Municipal and Community Empowerment Service] for Chuquisaca Department. When I made a pilot trip to Sucre in August 2006 to consult with Gregorio about my proposed project, he had just taken up this important regional government position. During my visit to his office he could scarcely contain his amazement about this turn of events. The last time we had met had been in his humble adobe hut in rural Tomaykuri; now here he was sitting behind the director's desk of a major government office.

This high-profile post involved responsibility for Chuquisaca Department (an area about 20 per cent larger than the Netherlands) and directing a team

13 This appeared first as an audio cassette.
14 See https://www.youtube.com/watch?v=NS4Fgz_gq5Y (accessed 10 Dec. 2017).

Figure 9.2. Gregorio Mamani Villacorta (1960–2011). Depicted playing the charango and wearing sika bota *leggings and a* tinku *[ox-hide] fighting helmet. Image used in music video productions. (Photo by Henry Stobart.)*

of more than 20 'technicians', most of whom were university-educated urban mestizos. Gregorio, by contrast, had left rural school in Tomaykuri at the age of 11, needing to help out with agricultural and herding work following the death of his father. The attitudes of some of the staff to their new boss can easily be imagined, as can the unpopularity of some of Gregorio's seemingly practical proposals. For example, he suggested that technicians re-locate to the provincial areas for which they were responsible, rather than living far away in the city of Sucre where lack of local knowledge and interactions often limited the impact of their work. Nonetheless, a few members of the team admired and strongly supported Gregorio, and were deeply committed to the political significance of his occupancy of this position. For example, Jenny Vargas reminisced:

> It was there [in the Municipal and Community Empowerment Service] that I got to know Gregorio. A very intelligent man. He memorised and learnt things very quickly. This surprised me as he had not had the opportunity to go to university. I saw how he was mistreated. [They'd say] 'this Indian' and used many other deprecating adjectives, not suitable to repeat. He was badly treated even by his own technicians. (9 January 2008)

After several months in this role, Gregorio was moved to the culture unit for Chuquisaca Department. Once again he encountered difficult working relations and in August 2007, a few months before I commenced my research in Sucre, he resigned from government employment in order to return to his career as an artist. His resignation was certainly in part due to the racist attitudes he had encountered. However, although immensely charismatic, his idiosyncratic personality – and sometimes acerbic response to opposition – may not always have served him well as a line manager. A lack of infrastructure, training and support in this challenging role was also probably part of the problem.[15] Following his resignation, Gregorio dedicated himself to producing music videos in his home studio in order to rekindle his career as an artist. Notably, this was the first time he had created videos entirely independently, without employing the services of a mestizo video editor. He approached the medium's creative opportunities with immense enthusiasm, despite the constant technical challenges it posed (Stobart, 2011, 2017).

Playing on the edge: structural racism in practice?

While in many respects Gregorio would seem to be well qualified to represent indigenous people, like other indigenous activists his positioning as regards race, class and culture was extremely complex, as was his relationship with the indigenous people he purportedly represented (see Lloyd, 2002). In different contexts, I heard his *originario* background invoked in admiration or as a means

---

15 By contrast, in more recent fieldwork in the chamber of deputies in La Paz, which formed part of a collaborative project with Michelle Bigenho, we discovered considerable support for indigenous representatives from the countryside which enabled them to occupy important government positions successfully.

to exclude or belittle him. I also witnessed Gregorio himself proudly assert his indigeneity, but in other contexts distance himself from it. Many of his music videos include speeches in which he explicitly presents himself as an *originario* politician, yet when telling me about his youth in the rural community of Tomaykuri he stressed how his family were 'different' from other community members. They often ate tins of sardines, he explained, and his sisters wore *pollera* skirts, rather than the embroidered *almilla* dresses worn by other local women. Notable, in the following excerpt from our discussion about this, is the way Gregorio directly relates race-based language to class, the two often being effectively inseparable:

> The [other people of Tomaykuri] never travelled and never wore *polleras*. … The people of the community gaped at us. 'They're mestizos', that's what they said about us, because my sisters wore *polleras*. It's as if [we were] half way to being a different class. (13 March 2008)

Gregorio's relations with his home community remained complex throughout his life. His career as an artist was locally celebrated and resented in almost equal measure. When he made his name in the mid 1980s, it was not by playing the indigenous music of Tomaykuri but though recording *huayño charangeada* [charango songs] identified with the *vecinos* [mestizo or *cholo* populations] of the provincial towns and villages – who would also have been seen as 'half way to being a different class'.[16] The sense that developing a career as a charango singer-songwriter meant transgressing his culturally and socially appropriate sphere, was communicated to me by the famous *huayño* artist Alberto Arteaga who referred to Gregorio as *indio*. As a youth, hearing recordings of Arteaga's charango *huayño* songs on the radio had originally inspired Gregorio to become an artist. However, his former idol's demeaning reference to Gregorio's rural origins suggests that Arteaga viewed him as 'jumped-up', and attempting to rise above his class and racial position. This same perception of Gregorio as jumped-up was also expressed to me by a *vecino* from the provincial town of Macha, some three hours' walk from the rural community of Tomaykuri. Bilingual Spanish- and Quechua-speaking provincial villagers from places like Macha – with their distinctive local musical traditions and where women typically wear *pollera* skirts – might well choose to identify themselves as 'indigenous' or *originario*. However, at the same time they may assert superiority over peasant people from the surrounding rural communities. This Macha *vecino* expressed particular annoyance about the way Gregorio had produced a recording of the village's carnival music:

> Here in the village what we don't like is the way that [Gregorio] sings and brings out certain pieces of music, exclusively from Macha, as though they were his own. The [village] authorities say they are going to pass him a note protesting about this situation; that he must not play the village music from here. He can sing [music] from his community, of his people,

---

16 For discussion of the concept of *cholo* see, e.g., Canessa (1998, p. 233).

that's fine. But beyond this, what we don't like is him appropriating what is sung here in the village of Macha. (9 July 2008)

A few moments later, another elderly Macha villager waxed lyrical to me about how in his youth he had played in a group called Los de Macha [the ones from Macha]. This group of Macha villagers had worn the distinctive peasant dress of the surrounding rural communities, like Tomaykuri, and had performed the distinctive rural *zapateo* [stamping] dance to great critical acclaim at the high-profile Lauro Festival in Cochabamba (Fernández Coca, 1994), on the back of which they toured widely as performers:

> We triumphed in the 4th Lauro Festival [1967] with the [*3 de Mayo*] *zapateo*. In those days, people didn't know about typical [Macha peasant] dress; they admired us. We toured all over the place ... even as far as Argentina ... it was a great time. (9 July 2008)

In these two examples, we see a common double standard derived from a structural racism that defines it as unacceptable for Gregorio, a peasant from Tomaykuri, to perform and record the village's carnival music, but as a matter for celebration when villagers achieve acclaim and commercial success through performing the rural traditions of peasant communities. It is not hard to see how such attitudes give rise to race- or class-based resentments.

In the late 1960s it had been unthinkable for people from rural communities in this part of Bolivia to own record players, but during the 1980s portable cassette players became more affordable, even if the high cost of batteries meant they were rarely heard (Stobart, 2006). In response to this technology, in the early 1990s Gregorio pioneered the commercial recording of music from Macha rural communities, such as Tomaykuri.[17] These diverse genres, which are closely linked to localised indigenous identity and agricultural practices, included distinct styles of charango songs derived from community festive practices and *pinkillu* flute music (2006). Other rural artists and community-based groups gradually followed Gregorio's example, creating a regional market among low-income, largely native consumers that expanded exponentially following the arrival of digital music video (VCD) technology in around 2003 (2010, 2016). Thus, in the lead up to Morales' rise to power in 2006, technological developments – alongside media piracy that hugely depressed prices – contributed to the spread of videos of rural music, featuring musicians and dancers wearing indigenous dress.

When in August 2006 Catalina Vargas told me how Morales' presidency had created new visibility, acceptance and opportunities for native culture she was undoubtedly correct. But this was also part of a longer story involving native entrepreneur activists, like Gregorio, and new low-budget digital audio-visual technologies. Catalina, a vendor of recordings of local music in the mining

---

17 Ponciano Mamani, the owner-producer of the Cochabamba-based label Borda that recorded most of Gregorio's early audio-cassettes, was also pivotal to this initiative.

town of Llallagua in northern Potosí, observed that before Morales' presidency rural native people used to hide their origins, by avoiding the use of local dress when they came to town, and would feel shame for the local musical traditions they played:

> Only recently are they valuing their musics. Previously they didn't value it, they were ashamed. A person who came from the countryside was ashamed because [s/he thought] 'they are going to call me Indian', whereas now they are not frightened, they don't have this shame. Now they say 'I'm an Indian, or whatever, but I am what I am', now they value this [identity], but only recently. (August 2006)

Despite ongoing silent and sometimes explicit racism, under Morales, indigeneity and ethnicity shifted from always being viewed as obstacles to being seen as economic, social and political opportunities, and even as a qualification for certain rights, privileges or government support. This situation has also given rise to hierarchies of indigenous authenticity, which can have exclusionary and discriminatory or *culturalist* aspects. For example, in our conversations, Gregorio sometimes described himself and his organisation CEMBOL (Centre for Bolivian Music) as representing 'true' *originario* culture, which in his view was a claim that most other organisations could not make. Indeed, Gregorio's *originario* credentials and his deep knowledge of rural indigenous Macha culture were beyond question. Few community members from rural Tomaykuri had his specialist musical knowledge and ability to multi-track all the parts of a *pinkillu* flute ensemble or to tune and to play the charango and *kitarra* [local rainy season guitar] in all the local variants. Music, for them, was a relatively small part of their lives and largely confined to festive occasions (Stobart, 2006). The sense that Gregorio was the bearer of a pure and original indigenous culture was conveyed to me by Heyson Adolfo, a young and highly educated mestizo musician also living in Sucre, who had toured internationally with the group Cantosur. He expressed huge admiration for Gregorio's cultural knowledge and abilities:

> What Gregorio does is very pure, it's very original, or rather it's very much *del pueblo* [of the people] and you notice this in the essence of the music, don't you? [In] its essence, its form, its variety of interpretation and this is what needs recovering. In our case ... we learnt in the town, from folklore, already a mixture. It is different and you can really see this. It's a bit difficult to explain perhaps, but you have to see this too, you have to live it. Thus, as I've said, [in the town] the culture is not left as it is. (2 January 2008)

But when Heyson asked for guidance about how to play the charango in rural style, Gregorio stated that this could only be learnt through extended immersion in the 'culture'. Heyson interpreted this very positively as an important lesson about culture as a totality, where charango technique and style could not be divorced from the cultural whole. However, there is also a sense that in this statement Gregorio was strategically essentialising his indigeneity and protecting his cultural capital. Thus, from being a source of shame, indigenous cultural expressions have sometimes come to represent valuable assets that need to be carefully protected and controlled.

Advocacy or appropriation?

Several of the urban mestizo folklore artists I got to know in Sucre perceived themselves as long-term advocates of native and national music. They were painfully aware that, like most of my children's classmates at the Sucre city centre schools they attended, urban mestizo youths tended to be far more interested in North American and European popular music than national folkloric styles, let alone native music. In this context, many of these urban folklore artists – all of whom, necessarily, combined their scant semi-professional work as musicians with other more reliable forms of income or 'day jobs' – were involved in activist projects to promote national folklore music or to support native or marginalised people of the region. For example, Los Masis, who periodically tour in Europe, run an immensely active performance group for young people, the Juch'uy Masis [little Masis], which rehearses almost every weekday evening. Young people from wealthier families pay a subscription towards the cost of running the group, but scholarships are offered to children from poorer parts of the city. This initiative, as Roberto Sahonero – the group's founder and director – explained to me, explicitly aims to break down social barriers by getting children from different social backgrounds to play music together. Los Masis, whose mission statement is 'to maintain, *reivindicar* [re-validate] and disseminate Bolivian cultural heritage', have also been running a bicultural education programme in the rural community of Mishkamayu, near Tarabuco, for many years (in part supported by international funding). The group were hugely supportive of Evo Morales' election campaign, but following his rise to power they came to feel increasingly ostracised due to their class position. From being advocates for rural people and native culture, they have found themselves being accused of appropriation – even by other urban mestizo folklore musicians. For example, according to Vicente Vargas, the director of the urban mestizo group Cantosur, which also tours internationally:

> Los Masis ... imitate autochthonous expressions and present them in public performances in the cities, around the world. [They] make a copy of what still exists in the [cultural] roots. But this is a bit limiting for a musician because it's simply copying that which is played in its place of origin ... it lacks respect because this music has an owner, right? It has origins which should be respected, it should be preserved as it is in its place and this is a bit difficult and a commitment too. (19 February 2008)

In reality, there is very little in the repertoire of Los Masis – much of which consists of original compositions – that resembles the aesthetic world of native rural music. However, some local jealousy may surround the group's relative success in attracting European funding to create a foundation and their acquisition of a centrally located rehearsal space. Their long-term dedication and advocacy cannot be questioned, even if there was sometimes a paternalistic aspect to their relationship with rural people; a general tendency – far from unique to them – not to treat rural native people as equals (Doxtator, 1988, p. 67–78, cited in Diamond et al., 1994, p. 44). Like Los Masis, Cantosur was also involved in charitable initiatives. Vicente ran a workshop in his home in which he trained adolescents from poor backgrounds to make a local guitar-type instrument that had fallen into disuse; a project that aimed both to revive this instrument and to provide skills and employment opportunities for marginalised youths.

In the context of the new government, Vicente was clearly highly conscious of potential accusations of appropriation, and was at pains to distance himself – discursively at least – from this. He explained:

> [In Canto Sur] one is given the liberty to make what one really wants to without ill-treating the traditional, typical, or autochthonous. But taking elements from that with which we have always coexisted. From here rhythms; from there melodies; from there instruments. So those things which can be used advantageously and built upon to express oneself freely in a composition. (19 February 2008)

As Sucre's representative for the national music royalties association, SOBODAYCOM, Vicente was also evidently concerned that authorship, and thus copyright, was neatly packaged and beyond contestation. His rhetoric may also reflect his interactions with Gregorio a few years earlier, when Vicente had helped Gregorio record his campaign songs for the election of Evo Morales.[18] He was probably well aware of Gregorio's outspoken criticism of urban mestizo musicians' appropriation of native identity. Indeed, Gregorio expressed this to me on many occasions:

> I don't like the way that Los Kjarkas and [other] folklorists distort [native] musics. They take them and stylise them with panpipes, quenas and bombo drums, finally making them into folkloric music. For us this is not *originario* ... When we analyse these pieces and find themes we have composed in them, [we repudiate the way] these groups feel they are artistic representatives to the world. (29 January 2008)

Many people, such as Jaime Robles (culture department, Chuquisaca Prefecture), described to me how rural music – 'as part of the expression of daily life' – was retrieved by people who are 'more knowledgeable about the artistic field', and then commercialised. Indeed, it is no surprise that educated, well-connected and cosmopolitan middle-class mestizo musicians are often better

---

18 However, by the time we spoke Vicente was strongly opposing the government and supporting Sucre's cause, and Gregorio – although entirely behind the 'process of change' – had become disillusioned by Morales and was looking to alternative indigenous political options.

positioned to commodify their work than their native counterparts (Brown, 2003). Nonetheless, in my experience, resentments over the appropriation of native dress – that is, the visual rather than the aural aspect – provoked the most heated objections and were directly related to perceived usurpation of indigenous identity. The contested nature of indigenous dress, and Gregorio's extreme position – which I suspect was more rhetorical than realistic – was communicated to me by Javier Ameller, a mestizo musician and restaurant owner, during my pilot trip to Sucre in August 2006:

> Gregorio told me 'we're going to create a law which makes it necessary to pay to use [indigenous] clothing, too'. Let's say, to use a poncho, trousers, *aksu* [back cloth], or *unku* [small poncho]. Well, this seems a bit exaggerated to me, to my way of thinking. If I'm Bolivian I can buy a poncho and put it on; nobody's going to charge me to use the poncho. And if I want to play in this poncho I'll go and do it. For one thing I'm a Bolivian, for another it seems a bit absurd. Fine, this article [of clothing] is part of a community. They would have to register their dress with SENAPI [National Intellectual Property Service] or whoever, and then somebody would need to be the owner.
>
> I think things are turning into a fever while we have a native president from a peasant background who is giving lots of attention to the peasants. They have the desire, I believe, to have power and do whatever they like, even [if this means] violating the rights of other people. (12 August 2006)

This example highlights how, in the face of long histories of discrimination, often buttressed by legal structures such as intellectual property law, native peoples are sometimes deploying the legal weapons previously used to exclude them; a kind of 'payback time'. There are many problematic aspects to locking up native heritage in an 'iron cage' of intellectual property protections (Brown, 2003). Besides creating a kind of essentialist cultural apartheid, which fails to recognise culture's dynamic, transformative and intercultural dimensions, practical questions surround which native 'owners' should receive benefits, what form these 'benefits' should take, and how royalty payments should be policed – especially given the Bolivian government's low-key approach to controlling the circulation of counterfeit goods and media piracy (Stobart, 2010). What is especially revealing about this example is Javier Ameller's insistence on his cultural rights as a Bolivian. Here he invokes a national culturalist discourse not dissimilar to some of those currently being expressed in Europe, where a critique of multiculturalism, alongside a belief in a post-race politics, ignores the discriminatory dimensions of what is perceived by majority populations as 'our culture' (Lentin, 2014). Nonetheless, in Bolivia's case – where, theoretically, indigenous culture has become state culture and where mainstream nationalist expressions are rooted in mid 20th-century *indigenismo* – this situation becomes very complicated and at times contradictory. Indeed, state decolonisation policy and discourse is often accompanied by nationalistic attitudes to heritage that resemble the folklore protectionism of the 1970s (Bigenho and Stobart, 2016; Rios, 2014). In the context of national folklore expressions, there is often little sense of moving beyond the notion of the *indio permitido* [authorised Indian] – according to which, native people are acceptable as long as they perform the part allotted to them by others. According to Silvia Rivera Cusicanqui, who coined this expression, 'This kind of racism is among the most tenacious because it is masked behind a discourse of valuing indigenous culture' (cited in Farthing, 2007, p. 7).

Concluding thoughts: an evening at Orígines

During our stay in Sucre, a new venue called Orígines [origins] opened a few blocks from the central square. It offered food and a culture show and has proved popular among tourists. When we attended the show in July 2008, a few months after the incident of 24 May, we witnessed a fashion show, and the crowning of Miss Sucre and Señorita Sucre by the mayor, Aydé Nava. The programme also included a video, featuring landscapes and tourist locations of Bolivia, and a choreographed dance involving about 15 performers.

The well-rehearsed and carefully choreographed dancers in this stage show were slick, energetic and highly professional, reflecting high standards and dedication to their craft as dancers. The distinctive costumes and percussive sounds produced by the men's wooden platform sandals, with rattling metal spurs, made this dance immediately recognisable as the *pujllay* of Yampara culture. This native group live in communities around the town of Tarabuco which is situated about 50 miles south east of Sucre. But the stylised dance moves, slick choreography and recorded soundtrack – which was much easier on foreign tourist ears than the *toqoro* flutes played by the Yamparas – incorporated little from the rural version of this genre. For many Bolivians, the *pujllay* dance represents a much-loved element of national folklore and heritage, which frequently appears in urban dance parades in Bolivia and beyond – even periodically in London and Paris. Yet, on this particular evening, the stark disconnect between what we were witnessing and my experience of the rural cultures of the region jarred. The culture of the region was being celebrated and nobody was being racist, but our proximity to the rural 'origins' of this dance – exacerbated by the name of the venue – and the 'exclusionary invisibility' of the culture bearers felt especially ironic (Ströbele-Gregor, 2011, p. 71). Maybe these sentiments were heightened by the knowledge that rural Yamparas had been among the victims on 24 May and that the mayor, as part of Sucre's inter-institutional committee, had actively fomented the mobilisations that led to the violence.

Early on in this chapter I discussed a 2017 speech by Evo Morales in which he insisted that recovering native-peasant cultural expressions – such as music and dress – was 'the only way to decolonise ourselves' and, by implication, to confront the structures of racism and discrimination. Morales' rhetoric is immensely attractive and in many ways reflects my own experiences of intercultural engagements through native Andean music. Similarly, most readers will have experienced how musical participation – as collective entrainment in melodic, rhythmic or affective sounds – can enable us to transgress social differences and achieve a sense of unity or *communitas*, as shared experience, identity and values. However, my ethnographic examples reveal how the dynamics that surround native cultural expressions – like music, dance and dress – often intensify and perpetuate the structures of discrimination or elicit resentments. It is hard to be sure how much extremist individuals like Gregorio Mamani – who expose, transgress or challenge these boundaries and structures – ultimately contribute to greater intercultural understanding or to polarising and hardening positions. Like many of the artists discussed in this chapter, his politics of indigenous emancipation was often compromised by professional interests: the need to acquire income as a performer and to protect his cultural capital. Accordingly, his vision for a 'cultural revolution' gave primacy to native expressions and artists, such as himself, but largely excluded middle-class urban mestizo artists – just as they have long marginalised native people. It was almost as if, for him at least, it was now 'payback time'. Nonetheless, I did encounter a few examples of intercultural collaboration in Sucre – such as in the context of creating music for the 2005 election campaign of Evo Morales.

Through the long presidency of Evo Morales, whose support of indigenous peoples has by no means been consistent (Postero, 2017), race-based conflict and debate have become more visible, as discriminatory practices and structures have been challenged. We might even wonder if the ugly and violent incidents of 24 May in Sucre were ultimately necessary in order to motivate anti-racist and anti-discriminatory legislation and policies. What is harder to assess is how effective this legislation and other initiatives – such as the smartphone app – are in reducing discriminatory attitudes and behaviour. In the households of Sucre that employ maids, nannies or gardeners, are native employees from the provinces now treated with greater respect and consideration than before? Or, more cynically, might apparent improvements simply mean that employers are being more careful about their behaviour as they are conscious that unfair or abusive treatment might be reported? Similarly, are domestic staff aware of their rights and do they feel empowered to assert them or to report discrimination? We might also wonder to what extent home owners and their domestic staff are sharing the same music. On this theme, Fiorella Montero-Diaz tells a striking story about the homework she set for a class of nine-year-olds while working as a music teacher in an exclusive school in an elite district of Lima, Peru. The assignment required the children to interview their maids about contemporary Andean (native) singers in Lima. Despite some initial awkwardness and resistance – 'Miss, my father will kill me if I talk to my maid' – the children undertook some interesting interviews and borrowed several CDs and videos.

Some were 'quite moved by sharing something with their maids again: "Maria was like my mother, she raised me, I don't know why I stopped talking to her"' (Montero-Diaz, 2017, p. 74). This cultural expectation that elite or middle-class children will learn to discriminate against the musical tastes of their maids and stop talking to them as social equals is by no means unique to Lima; the story is no different in Sucre. Thus, might transforming culture, by keeping up the conversation and sharing music, represent a step on the road to reducing racism and discrimination? What is for sure is that this road will be very long and arduous, and even if indigenous music, dance and dress can help ease the journey in certain ways, let's not forget that they carry heavy baggage and are no easy panacea.

Bibliography

Ballvé, T. (2005) 'Bolivia's separatist movement', *NACLA Report on the Americas*, 38 (5): 16–17.

Bigenho, M. (2002) *Sounding Indigenous: Authenticity in Bolivian Music Performance* (New York: Palgrave Macmillan).

— (2005) 'Making music safe for the nation: folklore pioneers in Bolivian indigenism', in A. Canessa (ed.), *Natives Making Nation: Gender, Indigeneity, and the State in the Andes* (Tucson, AZ: University of Arizona Press), pp. 60–80.

Bigenho, M. and H. Stobart (2016) 'The devil in nationalism: indigenous heritage and the challenges of decolonization', *International Journal of Cultural Property*, 23: 141–66.

Brown, M. (2003) *Who Owns Native Culture?* (Cambridge, MS: Harvard University Press).

Calla, A. and K. Muruchi (2011) 'Transgressions and racism: the struggle over the new constitution in Bolivia', in L. Gotkowitz (ed.), *Histories of Race and Racism: The Andes and Mesoamerica from Colonial Times to the Present* (Durham, NC and London: Duke University Press), pp. 299–310.

Calla, P. and the Research Group of the Observatorio del Racismo (2011) 'Making sense of May 24th in Sucre: toward an antiracist legislative agenda', in L. Gotkowitz (ed.), *Histories of Race and Racism: The Andes and Mesoamerica from Colonial Times to the Present* (Durham, NC and London: Duke University Press), pp. 311–17.

Canessa, A. (1998) 'Procreation, personhood and ethnic difference in highland Bolivia', *Ethnos,* 63 (2): 227–47.

— (2012) 'New indigenous citizenship in Bolivia: challenging the liberal model of the state and its subjects', *Latin American and Caribbean Ethnic Studies,* 7 (2): 201–21

Carrasco Alurralde, I. and X. Albó (2008) 'Cronología de la Asamblea Constituyente', *Tinkazos*, 11 (23–4): 101–24.

Centellas, M. (2010) 'Savina Cuéllar and Bolivia's new regionalism', *Latin American Perspectives*, 37 (4): 161–76.

Defensor del Pueblo (2008) *Informe Defensorial: Acontecimientos Suscitados en Sucre del 23 al 25 de Noviembre de 2007* (La Paz: Canasta de Fondos), available at: http://www.defensoria.gob.bo/archivos/sucre%20la%20calancha%20Inf.def.pdf (accessed 4 Dec. 2017).

De la Cadena, M. (2001) 'Reconstructing race: racism, culture and mestizaje in Latin America', *NACLA Report on the Americas,* 34 (6): 16–23.

Diamond, B., M.S. Cronk and F. von Rosen (1994) *Visions of Sound: Musical Instruments of First Nations Communities in Northeastern America* (Chicago, IL and London: University of Chicago Press).

Doxtator, D. (1988) *Fluffs and Feathers: An Exhibition* (Brantford, ON: Woodland Cultural Centre).

Dunkerley, J. (2007) 'Evo Morales, the "two Bolivias" and the third Bolivian revolution*'*, *Journal of Latin American Studies*, 39 (1): 133–66.

Farthing, L. (2007) 'Everything is up for discussion: a 40th anniversary conversation with Silvia Rivera Cusicanqui', *NACLA Report on the Americas* 40 (4): 4–9.

Fernández Coca, V. and unnamed authors (1994) *35 años de folklore marcando la soberanía patria: historia de 28 Festivales Lauro Records* (Cochabamba, Bolivia: Talleres Gráfico Lauro & Cia).

Gotkowitz, L. (2011) 'Introduction: racisms of the present and past in Latin America', in L. Gotkowitz (ed.), *Histories of Race and Racism: The Andes and Mesoamerica from Colonial Times to the Present* (Durham, NC and London: Duke University Press), pp. 1–53.

Lentin, A. (2014) 'Post-race, post politics: the paradoxical rise of culture after multiculturalism', *Ethnic and Racial Studies,* 37 (8): 1268–85.

Lloyd, J. (2002) 'Juggling knowledge, juggling power: the role of professional indigenous activists in San Pablo, Ecuador', in H. Stobart and R. Howard (eds.), *Knowledge and Learning in the Andes: Ethnographic Perspectives* (Liverpool: Liverpool University Press), pp. 127–40.

Montero-Diaz, F. (2017) 'YouTubing the "Other": Lima's upper classes and Andean imaginaries', in T. Hilder, H. Stobart and S.E. Tan (eds.), *Music, Indigeneity, Digital Media* (Rochester, NY: University of Rochester Press), pp. 74–94.

Peñaranda, K., X. Flores and A. Arandia (2006) *Se necesita empleada doméstica de preferencia cholita: representaciones sociales de la trabajadora del hogar asalariada en Sucre* (La Paz: Programa de Investigación Estratégica en Bolivia).

Plaza, L., L. Reinoso and V. Arciénega (2014) 'Racismo mediático en Sucre en el marco de la Asamblea Constituyente', in M. Ramos (ed.), *Ciencias sociales handbooks, Tomo I* (Sucre: ECORFAN), pp. 261–80.

Postero, N. (2017) *The Indigenous State: Race, Politics, and Performance in Plurinational Bolivia* (Oakland, CA: University of California Press).

Rios, F. (2014) '"They're stealing our music": the *argentinísima* controversy, national culture boundaries, and the rise of a Bolivian nationalist discourse', *Latin American Music Review,* 35 (2): 197–227.

Sánchez, W. (2001). 'Patrimonio, propiedad intelectual, autoría y "música indígena"', *Memoria: II Congreso Internacional sobre patrimonio histórico e identidad cultural 2001* (Cochabamba: UMSS–Convenio Andrés Bello–Instituto Internacional de Integración), pp. 359–69.

Stobart, H. (2006), *Music and the Poetics of Production in the Bolivian Andes* (Aldershot: Ashgate).

— (2010) 'Rampant reproduction and digital democracy: shifting landscapes of music production and "piracy" in Bolivia', *Ethnomusicology Forum,* 19 (1): 27–56.

— (2011) 'Constructing community in the digital home studio: carnival, creativity and indigenous music video production in the Bolivian Andes', *Popular Music*, 30 (2): 209–26.

— (2016) 'Dancing in the fields: imagined landscapes and virtual locality in indigenous Andean music videos', *TRANS–Revista Transcultural de Música/Transcultural Music Review,* 20: 1–29, available at: https://www.sibetrans.com/trans/article/527/dancing-in-the-fields-imagined-landscapes-and-virtual-locality-in-indigenous-andean-music-videos (accessed 12 Dec. 2017).

— (2017) 'Creative pragmatism: competency and aesthetics in Bolivian indigenous music video (VCD) production', in T. Hilder, H. Stobart and S.E. Tan (eds.), *Music, Indigeneity, Digital Media* (Rochester, NY: University of Rochester Press), pp. 127–55.

Ströbele-Gregor, J. (2011) 'Black day in the white city: racism and violence in Sucre', in O. Kaltmeier (ed.), *Selling EthniCity: Urban Cultural Politics in the Americas* (Farnham: Ashgate), pp. 77–93.

Index

aberrant readings, 15, 73–5, 76, 86, 89, 90, 92, 95
affect
    and art, 102, 109, 115–18
    and cultural production, 13–17
    and music, 209
    and race 1, 5, 13–17, 136
    and visual culture, 74, 76, 77, 85
affirmative action, 8, 125, 126, 128; *see also* legislation, anti-racist
Afroargentinian, 63, 68, 147
Afrobolivian
    cultural production, 147, 148, 151–7, 163
    history, 150
    recognition, 147–9, 151–3, 159–63
    relationship with Morales' government, 153, 159
    territory, 148–63
Afrobolivian king, 16, 17, 147, 148, 153, 157–60
Afrobrazilian
    education, 14, 125–7
    identity, 5
    history of, 8, 126
Afrocolombian
    activism, 9, 34–44
    and affirmative action, 32, 33
    discrimination against, 25, 26, 31, 44
    identity 35, 38
    politics of recognition, 25, 27–30, 32
    territory, 6, 35

Afrodescendant
    activism 5, 9, 17
    assimilation of, 101, 126
    authenticity, 148, 151, 153, 157, 161
    and gender, 15
    and *mestizaje* 5
    and racism, 1, 8, 9, 74
    pan-Africanism, 13
    see also enegrecer
Afroperuvian
    music, 178, 179, 182
    recognition of, 55, 56
agribusiness, *see* extractivism
Anderson, Benedict, 31, 32
Ano (artist), 15, 103, 104, 116–21
anthropology
    and photography 13, 52, 67, 82
    and film, 76, 86, archive, 17, 79, 86, 95
    and racism 75–7, 79, 85
    salvage tradition of, 77, 85
anti-racism
    activism, 28, 126, 128, 142
    agenda, 9, 14, 35, 128, 132, 142, 177, 185, 195
    alliances, 6, 18, 137
    and affect, 1, 5, 13–17, 136
    and art, 111
    everyday, 6
    and film, 73, 79, 90, 95
    institutional, 25–7, 34
    and the media, 44
    and music, 183, 185
    and photography, 49, 50, 58–69

and neoliberalism, 51
role of cultural production,
    12–17, 151
and the state, 5, 55, 147, 153,
    160
spectatorship, 75, 80, 95
see also appropriation, antiracist;
    education, anti-racist;
    legislation, anti-racist
appropriation
of Andean culture, 16, 171, 174,
    203, 205–7
anti-racist, 15, 17, 38, 66
consumerist, 16, 195
cultural, 13, 78, 93, 156
Argentina
racial formation of, 4, 10
racism in, 15, 63–5, 68, 77
Arhuaco community, 80–3, 85–9,
    94
assimilation
of Afrodescendants, 101, 126
of indigenous people 80
see also mestizaje
authenticity
Afrodescendant, 148, 151, 153,
    157, 161
indigenous, 16, 76, 89, 92, 161,
    204
racial, 179, 181
Avedon, Richard, 65
Aymara culture, 151, 156, 161

Baca, Susana, 178
Benjamin, Walter, 57
Bennett, Jill, 105, 109–10
black people; *see* Afroargentinian;
    Afrobolivian; Afrocolombian;
    Afrodescendant; Afroperuvian
body
and experience, 109, 174
and knowledge, 136, 143

as an archive, 81, 102–4, 105,
    108–20
female, 16, 61, 112–16, 133
racial politics, 15, 16, 65, 103,
    106, 108, 110, 133, 137
Bolivia
1952 revolution, 150, 194
1992 copyright law, 195
cultural heritage, 152, 194, 205,
    208
conflict around the capital city,
    193
elites, 170
Bonifaz Pinedo, Julio, *see*
    Afrobolivian king
Brazil
democratisation, 126
exceptions, 8, 9
public education system, 142
racial formation, 4, 5
racial terms, 133–5
recognition of racism, 126, 128
Butler, Judith, 57

cabildo (indigenous authority), 35,
    82
Cardoso, Fernando Henrique, 8
casta paintings, 6, 13, 75
Césaire, Aimé, 109
Chambi, Martín, 76
Chatterjee, Partha, 31, 32
chicha music, 173–5, 182; *see also*
    cumbia music
Chile, 4, 50
cholo, 5, 56, 174, 202
    white, 14, 167, 174
Cimarrón, 9
Clifford, James, 32
Colectivo Manifiesto, 15, 49, 51, 54,
    55, 63–7
Collins, Patricia Hill, 14
colonialism
    and archive, 95

and coloniality, 117
continuity of, 112
critique of, 7, 13, 15, 111
legacies of, 55, 104, 126, 171, 175
and *mestizaje*, 3, 4, 80
and racism, 2, 10–12, 74, 118, 120
coloniality, 2, 95, 117, 119–21
colour-blindness, 132, 152, 169, 181; *see also* post-raciality
commodification
of the black female body, 114
of the environment, 36
of enslaved people, 109, 119
of indigeneity, 16
of music, 207
of poverty, 53
CONAFRO (Consejo Nacional del Pueblo Afroboliviano), 147, 150, 154–9
CONAIE (Confederación de Nacionalidades Indígenas del Ecuador), 10
CONAPRED (Consejo Nacional para Prevenir la Discriminación), 10
constitutional reforms, 50
in Colombia, 25, 26, 30–3, 36, 37, 41
in Peru, 56
in Bolivia, 148, 149, 153, 155, 157, 191, 194, 195, 197, 198
see also legislation, anti-racist
consultation and consent, 39–40, 41
Convention 169 (International Labour Organisation), 39, 62
Córdoba, Diego Luis, 28
Cox, Oliver, 2
CRA (Casa Real Afroboliviana), 147
CRIC (Consejo Regional Indígena del Cauca), 10

criollo music (Peru), 178–80; *see also* Granda, Chabuca
cumbia music, 15, 16, 59, 61, 168, 173, 175, 183; see also *chicha* music

da Silva, Luiz Inácio Lula, 125
Davis, Kimberly, 179
de la Cadena, Marisol, 13, 62, 198
decolonisation, 103, 116, 117, 120, 193, 194, 207, 208
democracy, racial, 4, 14, 125, 126, 129, 133, 135
Dependency Theory, 2, 36
diaspora
African, 153, 159
Caribbean, 102, 103
Nordestina (Brasil), 138
Dioses (film), 177
discrimination, racial, 3, 8, 9–12, 28, 50, 56, 62, 102, 116, 132–42, 176
domination, matrix of, 14
Du Bois, W.E.B., 8
Dussel, Enrique, 117

Ecuador, 10
education, anti-racist, 12
in Bolivia, 205
in Brazil, 14, 17, 125–43
in Colombia, 25
in Peru, 170
Ehlers, Jeannete, 15, 102–4, 112–6, 120, 121
El valle de los arhuacos (film), 82
enegrecer (blackening), 14, 135–9
eugenics, 7, 8
extractivism, 17, 30, 33, 35, 36, 42

Fabian, Johannes, 76
FARC (Fuerzas Armadas Revolucionarias de Colombia), 30, 40, 42, 43

Fernández de Kirchner, Cristina, 63
Foucault, Michel, 31, 57
Frente Negra Brasileira, 8
Fujimori, Alberto, 55, 56, 58

gender
   and blackness, 14, 103, 114, 115, 119, 121, 132–9
   and class, 18, 73, 170
   equality, 141
   and indigeneity, 16, 59, 61, 62
   and race, 2, 18, 73
   and sexuality, 2, 15
Gilroy, Paul, 6
Ginsburg, Faye, 78, 95
Goldberg, David, 2, 10, 148, 152, 161
Gotkowitz, Laura, 193
governmentality, 31–3
Gramsci, Antonio, 29, 44; *see also* hegemony; revolution, passive
Granda, Chabuca, 178; *see also* Afroperuvian music; *criollo* music
Guevara, Ernesto 'Che', 7

Harvey, David, 30
Haynes, Jo, 182
Honduras, 7, 9, 28
huayno/*huayño* music, 168, 173, 174, 182, 202
Huni Kui community, 78, 79

identity
   Afrodescendant, 13, 37, 133–5
   cultural, 31, 36, 41, 56
   indigenous, 16, 78
   racial, 14, 128, 136, 137, 142, 143, 171
INADI (Instituto Nacional contra la Discriminación, la Xenofobia y el Racismo), 10
indigenismo, ideology of, 13, 74, 207
indigenous people
   archives of, 74, 75, 79, 89, 90
   and Afrodescendants, 125–7, 156–9, 182
   and *campesino* identity, 40–1
   cultural expressions of, 203–8
   cinema by, 15, 73–95
   and *mestizaje*, 5, 31
   and modern technology, 76, 87, 88
   politics of, 43, 74, 152, 195
   political representation of, 27, 32, 148–9
   racism against, 3, 9–11, 28, 50, 56, 79
   visual representation of, 76, 87
   rights of, 30, 204
   violence against, 44, 50, 56
indio permitido, 17, 208
indio, 11–12, 56, 195, 196, 202
inequality
   global, 10
   racial, 4, 12, 15, 31, 106, 107, 125, 126, 134, 136, 137, 162, 181
   reproduction of, 2
   social, 5, 18, 28–31, 36, 44, 127, 132
   socio-spatial, 61
Ingenieros, José, 7
interculturalism, 5, 16
   in Bolivia, 16, 148, 195, 207, 209
   in Colombia 43
   in fusion music, 168–9, 174–5, 185
intersectionality, 2, 14, 16, 28, 31

Já me transformei em imagem (film), 78, 79
justice
   reparative, 14, 32, 101, 104–11, 126
   transitional, 105–7

Kirchner, Néstor, 62, 63

legislation, anti-racist, 10, 12, 50
    in Argentina, 10, 62
    in Bolivia, 148, 151, 191–5, 209
    in Brazil, 14, 17, 125–43
    Colombia, 10, 17, 25, 27, 36–8, 41
    in Peru, 56
Lepecki, André, 115
limpieza de sangre, 6, 11
Llosa, Claudia, 177

Madeinusa (film), 177
Mamani Villacorta, Gregorio, 16, 196, 199–209
Marcha de la gorra, 51, 63–5
Masschelein, Jan, 57, 58, 69
Mbembe, Achille, 50, 68, 69
Méndez, Josué, 177
mestizaje
    anti-racist alliances, 5, 6, 18
    and denial of racism 3, 42
    as national identity, 4, 5, 194, 195
mestizo
    figure of 3, 11
    in Argentina 15
    in Bolivia, 17, 149, 151, 157, 159, 161, 194, 195, 209
    in Colombia 28, 31, 31, 35–8, 41, 80, 85
    in Peru, 14, 56, 61
    privilege, 6
Mexico, 7, 10, 13, 31
Mignolo, Walter, 2, 117
migration
    to Argentina, 62, 63, 68
    in Bolivia, 150, 199
    in Brazil, 138
    Peru, 61, 150, 167, 173
Molina Enríquez, Andrés, 7

Morales, Evo
    and Afrobolivians, 153, 159
    election of 16
    political reforms of, 147, 148, 193, 194
moreno, 5, 129, 133–5, 137
Movimento Negro Unificado, 9
multiculturalism
    critique of, 207
    in Argentina, 62
    in Colombia, 17, 25, 27, 30–2, 36–9
    in Peru, 180
    low-intensity, 17
    and the state, 5, 25, 152
    turn towards, 1, 4, 9
    see also legislation, anti-racist

Nabusímake (film), 74–5, 79–87, 95
Nanook of the North (film), 76, 77
négritude, 13, 108
negro
    in Argentina, 63
    in Brazil, 132–42
    in Colombia 37–9
    see also Afrobrazilian, Afrocolombian
neoliberalism
    and the arts, 13
    culture changes of, 50
    in Argentina, 51, 62, 63
    in Colombia, 28, 30, 36, 44
    in Peru, 51
    resistance to, 115
Noble Savage (trope), 76, 92, 94

O Mestre e o Divino (film), 74, 75, 79, 80, 90–5
originario, 148, 191, 196, 199, 201, 202, 204; *see also* indigenous people

palenquero, 34, 36, 37, 39
Paraguay, 28, 63
pardo, 5, 129, 134, 137
Peru
   antifujimorismo, 58
   hispanismo, 167
   indigenismo, 13
   mestizaje, 5
   military dictatorship of 1968–75, 55
   neoliberalism, 50, 51
photography
   anthropological, 13, 52
   anthropometric, 67, 75
   anti-racist, 15
   collectives, 49, 50, 54, 55
   digital, 53, 54
   documentary, 51–3
   indigenous uses of, 75–8, 83, 87, 90, 95
   participatory, 53
   see also Supay Fotos, Colectivo Manifiesto
Pinney, Christopher, 49
Piquet, François, 102–12, 120, 121
plurinationalism, 148, 149, 151, 153, 157, 159–63, 195
politics of identity
   in Bolivia, 151
   in Colombia, 28, 34, 38, 40, 43, 44
   in the Caribbean 101, 102, 105, 109, 112, 121
Poole, Deborah, 75
Portugal, Adrián, 15, 16, 49, 51, 57–62; *see also* Supay Fotos, *Retratos de peruanos ejemplares*
postcolonial
   capitalism, 2
   Caribbean, 101, 104, 111
   myths, 116
   nation-building, 3, 4
   racism, 10

post-raciality, 4, 5, 152, 195, 207;
   see also colour-blindness
preto, 5, 129, 134
Puerto Rico, 4, 101

Quechua
   culture, 156
   language, 55, 172
Quibdó MIA (development plan), 34–6, 38
Quijano, Aníbal, 2, 117
Quintín Lame, Manuel, 8

race
   and biology, 4, 7, 8, 11
   and class, 2, 3, 5, 14–18, 28, 31, 175, 178, 180, 196, 202
   classification, 2, 3
   consciousness, 14, 15, 102, 103, 137
   critical theory of, 2
   and culture, 7, 13
   deconstruction of, 75
   and gender, 2, 14–16, 59, 61, 62, 114, 115, 119, 130, 132–9
   history of, 3, 6–8
   and identity, 2, 16, 135–7, 143, 174, 179
   mixture, 3–5, 18, 31, 126
   and nationhood, 62, 101
   and neoliberalism, 50
   and racism, 6–10, 117, 125
   social constructedness of, 4, 12
   and the state, 152, 153, 161, 162
   and visual culture, 74, 75, 94
   see also mestizaje
racism
   and affect, 13
   and class, 2, 15, 27, 28, 31, 34, 42–4, 63, 66, 148, 117–8, 202
   and gender, 2, 14–16, 114, 138

and *mestizaje*, 4, 5, 31
and sexuality, 2, 15
definition, 2, 9–12
denial of, 31, 125
everyday, 26, 27, 102
history of, 3, 9–12
institutional, 132, 147
structural, 101, 105, 110, 132, 196, 201, 203, 209
visual, 1, 73, 74, 95
see also *mestizaje*
Raheja, Michelle H., 76, 77
raizal, 34, 36, 37, 39
recognition, politics of
advent of, 1
of Afrobolivians 17, 147–63, 153, 195
of Afrobrazilians, 129
in Colombia, 25, 28, 30–2, 42, 59
of mixed-race identities, 4
of difference, 4
Resistencia en la línea negra (film), 86–9
Retratos de peruanos ejemplares, 51, 58–63; see also Supay Fotos; Portugal, Adrián
revolution, passive, 29, 30, 33, 36, 40, 43, 44; see also Gramsci

Sangradouro (film), 74, 75, 79, 91, 92, 95
Sassen, Saskia, 49
Saya music, 147–62
Schwab, Gabriele, 105, 111
serialities
bound, 31–33, 35–8, 41, 44
unbound, 31–33, 36–37
Serra, Rafael, 28
sexism, 16, 114, 121
Sey arimaku (film), 74, 75, 79, 80, 86–91, 94, 95
Shohat, Ella, 74

slavery
in Bolivia, 149, 150, 157
in Brazil, 78, 134
in Colombia, 35
in the Caribbean, 14, 15, 101–26
history of 3, 4
rebellions against, 13
reparations of, 14, 32, 101, 104–11, 126
trauma of, 102–16
Solier, Magaly, 177
Sommer, Doris, 13, 55
sovereignty, photographic, 85, 86
Spence, Louise, 73, 95
Stam, Robert, 73, 74, 92, 94, 95
Supay, Fotos (collective), 49–51, 55, 57, 58, 68; see also Portugal, Adrián; *Retratos de peruanos ejemplares*

territory
Afro-indigenous, 6, 25, 30, 32, 33, 42, 44, 81
Afrobolivian, 148–63
Afrobrazilian, 6, 78
Afrocolombian, 9, 37, 39
campesino, 41
eviction from, 17, 56
indigenous, 56, 148, 156, 158, 162
see also extractivism
Trinidad and Tobago, 101, 112, 113
Trump, Donald, 5

Uribe, Álvaro, 30, 39, 43

Vargas Llosa, Mario, 55, 56
Vanishing Indian (trope), 76, 83
Vasconcelos, José, 7
Vídeo nas Aldeias, 74, 78, 79, 91, 94, 95
Vives, Carlos, 181

Wade, Peter, 74, 88, 94
Weismantel, Mary, 62
white ally (figure), 5, 143; *see also cholo*, white
whiteness
  and *mestizaje*, 5, 6
  in Argentina, 62, 63, 68
  in Bolivia, 148, 149
  in Brazil, 5, 125, 126, 132–43
  in the Caribbean, 15, 101, 104, 106, 107, 110, 112, 114
  in Peru, 13, 14, 55, 56, 61, 167–85
whitening, 63, 125, 126, 138

Zhigoneshi Centro de Comunicaciones (collective), 74, 80, 84–9, 94, 95

Founded in 1965, the Institute of Latin American Studies (ILAS) forms part of the University of London's School of Advanced Study, based in Senate House, London.

ILAS occupies a unique position at the core of academic study of the region in the UK. Internationally recognised as a centre of excellence for research facilitation, it serves the wider community through organising academic events, providing online research resources, publishing scholarly writings and hosting visiting fellows. It possesses a world-class library dedicated to the study of Latin America and is the administrative home of the highly respected *Journal of Latin American Studies*. The Institute supports scholarship across a wide range of subject fields in the humanities and cognate social sciences and actively maintains and builds ties with cultural, diplomatic and business organisations with interests in Latin America, including the Caribbean.

As an integral part of the School of Advanced Study, ILAS has a mission to foster scholarly initiatives and develop networks of Latin Americanists and Caribbeanists at a national level, as well as to promote the participation of UK scholars in the international study of Latin America.

The Institute currently publishes in the disciplines of history, politics, economics, sociology, anthropology, geography and environment, development, culture and literature, and on the countries and regions of Latin America and the Caribbean. From autumn 2019, the Institute's books, together with those of the other institutes of the School, are published under the name University of London Press.

Full details about the Institute's publications, events, postgraduate courses and other activities are available online at http://ilas.sas.ac.uk.

Institute of Latin American Studies
School of Advanced Study, University of London
Senate House, Malet Street, London WC1E 7HU

Tel 020 7862 8844, Email ilas@sas.ac.uk
http://ilas.sas.ac.uk

Recent and forthcoming titles published by the Institute of Latin American Studies:

A Return to the Village: Community Ethnographies and the Study of Andean Culture in Retrospective (2017)
edited by Francisco Ferreira and Billie Jean Isbell

Chile and the Inter-American Human Rights System (2017)
edited by Karinna Fernández, Cristian Peña & Sebastián Smart

Understanding ALBA: Progress, Problems, and Prospects of Alternative Regionalism in Latin America and the Caribbean (2017)
edited by Asa K. Cusack

Rethinking Past and Present: Essays in memory of Alistair Hennessy (2018)
edited by Antoni Kapcia

Shaping Migration between Europe and Latin America: New Approaches and Challenges (2018)
edited by Ana Margheritis

Brazil: Essays on History and Politics (2018)
Leslie Bethell

Creative Spaces: Urban Culture and Marginality in Latin America (2019)
edited by Niall H.D. Geraghty and Adriana Laura Massidda

Memory, Migration and (De)Colonisation in the Caribbean and Beyond (forthcoming 2019)
edited by Jack Webb, Roderick Westmaas, Maria del Pilar Kaladeen & Robert Tantam

A Nicaraguan Exceptionalism? Debating the Legacy of the Sandinista Revolution (forthcoming 2019)
edited by Hilary Francis

The Cultural Worlds of the Jesuits in Colonial Latin America (forthcoming 2020)
edited by Linda A. Newson

www.ingramcontent.com/pod-product-compliance
Ingram Content Group UK Ltd.
Pitfield, Milton Keynes, MK11 3LW, UK
UKHW061834210426
5322IPUK00026B/669